# THE CIVIL WAR

# THE CIVIL WAR
## A COMPLETE MILITARY HISTORY
## DOUGLAS WELSH

Bison Books Limited

Published by
Bison Books Limited
4 Cromwell Place
London SW7

Library of Congress Catalog Card Number:
81–80451

ISBN 0 86124 079 0

Printed in Hong Kong
Reprinted 1982

# CONTENTS

# INTRODUCTION

Over a century after the end of the American Civil War, secession and its causes are still a matter of controversy. The sequence of events leading to the opening guns at Fort Sumter may be said to start before the founding of the new nation. The economic differences which would eventually divide North and South developed through the period of colonization. The smaller farms of New England and the Middle Atlantic states flourished beside the growing industries of manufacturing and commerce. In the South, however, the bulk of the wealth was founded on the plantations growing tobacco, rice, indigo and cotton, which required cheap labor. This eventually meant slaves.

By the middle of the nineteenth century slavery had been abolished in most of the 'civilized world.' Following an agricultural depression the South might have done likewise, but for the impetus given the cotton industry by the invention of the cotton gin and the development of the English cotton trade. Slavery became profitable. It also became the rallying point of a discontent that had nothing to do with its morality. The economic sectionalism of the United States turned political. The issue of States Rights which had its roots in the Constitution and the very union of the United States, questioned the power of the Federal Government to determine the destiny of the individual states. The controversy over slavery was considered an attempt by the North to dictate policy to the South.

Equally the economic differences between the industrial North and the agricultural South were not aided by their commercial practices. Traditionally the South looked to Europe as a market. To protect their own interests the Northern industrial states sought to impose tariffs on European trade goods. The South demanded free trade to maintain an open market for their own produce abroad.

With the imposition of these tariffs assured by the election of Abraham Lincoln, who took an equally stern position on the abolition of slavery, balance and compromise were no longer felt sufficient to bridge the gap that divided the country. The southern states, led by South Carolina, broke away from the Union, believing that they must exercise their 'right' to remove from the union which was no longer beneficial.

Setting aside the major differences, certain issues determined whether one faction could possibly win a war. Speeches, hysteria and a determined belief in one's rights do not assure victory. The primary problem is the capacity of the society to raise and maintain armies in the field.

Population played a key role during the Civil War. In 1861 the population of the United States was approximately 30 million. The 22 states which remained in the Union accounted for more than 21 million citizens. By contrast the 11 states which ultimately joined the Confederacy had only five and a half million white citizens and three and a half million blacks. The North had a definite advantage in manpower. The population issue had been a key factor in the events before the war. The states in sympathy with the Union were represented by three times the number of Congressmen as the Southern states. In the Senate, of course, there were two representatives from each state. During the war, the only redeeming factor of the difference in population was the slave-based Southern labor force. Consequently more white males could be released for military service in the South. Even so, for every two soldiers the Confederacy could field, the Union could field five. That ratio would become critical the longer the war lasted.

Soldiers in the field require arms and supplies. Again the balance favored the North. The majority of the American army and navy remained loyal to the Union. Though small, those numbers formed the core of the personnel and kept much of the modern equipment, rifles, cannon and ships, in Union hands. Most armories were Northern based. The ability to produce war materials definitely favored the more industrialized North. In the early stages of the war Southern troops had to rely heavily on weapons seized from military arsenals in the South, which were primarily used to equip the militia and these were generally not first quality. To improve the situation the South was forced to capture equipment or import it

from England or France. In either case, supply and demand were critical factors.

Another consideration was the railroad. In the North, the railroad had expanded to allow easy access throughout the 22 states. The movement of troops and supplies would not be a major problem for the Union. In the South, the rail lines ran to the few major cities and ports from depots in the interior of the country and existed for the primary purpose of transporting goods. The Southern railroads were in deplorable condition, and would prove virtually worthless in the war.

The South did have an advantage in its leadership. The pick of the American officer corps, southerners by birth, were sympathetic to the Confederate cause and rallied immediately to the Confederate standard. These included Lee, Jackson, Johnston, Beauregard, Longstreet and Stuart to mention only a few, all serious students of the art of war. It would take the North nearly three years to find leaders who could compare with them. That single factor counterbalanced the disadvantages to such an extent that leadership came near to determining the outcome of the war at its beginning.

From the Confederate viewpoint time was all important. On 12 April 1861, when the first guns roared in Charleston against Fort Sumter, Southerners and Northerners alike looked upon it as a great adventure where honor and glory were only moments away. A quick skirmish, a few swift victories and the war would be over. Little did they realize the death, destruction and bitter fighting which lay ahead.

*Far right:* South Carolina made the decision to secede following a vote in the State Assembly.
*Left:* Slave auctions continued to be held during the early years of the war.
*Right:* Abraham Lincoln (1809–65), 16th President of the United States. Secession was a result of his election in 1860.
*Below:* After secession, Federal arsenals were captured in the name of the new Confederate States and used to equip the army.

CHARLESTON

MERCURY

EXTRA:

*Passed unanimously at 1.15 o'clock, P. M. December 20th, 1860.*

**AN ORDINANCE**

THE

UNION

IS

DISSOLVED!

The path of retreat from Bull Run became more
difficult as the Union forces moved back across
the many creeks near the battlefield

# THE OPENING
# DAYS (1861)

On the morning of 12 April 1861 the sentiments and rhetoric which had propelled the American nation down the path of inevitable conflict erupted into action as a howitzer shell exploded within the compound of Fort Sumter, South Carolina. The sense of confusion which accompanied the outbreak of war was coupled with mixed emotions and conflicting beliefs. Although a major rift had developed between the North and South, on both political and social issues, there were few who truly believed that Americans would indeed take up arms against one another.

The actual war began when Major Robert Anderson, commander of the 70-man garrison at Fort Sumter, received a request for unconditional surrender from General Pierre Gustave Toutant Beauregard, commanding officer of the Confederate battery in Charleston. If the garrison did not immediately capitulate it would be bombarded and taken by force. Having replied that Fort Sumter was the property of the United States Government, Anderson refused to comply and ordered his officers and men into the fort's protective bunkers.

The threatened bombardment did indeed follow, but with little effect on the Union forces within the fort. It was an assault on the nerves of the occupants rather than an actual siege attack. Ander-son gave orders that return fire would be given, to be directed only at the immediate shore batteries, the principal of which was Fort Moultrie. Union counterfire was to be limited to the silencing of the opposing guns and all efforts were to be made to inflict the minimum of damage to other sections of the harbor.

The two days which followed the initial shots saw intermittent Confederate shelling, while the Union batteries, who were severely handicapped in manpower and munitions, returned token fire which merely gave an illusion of defense.

For the Confederate command the surrender of the fort and a rapid solution to the situation were of the utmost importance. Anderson for his part applied delaying tactics as he awaited supplies and reinforcements from Northern ships. The highlight of Union activity revolved around the misadventures of two unnamed sergeants who decided that Anderson was not striking with enough resolve against the Rebels. The two men selected their own targets for shelling, and in two

*Right:* Brigadier General Pierre Gustave Toutant Beauregard, CSA, (1818–93) also commanded at the First Battle of Bull Run.

*Below:* The citizens of Charleston crowded along the Battery to watch the shelling of Fort Sumter.

separate incidents managed to damage a house along the shore near Fort Moultrie. In their first volley they succeeded in effectively scaring off a crowd of curious Carolinean onlookers. In their second attempt they scored a near miss on one of the Confederate floating batteries, yet succeeded in destroying their own gun by attempting to employ it in an unfirable position. Their activities were never made known to Major Anderson, but the zeal of their efforts clearly demonstrated that there were those in the Union army ready and willing to do battle.

By 14 April Anderson realized that a prolongation of the situation would prove increasingly less profitable, as the Confederate batteries had driven off all Union attempts to relieve or resupply the fort. He agreed to surrender the garrison to General Beauregard. In a style symbolic of those early days of the war the fort was permitted to fire a 50-gun salute as the Union flag was lowered and the entire force was given permission to board ships bound for Northern ports.

During the actual exchanges of fire neither side had sustained a casualty, though one Union soldier met an accidental death in a powder explosion during the salute. Both commanding officers saluted and praised each other, parting in mutual regard. The Battle of Fort Sumter was over, ending the first recognized armed conflict of the American Civil War.

Those initial shots gave rise to various Southern reactions and brought several issues into focus. Primarily it demonstrated that the convictions and sentiments of the Southern people were such that they were prepared to launch the country into war to substantiate the validity of their cause. They believed that their grievances and cause were just, and that the issues were divided along party-

*Above:* The distance between Fort Sumter and the mainland necessitated the use of floating batteries by the Confederates.

*Below:* Fort Sumter was defended by a small Union force commanded by Major Robert Anderson.

political rather than economic, social or geographical lines. Equally they were convinced the dedicated Northern Democrats would rally to their cause. The support of Northern party members would increase the turmoil and make their break from the current system that much easier. There was also conviction that the previously active Northern peace movement would influence the reaction of the government in Washington, as few believed that either the North or South desired an actual armed conflict.

Those various ideals were shattered as the first shells landed at Fort Sumter.

*Below:* After Fort Sumter, the restoration of the Union became a Northern crusade.
*Left:* General Winfield Scott, USA, (1786–1866) commanded the Union army until October 1861, despite his age.

Those volleys separated the nation, as the majority of the population rallied with great vigor around their individual states.

Although the early days of the war were among the most chaotic, they were also the days which set the definite pattern of the war and the manner in which it would be fought. Eleven states seceded to form the Confederate States of America. The governor of Missouri declared himself in sympathy with the Confederate cause although subsequently that state would be deeply torn by the conflicting loyalties of its inhabitants. Virginia declared for the Confederacy, but the part of the state which marched with Ohio, Pennsylvania, and Maryland broke away in support of the Union. Maryland itself remained under Union control, yet a great deal of Southern support could be found within its borders.

Men of all states rushed to join local militia and volunteer units. In the years prior to the war the United States Army had been composed of a relatively small number of regular soldiers who usually found themselves relegated to frontier and border duties. Thus at the outbreak of war the available troops were of little benefit to either side. The North was also faced with the fact that the armories and arsenals located within Southern states had been confiscated by those states in the weeks following secession. The contents of those arsenals had immediately been put at the disposal of Southern volunteers. More significant to the stability of the regular army and the Union government was the division of its trained officer corps. To a large degree the better,

# VOLUNTEERS WANTED!

## 1776!    1861!

## AN ATTACK UPON WASHINGTON ANTICIPATED !!

# THE COUNTRY TO THE RESCUE!

## A REGIMENT FOR SERVICE

### UNDER THE FLAG          OF THE UNITED STATES

IS BEING FORMED          IN JEFFERSON COUNTY.

## ☞ NOW IS THE TIME TO BE ENROLLED!

Patriotism and love of Country alike demand a ready response from every man capable of bearing arms in this trying hour, to sustain not merely the existence of the Government, but to vindicate the honor of that Flag so ruthlessly torn by traitor hands from the walls of Sumter.

## RECRUITING RENDEZVOUS

Are open in the village of WATERTOWN, and at all the principal villages in the County, for the formatiom of Companies, or parts of Companies.   ☞ Officers to be immediately elected by those enrolled.

WATERTOWN, APRIL 20, 1861.    WM. C. BROWNE, Col. Comd'g 35th Regiment.

Ingalls, Brockway & Beebee, Printers, Reformer Office, Watertown.

more experienced regular officers were Southerners. The most famous example was the former Superintendant of West Point, Colonel Robert Edward Lee.

With the outbreak of hostilities Virginia had not yet seceded from the Union and Lee remained in the Federal army. Army Chief of Staff General Winfield Scott, brilliant hero of the Mexican War, suggested that Lee assume principal command of all Union forces. Scott realized that he himself was too old for such a command and felt that Lee was without a doubt the most professional and promising officer from the qualifying ranks. Lee considered the offer unofficially, yet declined the position when his native Virginia seceded and he was offered the command of her land and naval forces. Scott's sentiments were amply expressed when he equated the loss of Lee's skills to the sudden loss of 50,000 veteran soldiers on a battlefield. On 23 April 1861 Lee officially accepted his command as a Confederate general.

By contrast the reaction of the regular enlisted troops was somewhat surprising. As the 'gentlemen of the officer corps' were resigning their commissions in the United States Army and Navy to return to their home states, the majority of the enlisted troops, whether of Northern or Southern birth, remained loyal to the Federal army. Accepted figures account that of the 16,000 regular soldiers, less

*Right:* General Robert Edward Lee, CSA, (1807–70) became Commander in Chief of the Confederate forces two days after resigning his commission in the US Army.
*Below:* At first recruits were easy to find.

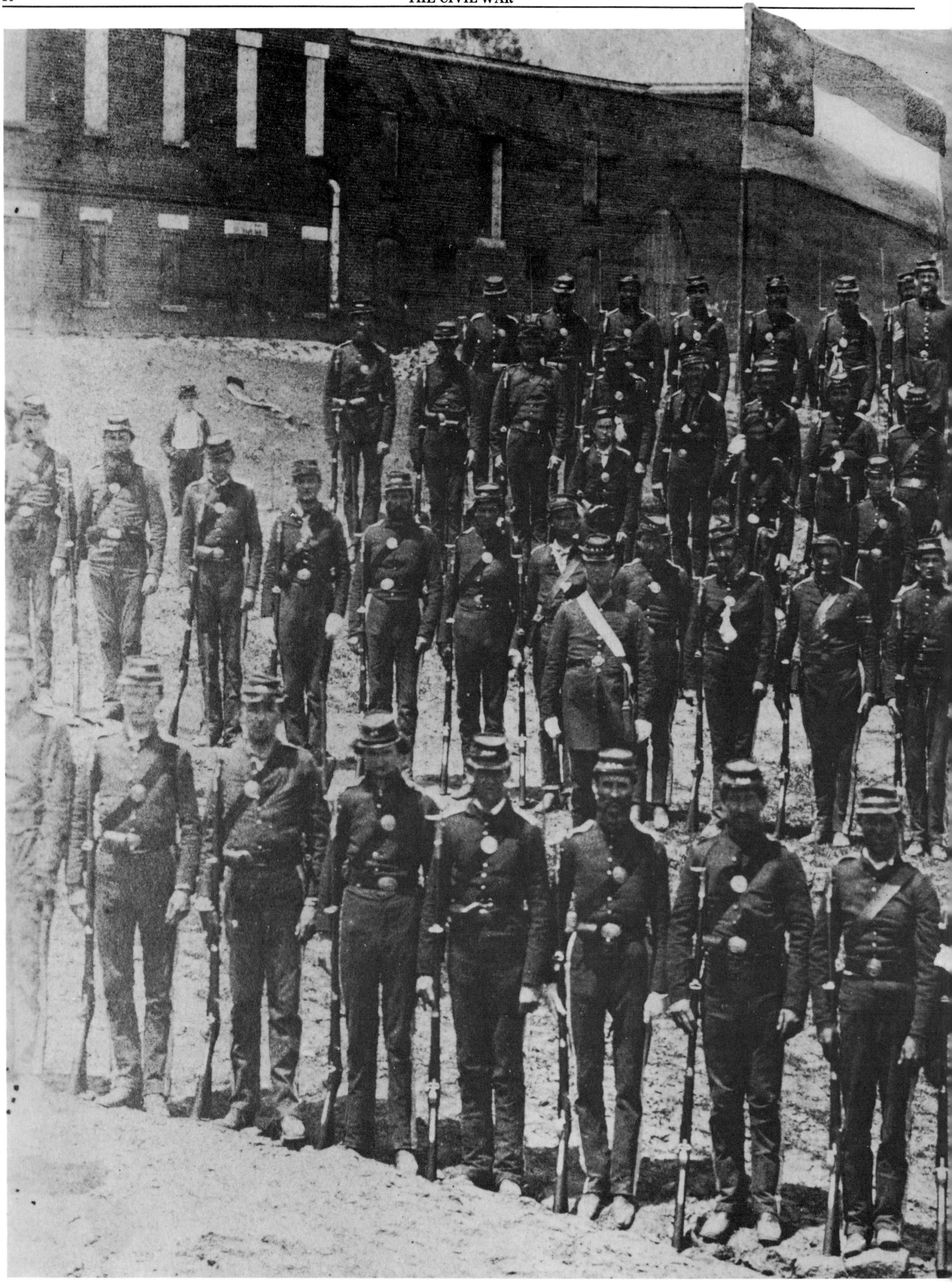

than one percent sought release to heed their states' calls to arms.

The key issue in those early days of the war was undoubtedly the creation of armies. Both the North and South were forced to train militiamen and volunteers into some sort of an army. The outcome of the war could possibly depend on the success of converting the eager rabble into an effective fighting force in those initial days.

Several days after Lee assumed command, another officer Thomas J Jackson from the state of Virginia emerged. A relatively unknown colonel who taught at the Virginia Military Institute, Jackson realized that regardless of spirit or the will to fight, a man was useless on the battlefield until he was trained to accept and carry out orders. His first command was the Confederate force forming ranks near Harper's Ferry, Virginia. Jackson immediately reduced all officers above the rank of captain by one or two grades and set about finding the best men to command his units. His actions created a terrible uproar among the new recruits, as it had been traditional for volunteers and militia to elect officers from their own ranks. Such elected officers had scant military experience with little knowledge of the art of soldiering.

In spite of his early lack of popularity, Jackson initiated the three procedures, in which he believed most emphatically drill, discipline and administration. The nucleus of the army which Jackson created at Harper's Ferry proved to be one of the best examples of trained fighting troops to appear in the war. Although Jackson soon lost his command to Brigadier General Joseph E Johnston, there is no doubt that in his time Jackson performed miracles with raw recruits.

Command and reserve officers and their appointments consistently plagued both North and South during the opening days. Disregard of military experience and the appointment of officers through political influence kept many first-class officers from proving their abilities. The early career of Ulysses Simpson Grant is a typical example of this practice. When war broke out, Grant, then a civilian, wrote to the Adjutant General giving his qualifications as a regular officer with the army during the Mexican War and on the frontier. His request for recommission was ignored as he lacked the necessary political connections to exert influence on his own behalf. Several weeks later, having given up hope of a regular commission, Grant accepted a commission from the state of Illinois, beginning his new military career as a command drill instructor. Numerous cases similar to Grant's demonstrated a lack of preparation and forethought on both sides.

*Left:* Typical of the untried Confederate States Army was Company K of the 4th Georgia Volunteers, 'The Sumter Light Guards' seen parading under their new flag.

The war gained momentum slowly. Many political figures made vain yet vigorous attempts to provoke their armed forces into action against the enemy. Weeks passed as cautious field commanders pondered the situations, not wishing to take responsibility for hastily committing troops who were neither ready for battle nor sufficiently assured of a victory. An air of unease prevailed, for neither side believed that the war would last very long. When President Lincoln called up the militia, the mustered troops were committed for only three months. Eventually the period of national service was extended to cover the duration of the war.

In those early days three areas seemed the most volatile. In the East the area around Washington appeared potentially the hottest as many Northerners feared the loss of the nation's capital. Such a loss was equated with the complete collapse of Northern spirit and victory for the Confederacy. Although militarily that fact was disputed, the psychological implications of the loss could indeed have proved to be too great a burden for Northerners to overcome.

Another prime area was the region of West Virginia. Politically the Northern hold on West Virginia was of major psychological importance, since that area had remained loyal to the Union despite the secession of the state of Virginia. It was important to keep the area's ties with Ohio and Pennsylvania intact. Those surrounding states also looked upon West Virginia as a battleground on which to halt the Southern advance, rather than allowing the war to cross their own boundaries. Strategically West Virginia was viewed by both the Union and Confederacy as a key position which could be used as a base for strikes deep into enemy territory.

The last of the three key areas was Missouri and the West. The state was known to be divided in its sentiments. Though declared as a Confederate supporter, many of its political and military leaders were strong supporters of the Union. The West, including the Mississippi River Basin, would prove to be an area of crucial controversy.

Of those areas, West Virginia was of primary concern as the war began. The governor of Ohio was pressuring for a Federal invasion of that state, on the grounds that it was necessary not only to deny the use of the area to the Confederates, but to support the Union sympathizers there. The military commander of that district, General George Brinton McClellan, agreed that in the current atmosphere some sort of campaign was warranted. However, he was also aware that in taking the initiative his army of less than 5000 was insufficiently prepared to do immediate battle on a major scale. McClellan was also undecided as to whether he should strike directly at the

Confederate force located at Grafton, or move down the Great Kanawha Valley, which he considered the better avenue of approach in the conquest of the area. As McClellan tried to buy time for his army, Confederate activity, in disrupting the Baltimore and Ohio Railroad, brought demands from the governor and President Lincoln for prompt action.

On 27 May McClellan dispatched a small force, commanded by Colonel B F Kelley, with instructions to drive off the Confederate forces and protect the railroad. At the same time a group of volunteers from Indiana, under Brigadier General Thomas A Morris were sent to rendezvous with Kelley's forces in West Virginia. When the two forces were united, Morris set out to dislodge a contingent of Confederate volunteers commanded by Colonel G A Porterfield.

On the night of 3 June Morris launched a three-pronged attack on the Confederates who were then located at Philippi. The assault was an astounding success since the Southern volunteers were totally unprepared, failing even to have mounted pickets. In a minor skirmish the Confederates, offering a little resistance, retreated to the nearby town of Beverly. The quick victory with no casualties other than a few wounded, of which Colonel Kelley was one, gave both Union troops and General McClellan an overwhelming air of confidence. 'The Philippi Races' as it became known throughout West Virginia, led Union troops to assume that the Confederates did not have the resolve to fight, and that the war

*Above:* Guerrilla bands, such as Quantrill's raiders terrorized the Western territories after the declaration of war.
*Above left:* The Civil War saw the first use of the railroads for troop transport in wartime.
*Below:* The early campaigns in West Virginia were a series of marches and skirmishes with few casualties.

would soon be over. However McClellan still was not wholeheartedly in favor of heated pursuit and direct confrontation, preferring to launch a two pronged thrust which would include the Great Kanawha Valley. In that manner he felt certain he could secure the state and drive out Porterfield's forces.

As a result of that Union victory, Confederate troops were withdrawn from Harper's Ferry, and as commander of the Virginian forces, Lee sent two contingents, the principal of which was commanded by General Robert S Garnett, to stabilize the situation. Garnett's route took him to Beverly where he assumed command of Porterfield's disorganized units. Garnett also attempted to carry out his orders to recruit local troops to expand his army. By the first of July he reported that his force consisted of 4500 troops, only 23 of whom had joined the ranks since his arrival in Beverly. He wrote to General Lee, exclaiming that 'the West Virginians were totally imbued with an ignorant, bigoted, Union sentiment' necessitating reinforcements from other areas.

With Union forces moving closer, Garnett believed that the pass over Rich Mountain offered his most effective defensible position. He entrenched 1300 men and a battery of guns to secure it. The remainder of his force, which he would personally command, was similarly positioned near Laurel Mountain. Garnett began his watch for McClellan's forces, whose arrival he anticipated by 8 or 9 July and whose numbers he believed to be five times his own army's strength.

By 6 July the Union Army was within striking distance of Garnett's defenses. McClellan's main problem lay in the fact that he had no true knowledge of the actual number of Confederate troops in the area. From the little reconniassance information he had obtained McClellan

Major General George B McClellan, USA,
(1826–85) was the first commander of the Union
army.

knew that his enemy had taken up well-fortified positions and would be virtually impossible to dislodge through frontal assaults without incurring heavy Union losses. McClellan's strategy was to divide his force in two. One force, under General Morris, faced Garnett to the north in the Laurel Mountains. The second under McClellan's direct command, confronted Lieutenant Colonel John Pegram in the Rich Mountains.

On 10 July a local man named Hart, sympathetic to the Northern cause, offered to guide part of McClellan's force around the left flank of the Confederate defenders. The path which they were to follow was a narrow one, allowing only infantry and a small number of cavalry to undertake the mission. Although the artillery would have to be left behind, McClellan and his staff decided that the risk was worth taking.

On the morning of 11 July McClellan dispatched troops commanded by General William S Rosecrans on the flanking mission. Upon Rosecrans engaging the enemy, McClellan would begin a frontal assault. Their combined efforts would dislodge the enemy. Pegram was alerted to the fact that McClellan intended a flanking maneuver, but he misinterpreted the direction of the assault. Expecting McClellan's forces to strike on the right flank to separate the two main Confederate forces, Pegram's preparations acted as perfect cover for Rosecrans' approaching troops.

After some 10 hours of marching and climbing the Union contingent appeared on Pegram's left flank. For almost three hours the two forces battled as each awaited reinforcements. By evening Rosecrans had a firm hold on the mountainside, yet neither force seemed able to get the upper hand as fighting broke off in the darkness.

By dawn 12 July the Confederate forces had abandoned their position without alerting the Union troops. Fewer than 100 sick and wounded Confederate soldiers were captured, which was small consolation to Rosecrans, as the enemy's whereabouts could not be discovered. Rosecrans blamed McClellan, furious that he had failed to support the assault as had been arranged. McClellan replied that he had received no word from Rosecrans that they had gained the summit and were in need of reinforcements.

Through McClellan's indecisiveness the Confederate forces on Rich Mountain slipped away. Garnett, hearing that Pegram had been outflanked and then had evacuated, moved as well. Realizing that Garnett had abandoned his position, General Morris's troops followed as quickly as possible. On 13 July they engaged Garnett's rear guard near Carrick's Ford. That small, lively action would have had little military importance beyond the skirmish level had it not been for the fact that General Garnett, who had taken personal charge of the evacuation of his army, was killed in the engagement. His death and the outcome of the encounter constituted a victory for the Union forces. McClellan remained in pursuit for several more days, but no further opportunity presented itself to block or seriously engage the departing Confederate army. On 22 July, as a result of his apparent success, McClellan was summoned to Washington and offered supreme command of the Union Army.

Although the battle at Rich Mountain was by no means important, it did give Northern newspapers the opportunity to write something that Northern citizens could cheer about. It gave many the elated notion that the Southerners were unable to withstand the Union pressure, and with the war movement getting into full swing the Confederacy would be brushed aside.

At the time McClellan was securing West Virginia, the stage was being set for the first major battle of the war. The First Manassas Campaign began on 2 July when Major General Robert Patterson's Union Army crossed the Potomac River and engaged a small Confederate force commanded by Colonel Thomas Jackson at Falling Waters. Like so many early encounters, little military significance was attributed to the engagement except for the attention attracted by the young lieutenant colonel of the Confederate cavalry, J E B Stuart, and the promotion of Colonel Jackson to the rank of brigadier general by the state of Virginia.

Neither the North nor South was prepared to take the initiative in what each considered might be the single decisive engagement of the war. The respective capitals of Richmond and Washington lay only a hundred miles apart and both sides believed that if their capital fell to the enemy, defeat would be imminent.

Neither army was anxious to engage without a positive chance of victory and numerical superiority over the enemy.

Brigadier General Irwin McDowell, field commander of the Union forces, was beset by the problem of commanding an army of three-month volunteers, whose period of enlistment had almost expired. Worse yet, their training was minimal. His greatest enemy was not the Confederate force on the opposite bank of the Potomac, but the administration and newspaper critics who pushed for action. Finally McDowell succumbed to their urgings and prepared to move against his enemy in mid-July.

Similarly, the Confederate commander General P G T Beauregard, faced grave difficulties as he confronted his one-time West Point classmate across the river. In an engagement where numerical su-

periority seemed all important, his 20,000 man army was opposed by a Union army of 50 to 60,000 strong. There were less than 14,000 Confederate troops in the immediate area as a reserve, of whom 11,000 were General Joseph E Johnston's troops countering Patterson's threat in West Virginia. Beauregard, like McDowell, struggled with the training and discipline of his men, yet with each passing day of preparation McDowell's army grew in strength. Realizing that it was impossible for his Confederate troops to initiate action, Beauregard contented himself with the knowledge that he could at least block any attempt to strike at Richmond.

On 15 July Patterson's army was ordered to advance against Johnston's troops in West Virginia. Direct contact was to be avoided, as the maneuver was simply an attempt to keep Johnston's forces in their present position near Winchester. Patterson's overt avoidance of confrontation lacked the subtlety required, and his obvious unwillingness to engage the enemy revealed the Union intentions.

On 16 July McDowell began his march toward Manassas Junction. His strategy was simple. He would take a numerically superior army of 35,000 troops, leaving the remainder behind to guard Washington, to engage his enemy's smaller force, and destroy it swiftly in one encounter. Although such an operation seemed simple enough, as the army began its march McDowell's nightmares became reality. It took two and one half days for his army to cover 20 miles. So slow and disorganized was his progress that Beauregard learned of the Union action and proceeded to march against them.

Those two days gave Beauregard the opportunity to make several key decisions. He called for reinforcements and within a day 3000 troops which had been encamped to the southeast had marched forth join him near Manassas. Acutely aware of the imbalance in troops strengths, Beauregard sought to even the odds, calling on Johnston to leave Winchester and march to meet him 'with all due haste.'

Johnston for his part realized that if Patterson discovered that the Confederate forces were on the move and went to McDowell's aid the Union superiority would be overwhelming. Having displayed himself advantageously at Falling Waters, Colonel J E B Stuart and his cavalry were called upon to screen the army as it moved

The Union forces were victorious at the Battle of Rich Mountain, a skirmish with the rearguard of the retreating Confederate army, commanded by General Robert S Garnett.

away from Winchester. Despite other mishaps, Stuart's activities were carried off to such perfection that two days passed before Patterson realized he had been duped.

On the Confederate side, Johnston too was plagued by the slow movement of his troops. Jackson's brigade, which led the army, was moving well, yet as a result his troops were beginning to tire. Knowing that his troops would be useless to General Beauregard if they arrived too exhausted to give adequate support, Jackson and a selected group of officers stood watch at night that no soldier would be denied his much needed sleep. Such added concern for the welfare of the average soldier was the trademark of Southern leadership and would be largely responsible for the fact that Confederate soldiers always seemed willing to tackle the impossible.

On 18 July a minor skirmish occurred outside Manassas, but McDowell, lacking confidence, decided not to press the issue. Two days passed as McDowell sought to assemble his army for a proper engagement. In his hesitation he gave the Confederates the vital time they needed for Johnston's forces to arrive. Had McDowell initiated an assault to follow up the skirmishing of 18 July he might not only have

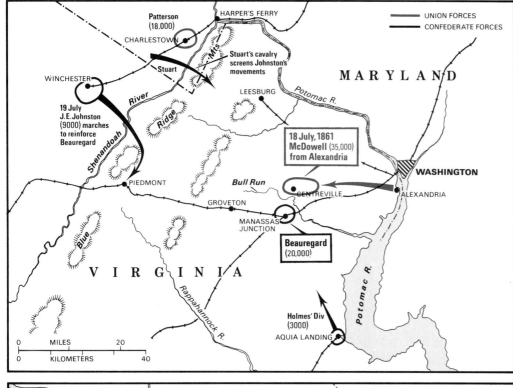

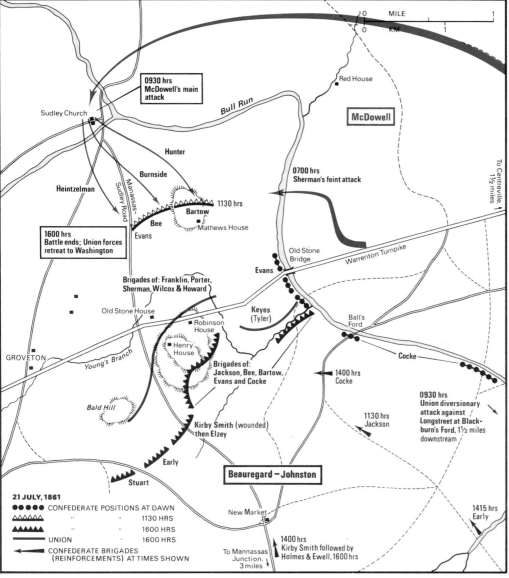

had a chance for victory over Beauregard, but might also have caught Johnston, on the move, between Patterson's forces and his own.

On 21 July 1861 Johnston's army arrived on the battlefield. Although unfamiliar with the terrain around Manassas and Bull Run Creek, he was prepared to carry out Beauregard's plan. Oddly enough, both the Union and Confederate commanders' primary strategy was to attack the enemy's left flank.

However, as the Confederate troops began to execute their plan of attack Johnston recognized the vague and confusing nature of his orders and chose to suspend operations before the entire army was in complete disarray. In doing so he handed the initiative to his opponent.

The Union army's plan was quite simple. A small diversionary attack was to be made down the Warrenton Turnpike toward the Old Stone Bridge, while a two-pronged sweeping maneuver, commanded by Brigadier General William Tecumseh Sherman and McDowell himself enveloped the Confederate left flank. As the Confederate forces had deployed to the south of the pike along the banks of Bull Run, the Union maneuver was intended to force them to leave their defensive positions in an effort to support their left flank. McDowell was relying on the fact that such an attempt would be virtually impossible to execute owing to the poor quality of troop discipline. He felt confident that he would be able to achieve a victory, in spite of the fact that several

volunteer regiments had left the field just before the impending battle because their enlistment periods had ended.

At seven in the morning Union forces attacked near the Old Stone Bridge, drawing fire from the Confederate left flank. Less than two hours later the alarm was raised that the left flank was endangered as the main Union assault force began to cross Bull Run Creek near Sudley Church. Simultaneously a Union diversionary attack began, aimed at General James T Longstreet's brigade. As Confederate troops near the stone bridge attempted to turn and face the threat on

The first battle of Bull Run, or Manassas, was a matter of confusion partly because of the similarity of flags and uniforms on both sides.

*Above:* The open terrain of eastern Virginia lent itself to the traditional form of infantry attack.

*Above:* Ambrose Everett Burnside, USA, (1824–81) a colonel at the first battle of Bull Run, rose to supreme command of the Union forces.

their left flank, McDowell launched his main attack.

The Union 2nd Division, led by Colonel Ambrose Burnside, along with part of the 3rd Division, began to disperse the heavily outnumbered Confederate defenders. Although it appeared that Union troops would soon have the enemy on the run, two Confederate brigades under General Barnard Bee and Colonel Francis Bartow, held their ground and offered staunch resistance. As McDowell's initial assault began to lose impetus, Sherman's forces caught the defenders in an attack on their right flank, throwing the two brigades into flight. It appeared that Sherman's brilliant tactical maneuver had won the day.

Confederate forces fled across Young's Branch past the Old Stone House. The sloping hills over which they retreated had two prominent landmarks, the Robinson house and the Henry house. As they approached those hills, Bee sought to rally his force to prevent their disorder from giving way to full rout. Cresting the hill Bee caught sight of a long, steady line of Confederate soldiers on 'Henry House Hill.' The presence of such a force took Bee by surprise, as the Confederate general commanding those forces had marched to the sound of gunfire, taking up what he considered the best defensible position. Bee took heart and it was at that moment one of the legendary figures of the Civil War was recognized. As Bee saw the flags of the Virginia regiments he was said to have pointed toward them shouting, 'There stands Jackson like a stone wall! Rally behind the Virginians!' At his cry, Bee's forces rallied and Bee himself was struck dead by a musketball. From that time on Thomas J would be would be known as 'Stonewall' Jackson.

It was also at that moment the tide began to turn and Jackson's training programs at Harper's Ferry began to show results. The Virginians stubbornly defended their hill as Union forces battered away in their assault. The situation grew desperate and a Union artillery battery was called forward to apply added pressure to the dislodging of the Confederate forces. As the battery exposed itself, Colonel Stuart's cavalry and one of Jackson's regiments counterattacked. In their swift retaliation they not only captured the guns but temporarily broke the impetus of the Union assault.

Confederate morale soared as for the first time since the attack began they appeared to have the advantage. However, the battle was not yet over. Although temporarily set-back by the loss of their guns, the Union troops rallied to renew their assault on Henry House Hill with increased ferocity. As the fighting continued, it became apparent to both the Union and Confederate commanders that the first to receive reinforcements would carry the day.

Union troops were surging to the critical left flank area and Jackson's own left flank was almost lost when support in the form of Brigadier General Kirby Smith's brigade arrived to strengthen the Confederate position.

No break in the stalemate was achieved. The reserves available were almost exhausted when in the distance a massive troop movement was observed. In the confusion neither of the opposing commanders could tell whose troops were advancing. This typified early battle conditions, since both armies arrived on the field with a multitude of uniforms, flags and paraphernalia. It was often difficult if not impossible to judge whose troops were whose, and not at all uncommon for units to inadvertently fire on friendly troops.

As the troop mass moved closer a sudden calm in the breeze seemed to accentuate the tenseness of the moment. A sudden gust of wind unfurled the approaching flags and revealed the force as Colonel Jubal A Early's Confederate brigade. They had marched the length of the battlefield in response to the sound of heated battle. All along the line Confederate troops took heart, surging forward with the rebel yell which became a prelude to all Confederate attacks throughout the war.

At the sight of reinforcements and the revitalized Confederate assault the Union attack collapsed. However the Confederate advance lacked organization and the Union troops were able to retreat in relatively good order. For the most part the Confederate troops were too exhausted to attempt to follow up their counterattack.

The events which followed would prove crucial to the ultimate results of that fateful encounter. As Union troops withdrew they discovered the road toward Washington blocked by crowds of Sunday onlookers, socialites and politicians from the capital. When Confederate artillery fired on the road upsetting wagons and causing a few casualties, the civilians panicked. In near hysteria they swarmed down the road. As quickly as the panic seized the civilians it spread to the Union troops. Before Union commanders could establish order, the army, which had fought so bravely throughout the day, was engulfed in an hysterical rout to Washington, never slowing in its flight until the city was reached.

Of the Union forces at the scene of the battle, only half had actually engaged in the fighting, with 3000 killed, wounded, captured or missing. The Confederates had engaged almost an equal number of troops, yet with 1000 fewer casualties.

Although neither side had inflicted great losses, the final result was without doubt a victory for the Confederacy. The Confederate forces were still in possession of the field. An additional factor with grave psychological effects was the rout to Washington led by the 'Sunday onlookers.' It would in fact be several months before the Union Army recovered from the events of that day.

Three months after McClellan's promotion to the command of the Union forces, General Winfield Scott retired, leaving the Army General Staff in complete disarray. Scott, though aged and in the opinion of some approaching senility, had managed to keep firm control. The

*Right:* The Southern forces managed to withstand the Federal onslaught until relieved by Early's brigade.
*Below:* The Union army began an orderly retreat which became a rout when the civilian bystanders panicked.

loss of his experience would be obvious in many subsequent command decisions and placed much of the decision-making power in McClellan's hands. The West Virginia campaign had focussed public attention on McClellan. In spite of the fact that his subordinate officers were truly responsible for the victories achieved in that campaign, McClellan used the newspaper publicity to his own advantage. Claiming that he alone was responsible for the winning strategy, tactics, and execution, McClellan went so far as to dub himself the 'New Napoleon.'

Little action of any consequence took place during the remainder of the year in that eastern arena. Although many attempts were made to establish a Union stronghold across the Potomac in Virginia, each met with failure. Confidence within the army was visibly shaken and although it had been thought that Mc-Clellan would be the solution to their problems, his results were disputable. To his credit McClellan was a genius at administration and organization. He demonstrated great skill in converting the eastern forces into the organized body of men known as the Army of the Potomac.

The railroads faced continual sabotage by both armies.

McClellan and his staff implemented training programs and gave true cohesion to the divisions being formed from the new recruits who filtered into the capital. He concentrated on establishing a supply system which would not only maintain the large force but which could travel with the army, ensuring that the troops did not lack equipment, uniforms or food.

By the end of October, although the army appeared well organized, many were beginning to question whether or not its commanding general intended to use it to fight the enemy. Most Confederate commanders began to view McClellan as some sort of Northern joke, referring to him simply as 'George.' The 'New Napoleon' did not seem to possess the fighting spirit that the name implied.

During that first year the war in the West, which was primarily confined to the state of Missouri, had been set in motion. The division of that state centered around the Southern sympathies of its governor and the Northern sympathies of leading congressman Francis P Blair and a captain in the US Army, Nathaniel Lyon. Northern support in Missouri was stronger than its Southern counterpart, due in part to the prompt action taken by Captain Lyon in the opening days of the war.

Before Southern sympathizers could

seize any of the state's arsenals, Lyon had blocked their attempts by seizing the supplies himself. There were many accusations that Lyon was overreacting to the situation. One particular incident involved the capture of Camp Jackson and some 700 Southern volunteers. The fall of the camp was of little consequence, but the following day Lyon's troops fired on a crowd of Confederate sympathizers, killing 28 men, women and children. The severity of the incident drove a deep wedge between the opposing factions in the state of Missouri.

By May 1861 the area around St Louis had been secured by the Northern supporters, and in June, Lyon had been promoted to brigadier general. During that month he defeated a Confederate force in a small engagement near Boonville. Boonville itself was of minor military significance, but the victory destroyed the hopes of the Southern Rights Activists' ability to swing enough political or military weight for Missouri to secede from the Union.

After Boonville, Lyon moved south to Springfield. Further south Confederate forces under Major General Sterling Price were assembling. Although Price commanded nearly twice as many troops, his army was almost entirely equipped with weapons brought from their own homes.

Nathaniel Lyon, a Union captain, led raids on Federal arsenals in Missouri to prevent their seizure by Confederate sympathizers.

Lyon and Blair's foresight in seizing the arsenals increased Price's difficulties. It was even reported that some of Price's units were not armed at all.

Artillery was another major concern for the Confederate commander. His batteries were composed of guns of every conceivable caliber, making it almost impossible to adequately supply the batteries with proper ammunition. Perhaps his gravest problem lay in the morale of his troops. They suffered greatly from a lack of confidence which had resulted from Lyon's ability to anticipate, outmaneuver and overpower all Confederate attempts. His exploits had become legendary throughout Missouri. Price was faced with the task of securing a desperately needed victory, or at the very least causing Lyon's forces to lose some of their momentum.

On 1 August Lyon received information that a large Confederate force was situated near Dug Springs, directly south of his own position. Lyon moved his troops immediately, hoping to catch the numerically superior Southern army off guard. If he could soundly defeat that army he could move against the other Confederate forces known to be operating in southern Missouri.

Throughout early August, Union and Confederate troops engaged in minor skirmishes as the opposing commanders vied for the best possible location from which to stage their own particular battle plans. On 10 August, Lyon and Price finally faced each other for what would become known as the Battle of Wilson's Creek. The strategies of each commander were basic. Price intended to hold the Oak Hills area, forcing Lyon to take the initiative. Lyon divided his army into two main assault groups. He sent 1200 men and six artillery pieces under Colonel Franz Sigel's command to swing around Price's right flank and approach the Confederate army from the rear. Lyon himself would then stage a frontal attack with the remainder of the army.

It was not long before Lyon sensed that the situation might develop into a costly stalemate. After driving Sigel's forces from the battlefield, Price turned his full attention to Lyon's frontal assault. The Confederate cavalry swept toward the Union lines. General Lyon, accompanying the 1st Iowa Regiment at that time, led a party of men to meet the attack. In so doing he was mortally wounded. Fighting continued for a short time but eventually Union troops were forced to retreat. Union domination of Missouri was halted and the pendulum swung in favor of the Confederacy.

In the middle of the conflicts in both the East and West, one state clung desperately to the hope of neutrality. Like the other states which bordered the new Confederacy, Kentucky and its inhabitants were divided in their sentiments. Socially, Kentucky was bound to the agrarian traditions of the South. Economi-

The Union losses at the Battle of Wilson's Creek totalled 1235, including General Lyon.

Brigadier General Franz Sigel, USA, a German immigrant, trained at Karlsruhe and served in the rebellious army in the German Revolution of 1848.

1861 were ended, punctuated by minor activity between the Union and Confederate armies. However Lincoln also ordered a naval blockade of the Southern coastline. In the early days the Northern press had put great emphasis on the fact that the Union navy was blockading Southern ports, prohibiting the South from trading with or being supported by European countries. Such propaganda encouraged Northerners in the belief in a swift victory. It was soon apparent however that the isolation attempt was a blockade in name only. The Union Navy was ill-equipped and unprepared for the duties it was called upon to perform. At best the navy could merely inconvenience Southern shipping between its European and home ports. Southern newspapers, particularly those in Richmond and Charleston, openly ridiculed the meager attempts. They scoffed at the idea of the Union navy blockading the entire coast-

cally, the state was influenced by the industrial strengths of Pennsylvania, Ohio and Indiana. Although the state attempted to remain officially neutral, many young Kentuckians went to war, on both sides.

Until September both the Union and the Confederacy tolerated Kentucky's position. However on 3 September a Confederate army commanded by Major General Leonidas K Polk seized the Missis-

*Harper's Weekly* mocked the Union Secretary of the Navy Gideon Welles for his inability to stop the blockade runners.

sippi River city of Columbus, Kentucky. Kentucky was forced to decide whether it would openly declare itself for one cause or the other, or protest to the new Confederate government over the behavior of its general in seizing the town. The decision was a division similar to the one in Missouri. The governor declared his support of the Confederacy while the majority of legislators favored the Union.

As a result of Polk's initial action a Union brigadier general, Ulysses S Grant, seized the town of Paducah, Kentucky. The remainder of the year was spent vying for advantageous positions within the divided state with little actual conflict between the opposing armies.

For the most part the land campaigns of

line, considering such efforts of little consequence or cause for alarm to the Confederate cause. Although the Union navy was small and undisciplined there was indeed a naval presence. The Confederacy had no naval force whatsoever. In future the combined efforts of the Union army and navy would be a force to reckon with, becoming increasingly important as the war progressed.

As the year drew to a close neither the Union nor the Confederacy had a clear advantage. Lines of opposition were being drawn, strengths were being measured, and strategies were being formulated. All indications augured a long and bitter conflict ahead.

*Below:* The Battle of Wilson's Creek marked the opening of the war in the west.
*Left:* The Union naval blockade of the Southern ports was ineffective in the early years of the war.

General Grant attacked at Shiloh as Beauregard retreated. The casualties on both sides were high, and the battle was considered a draw.

# THE RISING TIDE (1862)

January 1862 found the North and South tentatively exploring the enemies positions. Confederate operations included Jackson's campaign into West Virginia, to destroy and disrupt the Federal lines of communication. Although there was seldom any conflict during this offensive, three important factors were brought to light. First, Jackson was moving his force with relative ease over long distances, through inclement weather. His training programs were indeed showing results in the behavior of his troops. Second, his disruption of rail and telegraph lines was hindering Union communication. To a certain degree that not only increased the confusion but influenced the Union's ability to set a definite policy for cooperation between the commanders in the East and West. Finally, Jackson's forces managed to capture large quantities of the military

The capture of Fort Donelson in February 1862 was an early victory for Ulysses S Grant. Grant demanded an unconditional surrender of the fort.

supplies so desperately needed by the South.

At the height of this offensive the Confederate Secretary of War Leroy Pope Walker inexplicably changed Jackson's orders, demanding that he cease operations and return to Winchester, Virginia. The sudden change nullified the gains which had been made by Jackson's army, and the recall confused and angered Jackson. He could neither understand the reason for the abrupt change nor why such orders had been sent directly to him and not through the chain of command via General Joseph Johnston. So infuriated was Jackson over the set-back in his operations and the manner in which the recall occurred that he resigned from the army.

Although that incident was of minor significance, the implications were crucial at that particular time. Both Union and Confederate commanders suffered from the meddling of politicians and the powerful influences of persons outside the military. What happened to Jackson was not an isolated incident but occurred all too

frequently to the officers of both armies. However, since Jackson was such a respected figure, his resignation brought the issue to a head in the South. The Confederate government realized that the military and the populace would not tolerate such interference with its generals. From that time on a concerted effort was made to keep matters of strategy and the mechanics of war in the hands of the professionals, and away from the politicians whose whims and viewpoints were so easily swayed.

Through the combined efforts of both the government of Virginia and General Johnston, Jackson was persuaded to withdraw his resignation and resume command of his forces. A much needed lesson was well learned by the Confederacy with a minimum of damage. Northern generals were less fortunate and the adverse effects of an overabundance of meddling in military affairs would continue well into 1863. The rapid succession of commanders and the conflicting strategies were clearly evidence of that interference.

During that first month of 1862 Confederate forces were again defeated in a battle at Mill Springs, Kentucky. Although less than 4000 troops participated in that action, eastern Kentucky was 'effectively secured' by the Union. By February parts of western Kentucky had also succumbed to the combined operations of river assaults, led by Commodore Andrew H Foote, and the forces of Brigadier General U S Grant, who sailed up the Tennessee River and captured Fort Henry. The fort surrendered on 6 February, though much of the garrison escaped to Fort Donelson on the Cumberland River.

The situation was critical, prompting the Confederate commander in the West, General Albert Sidney Johnston, to send reinforcements in an attempt to bolster the Confederate position at Fort Donelson. In spite of the fact that the last key fortification was at stake, Johnston seemed more preoccupied with extracting his troops from central Kentucky. The command at Fort Donelson was left much to

chance as three Confederate generals appeared at the scene, all of whom lacked the experience and confidence necessity demanded. The command ultimately fell to General John B Floyd, former Secretary of War under President James Buchanan. Although a well-known figure, Floyd's inability to be assertive in leadership would eventually lead to defeat.

In less than one week the Union army and river fleet had isolated the fort, applying the same basic strategy used at Fort Henry. However, their attempt to achieve capitulation through an extensive naval bombardment led to near disaster as the heavy guns of Fort Donelson inflicted serious damage on the Union gunboats. As the Union forces regrouped, the garrison made a bold attempt to break

*Right:* John B Floyd, the Confederate Commander at Fort Donelson had been Secretary of War in President Buchanan's Cabinet.
*Below:* At the Battle of Pea Ridge, the Confederate losses were four times that of the Union. The Confederates were led by Earl Van Dorn and the Union by Samuel Curtis.

out and lift the siege. Had a more competent leader commanded the Confederate troops such an attack would have had a far greater chance of success. As it was, the assault was repelled.

With his one attempt thwarted, Floyd decided that the situation was lost. After holding council with General Gideon J Pillow and Brigadier General S B Buckner, Floyd decided to evacuate his brigade via steamboat. He believed himself to be too important to risk capture, owing to his former position as secretary of war and the treason charges pending against him in Washington. Pillow, second in command at the fort, decided that he too would evacuate, leaving the task of surrender to General Buckner. On 16 February Buckner surrendered Fort Donelson, its 11,000 men, and 40 heavy guns to General Grant.

The victory resulted in Grant's promotion to major general and A S Johnston's removal of the Confederate army to Murfreesboro, Tennessee. Southern hopes for the successful defense of Kentucky were crushed and with Johnston's retreat Union troops could march as far as Nashville without interference.

In early March a decisive Union victory, the Battle of Pea Ridge, Arkansas meant an end to Confederate hopes for the recapture of Missouri and served to deepen the gloom felt within the Southern states.

The battle between the *Monitor* (USA) and the *Virginia* (CSA), rebuilt from the *Merrimac*, marked the first combat between ironclad vessels.

It seemed that everywhere Union forces were on the move. On the Atlantic coast Union forces in conjunction with the navy occupied St Augustine, Florida and seized Roanoke Island and New Bern, North Carolina. Although no great territorial gains were made by such coastal actions, they served to demonstrate the Union's ability to successfully strike against the Confederate coast.

Early March was also the time of another naval engagement. Although the battle between the *Monitor* and the *Merrimac* at Hampton Roads off Norfolk, Virginia was a draw, it demonstrated that ironclads were the vessels of the future and that the era of wooden naval ships was at an end.

That same month the Army of the Potomac, under General McClellan's command, took up a position in the region of Yorktown and Fort Munroe, Virginia, and began the Peninsular Campaign, the goal of which was the capture of the Confederate capital, Richmond. Later in March Jackson's forces were defeated, at the Battle of Kernstown. However, Jackson attained a strategic victory by keeping General Nathaniel Bank's Union troops in West Virginia. Banks was thus unable to break off and employ his forces in the Washington defense and free troops for McClellan's Richmond Campaign.

At the same time another sector of the Union army rocked with uncertainty. After Grant's victory at Fort Donelson, his immediate superior, Major General Henry W Halleck, claimed that it was he

Major General Don Carlos Buell, USA, commanded the Union Army of the Ohio.

and not Grant who had initiated the winning strategy. He accused Grant of neglect of duty, inefficiency, drunkenness and disobedience to orders. Only one of those claims, disobedience, had any foundation of truth. It was said that Halleck sent orders which Grant failed to reply to or take action upon. Grant claimed that he never received the telegraphed orders. One explanation was that a Confederate spy intercepted the orders and fled with

them to his superiors. More likely, Grant did receive the orders but felt that no action was necessary.

There had never been any love lost between the two officers. Before the war Grant was known to have referred to Halleck as an 'emptiness surrounded by education,' while Halleck could not even bring himself to congratulate Grant on the Fort Donelson victory. During the confrontation in March, General Halleck sent an urgent message concerning Grant to General McClellan, McClellan replied that Halleck should pursue measures in the best interest of the army. From Halleck's perspective those measures resulted in Grant's immediate arrest, the loss of his command and replacement by Brigadier General C F Smith.

Shortly after the Union command structure was again revised and Halleck was put in full command of all Union forces in the West, including those of Brigadier General Don Carlos Buell's forces at Nashville which had previously been responsible to General McClellan. By mid-March the army occupied the area around Pittsburg Landing, a site which Brigadier General William T Sherman had selected as a suitable base for raids against the Confederates. At that same time General Smith fell prey to a fatal attack of tetanus. Having no alternate commander available, and because Halleck preferred to command through subordinates he could find culpable, Grant's alleged misbehavior was overlooked and he was reinstated.

By the end of the month Grant had arrived to resume his command at Camp Shiloh, Tennessee. The camp sprawled across the countryside surrounding the Old Shiloh Meeting House and bordered the Tennessee River. The army had not dug itself in nor overly concerned itself with military duties. Everyone, including Grant, seemed convinced that the Confederate morale was broken and that General A S Johnston could not have sufficiently recovered from his recent losses to mount an offensive.

In the West, General Johnston was rapidly losing control of the situation. To bolster the efforts of the army, General Beauregard was transferred from the East with the purpose of reassembling the scattered Confederate forces. Although time was limited, Beauregard managed to assemble an army of more than 40,000 near Corinth, Mississippi by the end of March. To that end he drew together 15,000 men previously commanded by Johnston, 10,000 from General Polk's command, and another 15,000 men from as far away as Texas and the Gulf of Mexico.

With consolidation of those forces, Major General Braxton Bragg was appointed Chief of Staff for the Army of the West. His name was well respected among Southern generals for his abilities in administration and discipline. Both Johnston and Beauregard were aware that although morale of the troops was rising, the army would stand little chance against its Northern counterpart. Johnston struggled to correct the grave situation

concerning supplies and arms. The battlefield had already claimed many lives, yet malnutrition and disease took an even greater toll. Deaths attributed to those causes were increasing at an alarming rate as weakened men easily succumbed to the simplest ailments or the most minor wounds.

While the government in Richmond sought to provide the necessary supplies, arms and ammunition were also in demand. The arms of most of the army more closely resembled a collection of museum pieces than the weapons of a fighting army. To remedy the situation, Johnston's army was given some 18,000 new British rifles which blockade runners had recently brought from Europe. Less than half the total needed, it still could not help but improve the army's fighting capability. Artillery was still lacking and it was only through the capture of Northern weapons that Johnston could hope to fill his army's requirements.

Despite such disheartening circumstances, the Confederate Army was prepared to launch an offensive by the beginning of April. The situation within the Union Army had not gone unnoticed. In the South Beauregard urged Johnston to attack the Shiloh encampment and upon hearing that General Buell's forces had left Nashville to join Grant, became

The battle of Shiloh began with sniping by both sides, before the first massive Confederate attack. The Union was taken by surprise despite the previous skirmishes.

insistent that Johnston begin his offensive before the two Northern armies could unite. Beauregard chose 3 April as the day for the attack on the Union camp. However, through mismanagement and the effects of a spring storm, the attack was delayed until the morning of 6 April.

Johnston's plan was to catch Grant's forces by surprise and destroy them before they could evacuate across the river. Upon successful elimination of Grant's forces, Johnston intended to move against Buell's army. In that manner Johnston could effectively open the way to Kentucky and Tennessee.

As the Confederate forces began to move into position on 5 April they encountered skirmishers. Beauregard was certain that such activities meant his intentions had been discovered by the Union command, but Johnston refused to turn back. Surprisingly enough, neither Grant nor Sherman believed an attack was imminent and Grant himself was away attending a strategy planning session with Admiral Foote. Only one Union commander, Brigadier General Benjamin A Prentiss, whose division consisted of raw recruits, felt uneasy enough to assign pickets to a perimeter one and a half miles from camp.

At dawn on Sunday, 6 April, 40,000 Confederate soldiers, drawn up in four massive consecutive lines, attacked the camp at Shiloh. Although it seemed impossible after the sniping of the previous day, Union forces were indeed taken completely by surprise. The only alarm was that raised by the gunfire of Prentiss' pickets as the Confederate troops bore down on them from the forest.

Hastily the five Union divisions at Shiloh made efforts to form up and repel the attack. Troops under Sherman and Prentiss were the first to take the brunt of the Confederate assault. Although Sherman's forces stubbornly formed around Shiloh Church, Prentiss' recruits held their ground only briefly, giving way under a combined flank and frontal assault.

By nine in the morning both Sherman's and Prentiss' camps had been taken in the initial Confederate assault. Union troops fell back to secondary lines along the Purdy and Hamburg River Roads. By that time the firing had alerted the remaining

three divisions as well as a sixth division commanded by Major General L E W Wallace, camped five miles downstream at Crump's Landing, and the advance guard of Buell's army.

Even after reaching the camp Grant was unconvinced that he had an authentic battle on his hands. He remained confident that Johnston would not risk a full-scale attack on the Union encampment, but within the hour both forces were totally committed to battle. On the far right Union flank General Sherman's division was stretched along the Purdy

*Below:* A few weeks after the capture of Island No 10, Farragut captured New Orleans and opened the mouth of the Mississippi to Federal gunboats. *Right:* In March 1862 McClellan began his Peninsular Campaign to attack Richmond.

Road. Beside him the divisions of Major General John A McClernand and Brigadier General W H L Wallace were forming at Duncan and Ross Fields, next to the divisions of General Prentiss and Brigadier General Stephen A Hurlbut. The far left flank was being maintained by the scattered independent brigades of both W H L Wallace's and General Sherman's divisions. For the most part the defenses of the entire front were set along sunken roads, low hills, and dense thickets.

Confederate forces continued to surge forward in almost continuous waves. The Union position appeared hopeless. Although Union commanders had managed to set up a secondary line of defense, the morale of their troops had been severely reduced. The Confederate soldiers sensed victory. Johnston estimated that the battle would be quickly won by shifting his troops and directing them more fully against the Union left flank. He considered the forces under Sherman and McClernand no longer a serious threat to his army. In repositioning his force Johnston encountered staunch resistance at a point which the Confederates nicknamed 'The Hornet's Nest', where the Rebel attack

The loss of Island No 10 by the Confederates was the start of the Union campaign to capture the Mississippi River and split the Confederacy.

was opposed by the divisions of Hurlbut, Wallace and Prentiss.

The Hornet's Nest was the scene of one of the epic battles of the war. Johnston realized that securing that sector would bring about Grant's defeat. To achieve that end Bragg's forces attacked that position no less than 12 separate times. The battle raged with neither side accomplishing much beyond the wholesale slaughter of troops. Engrossed in the assault, Johnston himself was drawn into the combat area, leading multiple assaults into the Peach Orchard adjacent to the Hornet's Nest in efforts to dislodge Hurlbut's forces. So intent was Johnston that he and his aides failed to realize that he had in fact been severely wounded in the knee. Upon returning from an assault, Johnston grew suddenly pale, reeled in his saddle, and slumped over his horse's neck. He died that afternoon, having literally bled to death. The blood from an arterial wound had flowed unnoticed into his high boots. Ironically a field tourniquet, several of which he carried in his personal effects, could have saved his life if applied soon enough.

As Johnston lay dying the Confederate forces were regrouping for another assault on the position between Hurlbut and Prentiss. Beauregard assumed command and feeling that there was still a strong possibility of victory in that sector kept

the demoralizing news of Johnston's death a secret. An hour later Bragg was mounting another attack, employing no less than 60 artillery pieces to pound at the defenses.

In spite of the apparent stalemate at the Hornet's Nest, the Union flanks were beginning to falter. The weight of the Confederate advance had snapped the morale of Sherman's units and Hurlbut's force was left dangerously exposed in the Peach Orchard. Wallace's troops were also beginning to succumb to the Confederate pressure. However, Grant would not give up hope. He knew that fresh troops were on their way to reinforce the position and decided that he could delay by falling back to Pittsburg Landing. He would stretch the army to its limits to make a last ditch attempt to halt the Confederate advance.

While the rest of the army began its withdrawal Prentiss faced the fact that his position at the Hornet's Nest was no longer defensible and at four-thirty in the afternoon he and 2200 Union troops surrendered to the Confederates. At almost that same time W H L Wallace was killed as he led a break-out via Tillman's Creek in an attempt to rejoin the bulk of the army. Confederate forces trapped the confused Union soldiers in the ravine, shooting them down unmercifully. That ravine was later named 'Hell's Hollow.'

However the sacrifices of Prentiss and Wallace and their men were not in vain. With their lives and honor they bought Grant the precious time he needed.

As the situation seemed in danger of collapsing, another break in favor of the Union army occurred. The Confederate forces which had been hammering at the Hornet's Nest ran out of ammunition and had to await supplies before pursuing their attack. The two-hour delay caused by that supply shortage gave Grant more time to arrange his hasty defense. It also resulted in a loss of momentum and a degree of disorientation for the Confederates. Two brigades who found themselves out ahead of the main troop body attacked the Union guns supporting Pittsburg Landing. Virtually out of ammunition and near exhaustion from more than 12 hours of combat, the brigades managed to capture the guns only to be driven back by the vanguard of Buell's forces and the heavy fire of Union gunboats on the river.

Disregarding the factor of decreased momentum Bragg ordered preparations for a massive assault on the Pittsburg Landing defenses. To the astonishment of the Union troops and command the assault never materialized. Beauregard had vetoed the attack, deciding that nothing more could be gained at that time, and preferring to consolidate his

forces for the next day. Beauregard did not realize that Grant's defending force had been reduced to barely 7000. By morning however, he would be reinforced by both Major General L E W Wallace and Major General Don Carlos Buell, bringing his command to 25,000 strong as opposed to Beauregard's remaining 20,000.

On 7 April Grant counterattacked without success. Confederate forces stubbornly held the battlefield they had gained the previous day. By two o'clock in the afternoon Grant considered that he had little to gain by pursuing the attack, yet he remained undecided about his next course of action and in ignorance of the actual strength of his enemy.

Again fortune favored the Union. Less than half an hour after Grant began to consider abandoning the struggle, Beauregard decided that the chance of victory was lost and ordered his army to retreat from the battlefield. Watching the Confederate withdrawal General Sherman is said to have remarked, 'We had had quite enough of their society for two days and were glad to be rid of them on any terms.' For the Union those terms were not victory, nor could the Confederacy make that claim. Beauregard had chosen to leave the battlefield of his own accord rather than be driven from it by his opponent.

Shiloh was the scene of the first epic bloody land battle of the Civil War. Total casualties for both armies approached 24,000, including General A S Johnston the highest ranking officer to meet his death in battle during the war. As reports of the engagement reached Northern and Southern newspapers the populace were stunned by the details of horror and bloodshed, particularly at the Hornet's Nest, where fighting had been most vicious. It was said that the bodies of Union and Confederate soldiers were so numerous that one could walk over the entire battlefield and never set foot on the ground.

The outcome of Shiloh pointed the way to a long and bloody conflict ahead. More specifically it tempered the Union army in the West into one of the best fighting forces to date, and Beauregard's retreat opened the door to the entire Mississippi Basin.

The situation appeared extremely grim for the Confederacy in the West. Not only had they suffered a severe setback in the land campaign, but on the second day of battle Commodore Andrew Foote, with the aid of a military force commanded by Major General John Pope, succeeded in capturing the important Confederate fortification known as Island No 10. The loss of the highly effective batteries located on the island meant the opening of the Mississippi River to Union gunboat traffic.

After the success at Shiloh, 'Old Brains' as Halleck was known to his men, took command of the independent armies in the West. He consolidated them into

one force of nearly 128,000 men and marched from the region of Shiloh toward Corinth, Mississippi to engage what remained of the Southern army in that area. Short of actual command experience in battlefield situations, and cautious by nature, Halleck marched toward Corinth haltingly, squandering time digging-in after each day's march. His army did not reach Corinth until the end of May, by which time Beauregard's army had recovered and withdrawn from the area.

In late April as Halleck marched, Admiral David G Farragut struck at the mouth of the Mississippi and captured New Orleans. The victory opened the river to Union shipping from the Gulf to Vicksburg and was yet another example of the precarious position which was developing for the Confederacy in the West.

April and May of 1862 were dark days for the Confederacy. With Halleck's capture of Corinth and Farragut's possession of a large section of the Mississippi River, the South was in danger of being split in half. The entire Mississippi River basin was at stake and Union commanders were prepared to force the issue. Chattanooga was threatened. Memphis fell quickly. The only segment of the river still controlled by Confederate forces lay between Vicksburg and Port Hudson.

In spite of the odds in his favor, Halleck chose to divide his force. Rather than using a strong superior army to crush the Confederate resistance, Halleck scattered his troops in a multitude of individual campaigns. His decision accomplished nothing, and it allowed the Confederate army to again take an initiative against the smaller Union forces.

Through July and August Confederate cavalry under Colonels Morgan and Nathan Bedford Forrest struck at the Union supply lines. In mid-August Major General Kirby Smith won a key battle at Richmond, Kentucky, swinging momentum once more in favor of the South. A change in the Confederate command structure also occurred in August with the promotion of General Bragg to replace General Beauregard. Bragg's immediate reaction was to capitalize on Smith's victory in Kentucky by following up the attack and maintaining the momentum of the offensive. Only Grant and Sherman, who held western Tennessee and parts of Arkansas, appeared to hold their own during that time. Everything which had been so expensively gained at Shiloh was being allowed to slip away through Halleck's over-cautious tactics.

By the end of 1862 the Union progress made at Shiloh had been forfeited. The Confederate army in the West had recovered sufficiently enough that the bitterly contested war in the West was turning into a stalemate rather than the obvious Union victory which Shiloh had augured.

The West was not the only arena in

One of the major battles of the Peninsular Campaign, the battle of Williamsburg cost the Union forces over 2000 casualties.

Lincoln and his staff equally feared that a Confederate attack on Washington, would crush the North, and the Union would be in danger of collapse regardless of how favorably the war in the West was progressing.

To avoid that possibility Lincoln refused to allow McClellan to take some 150,000 troops for the Peninsular Campaign which McClellan felt were essential to overwhelm the Confederate army around Richmond. McClellan was convinced that he needed a large majority for a decisive victory and decided to rearrange the military disposition accordingly. He decided that a large portion of the troops in West Virginia were to march from their locations to reinforce Washington and allow McClellan the reinforcements for his army. At the same time Lincoln began to question the strategy behind McClellan's campaign, considering that the more conventional land route should be employed. That way troops could be easily drawn from West Virginia and the capital for the offensive, while at the same time representing a sufficient force to keep Washington out of jeopardy. Although this was a sounder military approach, McClellan believed wholeheartedly in his Peninsula strategy, perhaps because the success of his plan would bring him the most fame and glory.

McClellan failed to realize that in leaving Washington he was no longer in command of the troops of the capital. He left the city supreme commander of the Army of the Potomac, but Lincoln relieved him of his command of the capital city, indicating not only Lincoln's lack of confidence but his displeasure with McClellan's attitude.

which the war continued to rage fiercely. In the East General McClellan was concentrating on Lincoln's primary objective, Richmond. In March of 1862 the Army of the Potomac had been moved by water to Fort Monroe, on the peninsula below Richmond. The distance between Fort Monroe and Richmond was less than that from Washington to the Confederate capital and it was felt that that approach had certain advantages. Primarily the Confederate defenders had not positioned their forces to ward off a massive assault from that direction. The Confederate command would be forced to stretch the available troops to cover the new threat while at the same time maintaining an adequate defense of the more traditional avenues of approach. Union armies were now to be found in West Virginia, Washington and the Peninsula, and the Confederate command could never be certain of the direction from which the main offensive would come. Union hopes were to catch the defenders off guard and succeed in attaining a rapid victory.

Matters were still in favor of the Union in the East during early spring and Lincoln and his generals believed that an overwhelming victory and the capture of Richmond would sound the death knell for the Confederate States. However, the scheme had several significant inherent disadvantages. Convinced that the fall of Richmond would doom the Confederacy,

*Above:* Major General Richard Stoddart Ewell, CSA, (1817–72) led a division under 'Stonewall' Jackson throughout the Seven Days battle.
*Below:* Jackson's 'Foot Cavalry' harried the Union forces in the Shenandoah Valley throughout the early summer of 1862.

Although the Peninsular Campaign was one of the major campaigns of 1862, a smaller military sideshow was beginning in the Shenandoah Valley of Virginia which would not only deny McClellan essential troops and disrupt his time schedule, but would develop into one of the most remarkable campaigns of modern history. That particular arena would become known as Jackson's Valley Campaign. For three months, with a minimal force, Jackson managed to tie up an overwhelming number of Union troops, prohibiting them from participating in the defense of Washington or McClellan's offense on Richmond. Not only did Jackson inflict considerable casualties on the Union forces but in doing so convinced the Union command that a Confederate contingent of considerable size ruled the valley and threatened the capital. In addition Jackson managed to retire from the valley in time to aid in the defense of Richmond.

Operating from the Winchester area Jackson commanded a force of approximately 4200 men, opposing Major General Bank's army of 20,000. Although Jackson would later be reinforced the Union would retain a superiority of almost three to one. Basically the Valley Campaign was a succession of five major battles. Although each was in itself important, it was the overall effect of the campaign on the Union command and strategy which held the greatest significance.

The confrontation began in March as General Banks attempted to dislodge Jackson's forces from the valley and proceed to the defense of Washington thereby freeing McClellan's total forces for the Peninsular Campaign. Jackson's strategy was to keep Banks occupied as much as possible so that some degree of pressure was removed from the Richmond defenders. General Joseph E Johnston, commander of the Army of Northern Virginia in the defense of the Confederate capital, counted on Jackson to buy him the time necessary to develop an adequate defense against McClellan. The extent of Union superiority hinged on Jackson's success or defeat in the valley. If Banks swept aside Jackson's force it would mean that McClellan would achieve a three to one superiority over the Confederate defenders making the fall of Richmond a distinct possibility.

The campaign opened as General Nathaniel Banks surged into the Shenandoah Valley. Jackson tactically withdrew to give Banks the impression that the presence of the large Union army had forced the Confederates to abandon the area. Assuming precisely that, Banks began to move troops out of the valley toward Washington. At the same time Lincoln, who had held McDowell's corps in reserve in the capital, prepared to release them to join McClellan.

On 23 March Jackson struck north against Banks near Kernstown. After a fierce, daylong struggle Jackson was forced to remove from the battlefield. It was a Confederate defeat, but only on the tactical level. Banks could not believe that Jackson would risk such an attack unless considerable reinforcements were close at hand and recalled the troops which had begun their march toward Washington. Consequently, Lincoln, realizing the vulnerability of the capital, recalled McDowell's corps. He even went so far as to send one of McDowell's divisions to reinforce Banks. Although suffering a defeat, Jackson had succeeded in his strategic purpose of binding Banks' army to their present position.

By the beginning of May it was abundantly clear that the threat of Jackson must be removed if McClellan's campaign was to have any hope of success. The Union command embarked on a two-pronged attack against Jackson's forces. Once again Banks marched down the valley, while Major General John C Frémont, Union commander in West Virginia, led his command south toward Staunton at the southern end of the valley. Jackson, grasping their intentions, decided to attempt an artful deception. After receiving reinforcements in the form of Major General R S Ewell's division Jackson left a small force behind to counter Banks' offensive and moved the remainder of his army toward Richmond, as if giving-up the valley as a lost cause. So keen was his deception that even his own troops became convinced that Richmond was their destination. Disappointed by the apparent retreat the Confederate troops boarded trains disheartened by the fact that they were no longer defending their homes but were being committed to the defense of Richmond.

To their confusion the troop trains headed west rather than east, as Jackson set his attack on Frémont in motion. Surprise and joy were not confined to the troops when they disembarked at Staunton but were equally evident in the local citizens who had believed they had been deserted.

On 8 May, just outside the town of McDowell, Jackson's men attacked Frémont's army and soundly defeated it. After the battle Jackson's pursuit of the Union forces was so aggressive that the army managed to escape only after setting fire to the forest through which it retreated. Frémont returned to West Virginia.

At the opposite end of the valley and in Washington, preparations had again been undertaken for the movement of troops. Banks transferred a portion of his troops to the defense of Washington, and Lincoln, believing that all was secure, again allowed McDowell to march toward Richmond. Banks expected Jackson to make some move against him yet remained confident. However, when on 23 May Jackson attacked the small Union garrison at Front Royal, Banks was astounded.

Major General John Pope was typical of the second-rate commanders who plagued the Union army in the early years of the war.

He could not believe that Jackson's troops could have made such a march with such speed and became convinced that there had to be another Confederate force in the area. Banks retreated to make a stand at Winchester. Two days later his force was effectively defeated by Jackson, forcing him to flee across the Potomac River.

Jackson realized that pursuit and the possible destruction of his enemy would mean a great deal to the current situation and crossed the Potomac on Banks' heels. This action so alarmed the people of Washington that Lincoln again recalled McDowell's corps from its march to Richmond, sending half the corps to stabilize Banks' force and aid in subduing the Confederate army in the Valley. Again the troops which Banks had freed for the defense of Washington were ordered to rejoin their commander. Frémont was ordered to halt his retreat and immediately return to the valley, at Manassas Gap. There he was to link with Banks' division returning from Washington.

In the middle of the confusion Jackson's strategy was working beautifully, as an increasing number of troops were being drawn into the Valley Campaign and away from McClellan and Washington. With two major columns converging the Union command was confident that Jackson could not outmaneuver them.

On 8 June Jackson detached a division of troops to hold Frémont at Cross Keys. The following day he swung his remaining forces against General James Shields' eastern column as it approached to rendezvous with Frémont. In the Battle of Port Republic Jackson forced Shields to abandon his rendezvous and retreat northward. The resulting mass confusion enabled Jackson to slip from the Valley unnoticed to lend support to the battle for Richmond's defense.

Jackson's Valley strategy succeeded brilliantly allowing him to defend the Confederate capital, while not one of the Union units which fought against him ever managed to aid McClellan's attack on Richmond. The campaign earned Jackson's soldiers the title of 'Foot Cavalry' because of the speed with which they had maneuvered from one end of the valley to the other.

On 13 May several days after Jackson's confrontation with Frémont at McDowell, Confederate forces under General J E Johnston engaged the Union army at the Battle of Seven Pines. Not only were the Confederate forces defeated but Johnston sustained a wound which many believed would prove fatal. President Davis was faced with the task of finding a new commander to replace Johnston. He logically turned to the man who had been his military advisor. On 1 June 1862 General Robert E Lee became the new commander of the Army of Northern Virginia.

Lee was presented with a critical situation. If he were unsuccessful in stopping McClellan it could signify the end of the Confederacy. With little time in hand Lee began strengthening the fortifications around Richmond, sending a desperate plea for reinforcements from the Carolinas and Georgia. While Jackson stalled for time in the Shenandoah Valley, Lee sought the aid of another officer, the renowned cavalry commander Brigadier General J E B Stuart. Stuart would assist, as Jackson did, giving Lee the precious time he needed by harassing and raiding Union supply lines. Stuart's raids also screened Lee's activities with such success that McClellan and his staff had little first-hand information about Lee's plans. Ironically, Stuart's activities pitted him against his own father-in-law, Brigadier General Philip Cooke, a Union cavalry commander in McClellan's army.

By the end of June Lee had consolidated as many troops as possible in the Richmond area, including Jackson's forces which had by then arrived from the Shenandoah Valley. Lee's forces remained heavily outnumbered by McClellan's army. Rather than attack that force head on Lee would take advantage of the manner in which McClellan had chosen to place his troops.

The Chickahominy River divided McClellan's army. McClellan, still awaiting McDowell's corps, had placed Brigadier General Fitz John Porter's corps on the north bank to link with McDowell. The remaining four corps covered the area south of the river where he felt initial contact with the Confederate forces would most likely be made.

Lee's strategy was not overly complex. He hoped to effectively eliminate McClellan's army by attacking it piecemeal, beginning with Porter's corps. If he could remove the threat of Porter it would even the odds enough to enable Lee to engage the remainder of the Army of the Potomac with a higher possibility of victory.

On 26 June the engagement known as the Seven Days Battle began. Lee assaulted Porter's corps at Mechanicsville with Major General A P Hill's divisions making a frontal attack against the Union forces. By the second day of battle Union troops had moved to the Beaver Dam Creek where Hill planned to continue his offensive with the support of Jackson's reinforcements. However, events on that second day did not favor the Confederate forces. For the only time during his Civil War career Jackson arrived late, causing the attack to be postponed until afternoon. The delay gave Porter sufficient time to recover and his forces effectively repulsed the Confederate assault. Subsequently Porter was forced to withdraw toward the main army as his forces were facing a Confederate army twice their strength.

By the third day Porter was facing the troops commanded by Hill and Jackson, reinforced by the additional strength of Major General James Longstreet's forces who entered the fray near Gaines Mill. Although Porter was receiving fresh troops, the effects of the battle were taking their toll on his men. As the Union lines began to break Porter decided that the only course open to him was a retreat across the Chickahominy River where he could link with McClellan.

The following day brought little action yet McClellan's army was kept busy. Union supply lines, which had pushed forward before the Confederate offensive, were in complete disarray. McClellan had to find the means of rerouting his supply system before engaging the enemy again.

The final three days of battle McClellan fought a rear guard action as he sought to reach the James River. There he intended to regroup his army and reestablish his lines of supply.

During those three days the battles of Savage's Station, Frayser's Farm, and Malvern Hill took place. The Confederates sought vainly to pierce the Union rear guard, but were repeatedly repulsed. Lee's reckless attack at the Battle of Malvern Hill was unsuccessful, as the Confederate forces assaulted the strong Union position in vain. That failure, coupled with McClellan's continued retreat toward Harrison's Landing, prompted Lee to discontinue his offensive and return shortly thereafter to Richmond.

Although Lee did not emerge unquestionably victorious from the Seven Day Battle several items of extreme importance were accomplished. First and foremost, McClellan's threat to Richmond had been removed. Also, the Confederate forces had managed to capture more than 30,000 small arms and 50 artillery pieces. Perhaps of greatest significance Lee had tackled McClellan's army of more than 100,000 men and had succeeded in driving them back toward Washington. The morale of the Confederate troops had been restored and their confidence in Lee as a leader had been established. No longer were they an army of recruits but veteran troops becoming well versed in the mechanics of war.

The price Lee paid for the concentration of his forces against McClellan was the exposure of Richmond to attack from the north and the unguarded position of northern and western Virginia. Lincoln was quick to attempt to capitalize on the situation. He decided to consolidate the Union forces which had engaged in the Valley Campaign with those remaining in the Washington area into one army. His main problem, which would continue for many months, was to find an efficient, competent leader for the armies. To command this particular new army Lincoln appointed Major General John Pope who had achieved recognition in the West, primarily at the battle involving Island No 10.

Upon Pope's arrival General Frémont, who was senior in rank, resigned in protest over the apparent disregard of his seniority. Pope remained aloof from such 'petty squabbling' and immediately set about reorganizing his command along the lines established in the West. Pope informed his troops that he expected them to perform as professionally and heroically as had his western command, giving the general impression that he viewed the eastern soldiers as far inferior to their western counterparts. Pope also disliked large staffs and headquarters, remarking that 'his headquarters would be in his saddle.' That remark was publicly quoted by the northern press, prompting the South to retaliate that the '. . . only thing Pope could keep in his saddle was his hindquarters. . . .'

Pope's appointment coincided with Lincoln's decision that he needed an experienced military figure as Chief of Staff to help direct policy from Washington. During Jackson's Valley Campaign and McClellan's absence from the capital the Secretary of War had made vain, unsuccessful attempts to coordinate the armies and their actions. Once again Lincoln chose one of the commanders in the West, promoting 'Old Brains' Halleck to the position of Chief of Staff. It was a dubious choice. His exploits in the West had made him a popular figure but the credit for those successes was not truly his, being more rightfully attributed to the high military caliber of his subordinates.

Halleck approached the situation in the East with the same ideas of command and direction which he had applied in the West. He placed greater emphasis on geographical locations and cities rather than on armies. Halleck ascertained that McClellan could not take further action against Richmond from his current position and decided that the Army of the Potomac should return to Washington to unite with Pope's forces, which were located near Culpepper, Virginia. Had Halleck paused to review the entire picture he might have realized that McClellan and Pope had Lee trapped between them. A concerted effort between

Both sides used cavalry for scouting and raids during the Civil War.

the two commanders could have produced a coordinated attack which might have resulted in the destruction of Lee's army and the capture of Richmond.

Learning of the Union activity Lee decided that none of the Union commanders were aggressive enough to attempt an independent action which would counter an offensive Confederate maneuver. It was evident that McClellan would soon be moving from the peninsula, freeing Lee to shift all of his attention on Pope's newly formed army.

In early August Lee sent Jackson with 24,000 troops toward Gordonsville, Virginia. During that time Jackson encountered a segment of Pope's army, at Cedar Mountain. He soundly defeated the Union contingent, driving them back toward Pope's main force. Pope was somewhat surprised by Jackson's aggressive behavior, considering it a great risk, knowing his army to be twice the size of Jackson's force. Pope refused to believe that Lee would dare to leave the Confederate capital undefended to reinforce Jackson. However, it was Lee's intention to wrest the initiative from the Union armies through piecemeal attacks rather than wait for the Union to make its move. Lee and his remaining 30,000 men marched to rendezvous with Jackson. Such consolidation would mean a Confederate advantage which could finish Pope's army. Such a defeat would throw the Union armies around Washington into complete confusion.

Unfortunately for Lee, a Union cavalry detachment, after a minor engagement, almost captured Jeb Stuart. Stuart escaped but the Union cavalry had managed to secure one of his famous plumed hats and the orders and plans for the forthcoming

offensive. The details of that offensive clearly illustrated Pope's precarious position causing him to order an immediate retreat across the Rappahannock River.

At the same time McClellan's army had traveled on the Potomac River from the peninsula to join up with Pope. This consolidation would have placed 100,000 Union troops against Lee's 50,000. For reasons known only to himself, Pope chose not to move beyond his position to Fredericksburg. He felt secure in his location and apparently decided that McClellan could find him easily and bring up reinforcements. There was a flaw in Pope's delaying strategy. While McClellan was indeed drawing nearer, so was Lee.

Lee knew that McClellan was on the march toward Pope's army and decided that he had no alternative but to strike at Pope with the utmost speed. A raid commanded by Jeb Stuart on the Union rear area captured documents detailing Pope's placement and plans. During that raid Stuart also acquired one of Pope's best uniform coats, displaying it proudly as adequate compensation for the earlier loss of his hat.

Using the information thus acquired Lee's initial strategy was to keep Pope off-balance and guessing about the actual location of the Confederate forces. Lee intended to maneuver his army into a position of his own choosing while effectively freezing Pope in his current location.

Lee gambled, again dividing his army into two main forces, one under Jackson's command and the other under his own direction. The strategy called for Jackson to march around Pope's right flank in a wide sweep to assault the rear of the Union army. Lee hoped to entice Pope into attacking Jackson's smaller force, then reunite the Confederate army once Pope was committed to battle.

On 25 August Jackson began his march and by the following day had moved his units nearly 60 miles over poor terrain and through the blistering heat. From Bristow Station, Jackson continued on to Manassas where his troops captured a massive Union supply depot, and for the first time in many months the Confederate soldiers were fed, resupplied and refitted, courtesy of Mr Lincoln's army. Jackson's forces then moved into Manassas and Lee began his support maneuver.

By 27 August Pope was aware of the Confederate activity and prepared to retreat. As his troops began to fall back Pope saw before him a first rate opportunity to crush Jackson's force. With a superior force of four to one Pope decided to move his army to isolate Jackson from any attempted rendezvous or retreat toward Lee. Although Pope's actions were aggressive and appeared well founded, he lacked accurate knowledge of Jackson's actual location. Jackson on the other hand was well aware of Pope's latest move and began once again to exercise his tactical ability. He subtly began to maneuver Pope rather than allowing Pope the choice of battlefields. Jackson's troops openly appeared at Manassas and Centreville inviting Pope's vain attempts to catch the elusive Confederate forces.

Wherever Pope marched Jackson managed to evade him, causing Pope to literally run in circles. Finally on the evening of 28 August Jackson revealed his own location at Groveton by initiating an attack on Pope's forces as they passed in front of the Confederate position. By the morning of 29 August Jackson had positioned himself north of Groveton along what had been the westernmost boundary of the battlefield in the First Battle of Bull Run. Jackson knew that battle must be joined if the Confederate army hoped to defeat Pope before McClellan could arrive with his troop reinforcements.

Jackson had succeeded in placing Pope at a severe disadvantage. Pope's forces had become disorganized and certainly wearied by their fruitless hunting. Jackson also had the advantage of having forced Pope to come to a battle on Confederate terms with an army which lacked consolidation. He also relied on the fact that Pope believed the Confederates to be still in retreat toward Lee's main army, making Pope even less prepared for a Confederate offensive. Jackson only had to hold his army in check as they awaited Lee.

On that morning of 29 August Pope threw his army against Jackson's position. Under the mistaken assumption that Jackson was fighting a rear guard action, Pope sent his troops into the fray as they arrived on the battlefield, convinced that at any time the Confederate resistance would break and the chase would begin again.

In the middle of this engagement Pope

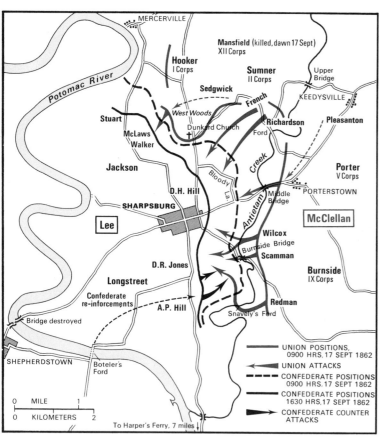

decided to send one corps in an assault on Jackson's right flank. As the Union corps began its attack Lee's forces arrived on the field, taking up a position directly in the path of the intended assault. Thwarted the Union corps commander, General Fitz John Porter, who had fought so valiantly in the Seven Day's Battle, called off the attack and prepared to set up a defensive position to block a possible Confederate counterattack. With daylight fading and the intended assault cancelled the first day of Second Manassas closed in stalemate.

The following day Pope, under the mistaken impression that Lee was retreating, ordered a second assault just north of the Old Warrenton Turnpike. The initial attack met with little success as Confederate artillery drove back the attackers. Union troops reformed and continued the assault, bravely trying to breach the Confederate lines. So rapid and numerous were the assaults that several of Jackson's units, running out of ammunition, resorted to using their muskets as clubs against their attackers. For a moment it seemed that the Union effort would be successful as Jackson's troops began to give way. In the moment of apparent Union triumph, Longstreet's Corps arrived on the scene to bolster the battered Confederate line.

Longstreet's approach revealed that the Union left flank had become exposed and he moved forward to capture Bald Hill, a site of heavy combat during the First Battle of Bull Run. The Union command, aware of their error, rushed troops to Henry House Hill to block Longstreet's advance. The Union position was in danger, for a defeat in that sector would

*Above far right:* Federal artillery taking up a position in the Blue Ridge Mountains.
*Right:* A Company of Union soldiers photographed by Mathew Brady during the Sharpsburg campaign.
*Above:* The Battle of Antietam began with an early morning assault by Hooker's division.

make retreat from the field virtually impossible. To counter the Confederate maneuver troops were pulled from the assault on Jackson's Corps. Jackson in turn quickly took advantage of the situation, launching a bold counterattack which buckled the Union lines.

With Confederate forces on the offensive Pope ordered a withdrawal. For the next three days his forces continued to retreat, stopping only when they were safely behind the defenses of Washington. Once again the battlefield at Manassas had yielded a Confederate victory, not through the superiority of the Confederate army but as a result of a multitude of misconceptions on the part of the Union command. Pope, unwilling to take responsibility for the defeat, blamed the loss on General Porter for failing to execute the initial attack on Jackson's flank. In spite of the fact that Porter would have faced certain destruction at the hands of Lee's reinforcements he was made the scapegoat and was courtmartialed.

Of the more than 70,000 Union troops at Pope's disposal, some 60,000 actually participated in that Second Battle of Manassas. Of that number 14,000 were listed as casualties or prisoners of war. Several thousand small arms and at least 30 heavy guns, including stores appropriated by Jackson's soldiers prior to the battle, were also lost by the Union. Although the figures were a blow to the

The Union attack at the Second Battle of Bull Run was met by Confederate forces commanded by General Lee.

Army of Northern Virginia, Lee had succeeded in keeping Confederate losses below 10,000.

Victory boosted the Confederate morale while that of the Union sank even lower. Capitalizing on his success, Lee took the opportunity to continue his offensive with a drive north. Although McClellan and Pope had suffered from a loss of Union prestige, their combined strengths in the vicinity of Washington were too great for Lee to challenge. Instead Lee launched an offensive north of the Potomac River, for political rather than military reasons. A Confederate victory in the Union territory would create vast repercussions not only in the North and South but internationally as well. Continued success might demonstrate the North's weakness and persuade the European powers, primarily England and France, to aid the Confederate cause and give the Confederacy the recognition it so desperately needed. Another factor was the increased protestations by the Northern Peace Movement to end the war which was becoming ever less profitable and ever more likely to result in a Confederate victory.

With those factors in mind Lee crossed the Potomac near Leesburg. Placing Jackson once more in the lead the Confederate army struck against Frederick, Maryland. It had always been felt in the South that Maryland was sympathetic to the Confederate cause, needing only the incentive of Confederate possession to swing in its

favor. Lee was convinced that large numbers of recruits would flock to his banners, increasing his army as it moved north. This was not the case as only a handful rallied to the Confederate camps. With no mass uprising of support Lee decided to turn his attention elsewhere.

On 9 September Lee issued his famous 'Special Order 191.' Through that directive Lee chose to divide his army into four parts. Three sections were to converge on Harper's Ferry to capture the Union garrison and the supplies located there while the remaining section would march westward across South Mountain. The division of his army not only displayed Lee's supreme confidence in himself and his commanders but illustrated his confidence in his ability to gauge his adversaries' reactions accurately. Knowing McClellan as a commander who was slow to act Lee felt assured that there would be no Union intervention.

Unfortunately for Lee on 13 September a unit of McClellan's troops discovered a copy of Lee's Special Order wrapped around a bundle of cigars at an abandoned campsite. McClellan was therefore aware not only of Lee's intentions but of the exact route his troops would be taking. The division of the army was also apparent and McClellan could see that it would be extremely difficult for any one section to come to the aid of another. The piecemeal destruction of Lee's army was a tempting possibility.

South Mountain appeared to be the key to the situation. If McClellan could move his army through the gap before Lee was aware of the maneuver the Union Army could defeat Lee or at the very least create

such chaos within the Confederate command that Lee would be forced to abandon his northern campaign. In spite of the advantages, McClellan decided to wait until the following morning to initiate any action. In the interim Stuart informed Lee of the possibility that McClellan had come into possession of the missing orders. Lee reacted immediately to block the pass at South Mountain.

On 14 September the battle of Turner's Gap took place with Lee's troops in a concentrated defensive position against the Union forces sent forward under Major General Burnside. Further south Major General W B Franklin marched his Union contingent toward Crampton's Gap where he also encountered considerable Confederate resistance. For the next day and a half Burnside and Franklin assaulted the stubbornly held Confederate positions. In that time Lee managed to keep his forces from suffering a disastrous defeat, in spite of the fact that the 19,000 men he had in the area were no match for McClellan's 90,000 available troops. Lee instituted an immediate withdrawal south with the town of Sharpsburg as his destination. As his forces reached Sharpsburg, Lee received a communication from Jackson informing him of a Confederate victory at Harper's Ferry, and that he would hurry to join Lee.

Upon receipt of that message Lee decided to attempt once again to take the initiative and prepared to give battle there at Sharpsburg. As before, McClellan failed to act swiftly. Had McClellan moved quickly Lee's forces would not have been capable of withstanding the pressure. Instead McClellan waited two days until

17 September, giving Lee not only the time to improve his position but Jackson time to arrive from Harper's Ferry.

The strategy of Lee's Sharpsburg campaign had often been criticized as a dangerously unnecessary gamble. The addition of Jackson's forces gave Lee command of an army which numbered some 40,000, against the 70–90,000 at McClellan's ultimate disposal. Also, Lee placed his army with its back to the Potomac River. That decision has caused many to question Lee's ability to chose a tactical battlefield. Lee formulated his strategy and took up a position facing a Union force twice the size of his own.

Lee was reacting to his knowledge of McClellan's character. McClellan's indecisiveness and apparent inability to carry through an attack may have caused Lee to consider the odds against him offset by his adversary's past record. It was above all a calculated risk. Lee had not given up the hope that a defeat of McClellan might well cause the Union to sue for peace.

In preparation for battle, Lee deployed his troops. His right flank was positioned behind Antietam Creek, although it was easily fordable and could offer little protection for his defending troops. His left flank occupied a wooded area north of Sharpsburg along the Hagerstown Road, which was also not an effective defensible blockade. Between those two flanks lay minor hills and farmland with scattered woods. Truly defensible positions were scarce and to make matters worse, Lee did not actually have the troops to defend the area properly. However the Confederate artillery could be posted on several higher hills east of the town, giving them dominance over the entire area. The army would therefore have the effective support of the artillery at any point on the central battlefield. The Confederate army stood with little defensive protection to the front and the Potomac River at its back. Defeat would most certainly mean the ultimate destruction of the Army of Northern Virginia.

By 16 September as Lee was stationing his troops, McClellan could easily have reached the potential battle site and defeated the divided Confederate army. Instead he continued to edge forward cautiously permitting the three Confederate divisions from Harper's Ferry to arrive. Again McClellan procrastinated, confirming Lee's assessment of McClellan's inadequacies.

By 17 September McClellan was ready to do battle, sending Major General 'Fightin' Joe' Hooker's troops to engage the Confederate left flank. Although Hooker's three divisions fought desperately for more than an hour to overrun the Confederate position and turn the flank, the Confederate troops under Major General John B Hood and Brigadier General Jubal Early held fast. Exhausted by the intense struggle Hooker's corps

began to back away. The Confederate defenders, who had barely repulsed that attack were almost immediately faced with another assault by General Joseph Mansfield's corps further down the line. Again the Southern troops fought toe to toe with their attackers and Mansfield's corps appeared to be making positive progress. As the Confederate line weakened Union troops began a drive to capture Dunker Church and in that attempt General Mansfield himself was killed. Although the battle continued to rage neither side seemed able to gain a clear advantage.

With the situation at the church becoming critical, Lee shifted troops to reinforce the left flank. Confederate artillery maintained an unmerciful assault on the Union forces which appeared to be the only thing which held them at bay.

A lack of ammunition forced Stark's brigade to fight with stones while waiting for support from Longstreet's Corps.

At nine o'clock in the morning the third Union assault on the left flank began as a division of General Edwin Sumner's corps attacked Dunker Church in an attempt to achieve the final breakthrough. It was pure chance which brought Confederate reinforcements, in the form of General Lafayette McLaws' division, to the exact point that Sumner chose to spearhead his attack. McLaws' Division stopped the new Union offense totally, effectively bringing the morning's attack on the Confederate left flank to an end.

Although one of Sumner's divisions had

The Second Battle of Bull Run resulted in a Union defeat and the loss of almost 8000 casualties.

been committed and halted, the remainder of his corps was prepared to strike the center of the Confederate lines. Opposing Sumner's corps were the troops of Major General D H Hill who had taken up a position along a sunken road. Fighting there was even more intense than the fighting which raged on the left flank. Slowly the Union troops began to gain ground and in the face of withering rifle and artillery fire managed to flank the Confederate defenders. As the advance continued Union troops prepared to fire down the sunken road, which had been dubbed 'Bloody Lane,' into the flank of the hard-pressed defenders.

At that point a Confederate regimental commander, who had been wounded no less than five times that morning, reacted to the Union maneuver. In a semi-conscious state of shock, he intended to give the command for his troops to wheel and face the Union threat. Instead he

*Left:* Confederate dead in the 'Bloody Lane' following the Union attack.
*Below:* The bridge over Antietam Creek shortly after the battle. In fact Union troops could have waded across the river.

cried out 'About face! Forward march!' The command so confused his disorganized troops that panic spread through the entire brigade and it began to fall back from its position. Had the Union forces pursued their assault Lee's army would have been split in two, leaving his left flank isolated without support or a path of retreat. However the intended attack never materialized. Union troops who had fought so bravely had reached the limits of their endurance. Not only had the battle taken a devastating toll of lives in the Union ranks but the Union chain of command along the front was in chaos. Union commanders struggled to maintain the cohesiveness of their independent units rather than focussing on the over all attack. Their failure to act and react spelled the end to their hard-fought offensive at Bloody Lane.

On the right flank Major General Burnside had been given the task of crossing Antietam Creek in an effort to breach the Confederate defenses. His ultimate goal was to reach Sharpsburg which would block the Confederate retreat. Throughout the morning Burnside concentrated his efforts on crossing a bridge over Antietam Creek which to this day bears his name. Each attack was repulsed as he tried vainly to funnel his troops across the bridge. The logic behind his attempting such a maneuver is a mystery. His troops could easily have waded across the creek anywhere along the front, making it impossible for the Confederates to defend their position. The defenders had already been weakened by the reinforcements for the left flank which had been taken from their ranks.

Finally at one o'clock that afternoon Burnside's forces secured the bridge, but it would be several hours before they pursued their drive toward Sharpsburg as Burnside halted to consolidate his units before moving on. It was four o'clock before they reached the outskirts of Sharpsburg. Although his movements were cautious, few Confederate troops opposed him and Burnside became confident of victory. Unfortunately he had delayed too long and the last of the Confederate divisions made their arrival from Harper's Ferry at a time and place which enabled them to strike the flank of Burnside's advancing corps. That Confederate division, commanded by General A P Hill, had marched 17 miles that day, but managed to drive the Union forces back across Antietam Creek, crushing all hope of a Union victory on that right flank.

The battle was over. Although McClellan had failed to achieve victory he had inflicted a severe blow to his enemy. A concentrated attack on the Army of Northern Virginia on the following day might have given him that victory. Such an attack never came. Lee was advised by his generals to leave the battlefield at once. Secure in his assessment of McClel-

lan's nature Lee kept his army in position, refusing to be chased from the field. On the night of 18 September, after baiting McClellan to attack for more than 24 hours by remaining in position, the Army of Northern Virginia safely withdrew across the Potomac River as McClellan stood idly by.

The Battle of Antietam was without a doubt one of the most costly and perhaps the bloodiest battle of the Civil War in spite of its brevity. Of the 40,000 Confederate troops who saw action more than 10,000 were casualties. For the Union some 12,000 casualties were sustained, 25 per cent of the total number of troops committed. McClellan had had the ideal opportunity to crush Lee's army and although he inflicted heavy losses on the Confederates he had not achieved a victory.

McClellan had committed numerous errors, but two had been crucial. Firstly he failed to coordinate his attacks, preferring to execute the three main assaults in succession along the front from the Confederate left to right. Those individual attacks gave Lee the opportunity to maneuver and reinforce each section accordingly. Secondly McClellan permitted two of his corps to stand idle, never committing them to the battle. As a result, rather than employing his entire army of 70,000 troops in the offensive less than 50,000 actually participated.

Lee on the other hand displayed a keen willingness to fight and an overt contempt for the questionable skills of his command opponent. He has often been criticized for the precarious position in which he put the army, and for the number of losses sustained in the battle, yet Lee was successful in his strategy. He stubbornly stood his ground afterward, and retreated from the battlefield in good order to

President Lincoln reviewed the Union army two weeks after the battle, accompanied by Allen Pinkerton, the chief of McClellan's secret service, and Major General John McClernand.

return to Virginia. Although his first attempted invasion of the North was not successful, the Army of Northern Virginia remained undefeated.

That same September Confederate commander General Braxton Bragg invaded Kentucky. His offensive continued into October but the hopes of a decisive Southern victory were finally dashed when Bragg's advances were halted at the Battle of Perryville. Although both the Union and Confederate forces suffered heavily in that battle, Bragg simply did not have the manpower to continue his activities.

Neither the North nor South was gaining any respectable advantage over the other in the two major combat arenas during the autumn. However, on the strategically valuable Mississippi River, the

Despite their gallant charge over the bridge at midday, Burnside's Division was pushed back across the creek by A P Hill's troops.

Union command was increasingly aware that the loss of the river would cause great damage to the Confederacy. One major obstacle continued to frustrate the Union hopes; Vicksburg held out as a Confederate stronghold.

Grant began the campaign to take Vicksburg by dividing his forces into two columns. His plan called for one column commanded by Sherman to be transported down the Mississippi River landing north of the Vicksburg fortification. At the same time Grant would march his troops overland hopefully keeping Confederate units in the area off balance until he met up with Sherman. The combined force would assault the heavily fortified position of Vicksburg.

From its outset the expedition was plagued with difficulties. Cooperation and assistance from Washington was constantly frustrated. Later Grant learned that one of his subordinates, Major General John A McClernand, had been pulling political strings with the Secretary of War in an effort to sabotage Grant's operation. McClernand felt he and not

Federal gunboats on the Mississippi were forced to pass below the Confederate batteries at Vicksburg.

Grant should have been given command.

Valuable time was wasted but Grant eventually managed to move both columns. On 29 December, Sherman's forces landed north of Vicksburg at Chickasaw Bluffs where they were promptly defeated. Grant, too, was suffering at the hands of two Confederate cavalry forces who harassed his forces and raided his supply lines. Grant was forced to place his army on half rations and relinquish his lines of communication and supply. The result of the Confederate interference and stiff resistance was the suspension of further Union operations. Both Grant and Sherman retreated, relinquishing all hope of capturing Vicksburg for the moment.

With the failure of the first campaign against Vicksburg the war in the West was virtually over for 1862. During the month of December only one other major battle took place in the West. At Murfreesboro, Tennessee, Major General William Rosecrans, who had replaced General Buell as commander of the Army of the Cumberland, faced General Bragg's Confederate Army of Tennessee. For all practical purposes Bragg won the battle. However, his failure to pursue the victory and his actual retreat from the vicinity placed

the city in Rosecrans' hands, giving him a victory by default. Casualties in the engagement were a staggering 25 per cent for both armies with the loss of a great many artillery pieces and a great deal of confidence. The hero of Murfreesboro was a young Union brigadier general, later to be associated with Grant in the East, Phillip H Sheridan. Sheridan proved to be a vigorous, energetic officer who was not afraid to take the lead in an assault. Even in impossible situations he had a talent for instilling trust and loyalty in the soldiers of his command. It was Sheridan's dogged resistance which kept the Battle of Murfreesboro from becoming an overwhelming victory for the Confederate army.

The late autumn and winter months of 1862 also produced one final battle of importance in the East. After the Battle of Antietam Lee returned to Virginia to reorganize his army and rebuild his strength. Although he had not won a significant victory nor maintained his Northern invasion the Confederacy itself had gained through keeping the Union in check. Each day that the stalemate continued meant a stronger case for the Northern Peace Movement, whose supporters continued to claim that the North could not win the

war without first being totally devastated by it.

To maintain the pressure Lee sent Stuart's cavalry raiding as far north as Pennsylvania. Their objective was not only to destroy supply and communication lines but to keep fear and uncertainty ever present in the minds of the people and the government in Washington. With Lee's first invasion repulsed, Lincoln issued the Emancipation Proclamation, to take effect in 1863, and began to consider a change in the military command. McClellan still had his retinue of staunch supporters and although he received credit for repulsing Lee's attempt Lincoln wanted him to push on immediately against the Army of Northern Virginia. Yet McClellan would not move against his adversary.

By the end of October McClellan was finally prepared to advance, but even after he had crossed the Potomac River he refused to engage Lee's army. That refusal angered Lincoln, who took action by appointing Major General Ambrose Everett Burnside as the new commander of the Army of the Potomac. Burnside's success earlier in the year in an independent operation in North Carolina and his position as a senior corps commander

gave Lincoln confidence that his competence was at least equal to McClellan's. Although the action in North Carolina had been a simple one, Burnside had been victorious against the Confederates.

When Burnside was notified that he was to command the Army of the Potomac his reaction was more one of shock than gratification. Burnside believed that he had reached the height of his career in the position of corps commander. Describing himself as unimaginative, with various weaknesses which would not suit an army commander, Burnside tried to decline the appointment. Lincoln took the refusal as simple modesty on Burnside's part and insisted that he take the command. He would perhaps have done well to listen to Burnside's honest self-assessment.

Upon assumption of command Burnside tackled the principal problem at hand; the rapid engagement of the Army of Northern Virginia. His plan was to march to Fredericksburg, capture the city, and from there launch an attack at Richmond. This straightforward plan had one major drawback. The Union forces would have to cross the Rappahannock River and seize the heights behind the city before Lee could retreat and escape. To achieve that goal Burnside would need to depend heavily on the use of pontoon bridges and the element of surprise.

As the advance units of the army appeared at Fredericksburg the Rappahannock was shallow enough to be forded. However, Burnside halted his advance, conscious of the fact that the river could rise without warning and divide his army. This delay cost Burnside the valuable time he needed to take his objectives before Lee could react. By the time Burnside's entire force had arrived a Confederate army of 78,000 waited in the heights above Fredericksburg.

On the Confederate left flank Longstreet's Corps was positioned on the Marye's Heights overlooking a wide canal and drainage ditch which would become a formidable obstacle should the Union

Major General Ambrose Burnside issuing orders to his staff upon taking command of the Army of the Potomac.

forces attack in that area. On the right flank Jackson's Corps took up a position on a less rugged piece of terrain. Lee dispersed his artillery along the heights which allowed them to cover his defenses and also put them within attack range of the Union guns. He also placed a brigade in the city itself, not so much as a defensive force but more as a harassing, disruptive agent against Burnside's efforts to cross the river.

Burnside organized his 120,000 men into three Grand Divisions. Sumner was to command the Union right flank which would cross the pontoon bridge and move into the city. General William B Franklin was to take the second Grand Division and cross three pontoon bridges further down the river from the city. The final Grand Division, under General Hooker was to support the other divisions as a general reserve which would not cross the Rappahannock unless it proved necessary. Union artillery was placed on the high ground opposite the city where, like the Confederate batteries, it could dominate the battlefield.

On 11 December Burnside began the construction of the bridges. Franklin's left flank had little difficulty with the construction in their sector, aside from the problems posed by ice on the river. On the right flank the situation was quite different. The Confederate brigade which operated from the city continually harassed the Union engineers striving to complete the bridges. Burnside would not cross the river with an advance force to counter the Confederate threat but he did finally employ his artillery against them.

By the evening of 12 December Sumner's division had managed to cross and were prepared to launch their assault. It was Burnside's intention that Sumner, supported by Hooker's reserve, would attack the Marye's Heights while Franklin's

forces kept the Confederate right flank pinned down. Early on the morning of the thirteenth Burnside reversed his previous battle plan, making Franklin's sector the main assault point. A heavy fog covered the region that morning and Burnside hoped to take advantage of that condition to move his troops. Franklin ordered General George Meade's division forward with two added divisions as flank support. It was not until the fog lifted that Confederate troops suddenly realized they were in fact under attack.

A state of confusion prevailed as the Confederate ranks attempted to form up to meet the advance. A young officer, Major John Pelham of Stuart's horse artillery, galloped his guns ahead of the line and began to engage both the advancing troops and the Union batteries. For half an hour he checked the advance and kept the opposing artillery occupied so that Jackson could organize his defenses. Then, as quickly as it had appeared, Pelham's force, which had almost exhausted its ammunition supply, galloped back to the safety of the Confederate lines.

The Union troops continued their assault. Jackson's batteries on the nearby heights opened fire. For an hour and a half an artillery duel took place between Jackson's batteries and those of the Union across the river. Outnumbered, Jackson's guns were eventually silenced and Meade pushed on. As Meade's division hit the Confederate lines it appeared that they would achieve success. Their contact

displayed a weak point in the defenses and they began to break through. However, as a result of a misunderstanding in the orders and the confusion caused by the artillery barrage Meade's forces found themselves unsupported in their attack. Confederate troops countered and Meade's lone division was driven back. The Confederate troops soon discovered however that it was impossible to pursue their assault beyond what had been their previous position. In spite of the exceptional manner in which both forces conducted themselves little had been gained.

At the opposite end of the battlefield Sumner and Hooker assaulted Marye's Heights no less than 14 times in their efforts to breach the defender's position. Their closest effort reached to within 25 yards of the stone wall which protected the Confederate position. The stubborn bravery of the Union soldiers in the assaults was phenomenal. Time and time again they threw themselves into an attack which had no possible chance for success. Lee watched from his vantage point on the heights unable to believe the carnage which was resulting from Burnside's tactics.

As night approached Union forces consolidated below the heights. The following morning Burnside ordered a renewal of of the attacks. Although skirmishing occurred his generals eventually persuaded him that further action was futile. Exhausted and disheartened the Army of the Potomac slipped back across the river

two days later under cover of darkness.

Although the Battle of Fredericksburg was considered a major Confederate victory it is often pointed out that Lee let pass an opportune moment when he did not counterattack the weakened Union forces in their positions pinned against the river. In fact he had come into possession of a copy of Burnside's battle plan and preferred to minimize his own losses by remaining in the strong defensive positions of the first day's battle.

The results of the Battle of Fredericksburg shocked Union sympathizers and badly damaged the morale of the Army of the Potomac. Confederate casualties were approximately 5000 killed or wounded as opposed to Union losses of more than 12,000. At the end of 1862 the Union was frustrated by the turn of events as the Confederacy remained in a stable position. The various situations which marked the autumn and winter months indicated that there was little hope of a rapid solution to the conflict. Battle lines were drawn as the armies took up their winter quarters. In Richmond the government was temporarily satisfied with the state of affairs. In Washington Lincoln hastened to find a new commander for his eastern army.

*Below:* The Confederate army was well positioned in the town and on the heights above Fredericksburg, before the Union forces were deployed.
*Right:* The Union army assaulted Marye's Heights over 14 times without success.

Although the Confederates held the best defensive positions at Chattanooga, the besieged Union forces were able to break out, even over the natural bastion of Lookout Mountain.

# THE CRUCIAL YEAR (1863)

At the beginning of the new year neither the Union nor the Confederacy had a decisive advantage. The Union forces were no closer to the heartland of the South than they had been the previous year. The seesaw of victory and defeat was taking its toll on both armies. The Northern opinion that it was not in the power of the Union Army to defeat the South was becoming more pronounced. Daily the Peace Movement gained momentum. Should 1863 follow the trends of the previous two years there seemed little doubt that political pressure would be brought to bear to sue for peace. For the South the new year was equally crucial. If Union forces could be kept at bay and the integrity of the Confederate States maintained the results would be as satisfying as any major military victory.

Foreign support for the Southern cause, particularly from France and England, continued to increase. The possibility of the United States becoming a permanently divided nation seemed ever more plausible. Until 1863 most of the European nations, like many Northern leaders, had not believed that the South could not hold its own against the Union, and that their claims as an independent sovereign nation would vanish as the Union armies reclaimed Southern territory. They had been disproved.

Lee continued to lead the Confederate forces in the East to victory in spite of the fact that his first invasion had been repulsed. It appeared as though Northern generals were incapable of dealing with him on the field of battle. A decisive turn of events was needed by one faction or the other if the war was to be brought to an early conclusion. The prime objective for Union commanders was not only the penetration of the Southern States, to occupy and hold strategic locations, but the elimination of the threat to Washington posed by Lee and his Army of Northern Virginia. For the South the continued occupation of the areas they possessed, a major victory in the East, and to a lesser degree in the West, could bring the war to a close by year's end.

After the stunning defeat of Burnside's Union forces at Fredericksburg, Lincoln knew that he must once again find a commander for his Eastern army. Several men were eligible for such a position, but it was Major General Joseph 'Fightin' Joe' Hooker, whose political influences were the strongest, who assumed command of the Army of the Potomac in January 1863. Hooker's main flaw was an exaggerated overconfidence in himself and his command abilities. He embarked on his career with the assurance that he would swiftly rout the Southern rabble.

In spite of his overconfidence and conceit, Hooker immediately began a necessary program of reorganization for the army. Morale was a primary problem. The defenses at Fredericksburg and the earlier battles were not responsible for the decay of the army's morale but the sense of never ending, never-broken con-

flict was. To counter the depression of his troops, they were sent on furlough following Hooker's assessment that it would be perhaps four months before any major activity on the battlefield resumed as both armies had taken up their winter quarters. During that same time he implemented an extensive staff training program. Mock battles were staged, conducted at brigade level. He set about restructuring the individual corps into self-contained fighting units which could sustain themselves in the field without having to rely heavily on the rest of the army. Hooker also reorganized the Union cavalry, patterning its structure closely on the Confederacy. Finally, but not the least of his innovation, was the development of an independent intelligence service, which would not only gather information but plant false information to deceive the Confederate forces. The group was strictly an army organization and it brought new direction and a higher degree of competence to the task of collecting essential intelligence information. Until that time Union commanders had relied on the Pinkerton Agency, whose misinformation often led to misinterpretation and disaster.

As the Army of the Potomac took on new shape under its latest commander the Army of Northern Virginia had remained in relatively the same condition. Both Lee and his army were in a very poor state of military readiness. The Confederate troops suffered from the same depression found among Union soldiers, but coupled with the morale problem was an inadequate supply of food and materials. Many Confederate soldiers still wore the uniforms they had been issued at the beginning of the war, which had, by that time, been reduced to rags. Arms and equipment were in short supply. The more modern equipment had been scavenged from the battlefield. Lee wanted to take the initiative again, yet found that he

*Right:* Despite his rank, General Lee usually wore the uniform of a Confederate colonel.
*Below:* Major General Joseph Hooker, USV, (1814–79) succeeded Burnside as commander of the Army of the Potomac.
*Left:* General McClellan's secret service, led by Allen Pinkerton, was replaced by organized military intelligence.

*Left:* The Federal engineers managed to keep the Union army moving over the numerous creeks and rivers of Virginia by a system of pontoon bridges.
*Below left:* General Reynolds' Corps marched through the night to rendezvous with the rest of Union army.
*Above:* Believing the Confederate army in retreat, Hooker's army moved toward Chancellorsville.

and his staff were unable to resolve a promising course of action.

Signs of activity were apparent elsewhere. In early March a Confederate captain, John Singleton Mosby, conducted one of the most daring operations of the Civil War. He and 29 of his men slipped behind Union lines within 20 miles of Washington. They captured a brigadier general, two captains, 30 men, and 58 horses, returning with their prizes to the Confederate lines. The episode received a great deal of publicity in both the North and South, with the obvious reaction of anger or joy dependent on public sympathies. Mr Lincoln found the entire business most irritating but was most annoyed at the loss of the horses. He was reported to have said that while he could always promote a new general, good horses were difficult to find.

In Tennessee, General Rosecrans was finding his position increasingly difficult as the Confederates continued to raid his lines of supply. In the West on the Mississippi River, Grant was again planning a campaign against Vicksburg with the support of Admiral David Dixon Porter. A Union cavalry raid into Georgia was also attempted at that time. However, the Union brigade of over 1600 men was finally captured by the forces of General Nathan Bedford Forrest, whose 500 troops so harassed and confused the Union cavalry commander that he surrendered, believing himself outnumbered.

The Union blockade of the Atlantic Coast was growing tighter, making blockade running more dangerous. Confeder-

ate fortresses on the coasts of Georgia and the Carolinas were being harassed by the latest addition to the Union navy, the 'Ironclads.' Although the new vessels could take a great deal of punishment, their seaworthiness, speed, and their ability to inflict serious damage was questionable.

In early April the Union and Confederate armies in the East remained separated by the Rappahannock River. The rains and resulting conditions had kept activity at a minimum, yet Hooker was eager to take control of the situation. He was confident that the Army of the Potomac, under his personal command could easily defeat Lee's army which was less than two-thirds the size of the Union forces. Hooker also thought of himself as the aggressive commander the army had long needed. Until his promotion other Union generals had allowed Lee to steal the initiative and choose the site of battle. Convinced that that was the primary cause of their defeats, Hooker vowed not to allow such a thing to occur.

As the weather began to break Hooker formulated his strategy. Knowing Lee to be in relatively the same deployment from which the Battle of Fredricksburg had been fought, Hooker conceived a strategy which he felt certain would accomplish one of two results. Either Lee would realize that his supplies were being cut off and he was being outmaneuvered by a superior force and retreat to the protection of Richmond, or he would remain to be crushed by that superior force. In either case Hooker could not envision a means of escape for Lee and his army.

The initial phase of the assault was to begin two weeks before the mass attack with the cavalry activities of Brigadier General George Stoneman. With a force of 12,000 he would raid the Confederate supply, communication and rail lines between Fredericksburg and Richmond. Those raids were intended to cause as much confusion and disruption as possible to throw Lee off balance and to decrease supplies in the Fredericksburg area.

In the second phase of action, pontoon bridges would again be constructed below Fredericksburg. With a masking force of three corps, the II, III, and Major General Sedgwick's VI Corps, Hooker would give the impression that he intended to engage Lee in a manner similar to the tactics employed by Burnside. However, two days prior to that event he would launch another three corps, the V, XI, and XII, under Major General Henry Slocum, in a massive flanking maneuver. That force was to use two major fording sites at Germanna's and Ely's Fords. From that position Hooker would pull the II and III Corps from their feint, leaving Sedgwick's VI Corps to hold its position while the entire army swung around to attack Lee from the rear.

The plan was fundamentally sound and Hooker had good reason to believe in its success. It was most certainly the most creative maneuver yet proposed by any of the Union commanders and Hooker saw little choice for Lee but to take his army and flee to Richmond or face certain destruction.

On 13 April 1863 Hooker gave the order for Stoneman to commence his raids. However, as he began his maneuver on 14 April a severe storm struck which lasted for more than 36 hours. Heavy rains made it impossible to cross the Rappahannock River and left one brigade of Stoneman's forces trapped on the Confederate side of the river. The result was a two week delay in the intended raids. Hooker confidently accepted the delay, deciding that he would continue with his strategy unchanged, allowing Stoneman to begin his activities as soon as possible.

On 27 April Hooker commenced his attack as the three Union corps moved to the fords which would allow them an access to the Confederate rear area. Coinciding with that maneuver Stoneman's cavalry crossed the river. However, it was several days before the cavalry was able to inflict any serious damage and their effect on the battle was minimal.

The advancing Union troops spent most of 28 April wading the fords of the Rappahannock. They encountered little opposition from the Confederate pickets and for the most part the fording action was accomplished in amused good spirits. By the morning of 29 April Lee was faced with a Union Army which appeared to be assembling for an attack similar to the one staged by Burnside the previous December. While Union troops maneuvered in an attempt to convince Lee of their impending assault Stuart's cavalry informed him that a large Union contingent had been spotted to the rear.

In spite of the great number of Union troops deployed before him, Lee could not accept that Hooker indeed intended to repeat Burnside's disastrous frontal assault performance. Convinced that a more involved strategy was being applied Lee focussed his attention on the flanking reports as the key to the Union plans. Although it was too early to totally commit himself to his theory, Lee sent a division under Major General R H Anderson to the Confederate army's rear left flank near Chancellorsville to give initial reaction to any possible development.

Also on the morning of the 29th, while Sedgwick's forces were taking up a position below the heights, Jackson approached Lee and strongly advocated the idea that a rapid assault should be made to drive Sedgwick's forces back into the river. Lee, confident that he was assessing the true scope of Hooker's intent, declined Jackson's suggestion.

On 30 April as Anderson's divisions were entrenching, their position reports confirmed that no less than three Union corps were approaching the crossroads at Chancellorsville, preparing to strike. Hooker assumed direct command of those forces. Except for the initial delays caused by the inclement weather, and a reduction in cavalry power due to Stoneman's absence, Hooker's strategy was progressing according to plan. His confidence increased. His intelligence system informed him that there appeared to be especially heavy rail movement along the lines between Fredericksburg and Richmond, which convinced Hooker that Lee was in fact attempting a retreat and that the forces facing the Union army were merely an effort to disguise that fact. He remained certain that Lee's primary concern was the defense of Richmond and that Lee, realizing the hopelessness of his current position, would choose to make his stand at the Confederate capital.

Feeling confident Hooker chose to slow his advance, believing the battle won without a major confrontation. After minor skirmishing Anderson's forces fell back from their position at Chancellorsville and it was there that Hooker chose to halt, consolidate and await reinforcements.

With Hooker's strategy obvious Lee considered his options. Heavily outnum-

Federal artillery attacking Jackson's column at Chancellorsville.

bered he examined the possibility that a retreat to reorganize elsewhere might be prudent. The more he reviewed that option the more apparent it became that such a maneuver would prove extremely costly with little hope of success. Equally, the thought of defense did not appeal to Lee. Hooker's over-confident halting of his main assault force was something Lee had not anticipated and he found difficult to believe.

Lee decided that if Hooker chose to surrender the initiative then he was more than willing to accept it. Lee and Jackson spent the night of 1 May discussing the possibility and chances of success in an attack on Hooker's forces. Surprise was the key. Lee would turn his army to face Hooker's threat. Lee placed every available man under Jackson's command, except for one division to offset Sedgwick's forces and a contingent which would remain with Lee to attempt a counter-flanking maneuver. Jackson would have to cross in front of Hooker's army before initiating his attack on the Union right flank. The operation had to be carried out in a limited amount of time and with the element of complete surprise. Only one man could hope to succeed. That man was Stonewall Jackson.

Jackson was fully aware of the fact that success hinged on crossing in front of Hooker's army and positioning himself at the weakest point of the Union right flank without alerting the Union com-

mand. As if the pressure of executing the maneuver was not sufficiently disturbing, Jackson also acted in the knowledge that while success would make a great victory possible, failure would mean the destruction of the Army of Northern Virginia. Any advance on the part of the Union army would reveal the scheme, yet Lee's assessment of Hooker's character gave reason to believe that the Union forces would remain inactive. Jackson hoped that by mid-afternoon or early evening he would have his forces in position.

On 2 May, Jackson's force marched. General Rodes' division led the column with Fitzhugh Lee's cavalry as a screen. It was hoped that if any contact were made between the cavalry and the Union army it would be construed as merely a scouting party. The march would cover approximately 15 miles before Catherine's Furnace and Brock Road were reached. Once there Jackson would turn his forces to face the Union flank. However upon reaching the area of Catherine's Furnace the Confederate troops were exposed in a large clearing. Union soldiers opened fire with rifle and cannon as the Confederate cavalry attempted to deflect the attack.

The element of surprise was apparently lost. The Union commanders in the area sent urgent messages to their corps commanders informing them of the large enemy troops concentration and the possibility of a major Confederate offensive. Such reports were immediately relayed

to Hooker's headquarters. After assembling the available information and conferring with his staff, Hooker came to two conclusions, both disastrous. The first was that the size of his army and the position of the right flank beside the heavily wooded 'Wilderness' was a more than adequate deterrent of a Confederate offensive in that area. As such, Hooker believed that the troops which had been spotted were nothing more than a decoy on Lee's part to shift attention from the main army and enable him to retreat. Hooker considered that he could deal with such a sacrificial pawn at will. Once again his confidence in his strategy and his belief that Lee would not stand and fight led him to deny the obvious.

Hooker's second error resulted from the fact that as night was almost upon them he believed he would not need to act against the Confederates until morning. It did not occur to him that the Confederate commanders might not have a similar inclination concerning a night attack.

At five o'clock on the afternoon of 2 May, Jackson swung his troops into a position parallel with the Union right flank, forming up in the Wilderness region of forest, brush and brambles which the Union command had considered an impenetrable barrier. He was amazed at the good fortune which allowed him to complete his maneuver with no sign of Union activity.

In less than half an hour a significant number of troops had been brought in line for the first wave of the attack. When Jackson gave the order the Confederate troops crashed through the Wilderness and burst out upon the unsuspecting soldiers of the Union XI Corps. The pickets posted by several commanders gave a belated warning but for the most part the corps was surprised in preparation for supper and the night's bivouac.

The Confederates attacked like madmen. By the time they had cleared the thickets many had literally been stripped of their clothing by the thorny undergrowth. In the face of the assault Union troops panicked and began to flee. The situation became so desperate that several Union officers resorted to the drastic measure of shooting several of their own men in an effort to keep the others from fleeing, but the onslaught of the Confederate soldiers was so fierce that even such extreme measures did not suffice.

As night fell Confederate forces were rolling up the entire right flank. Union troops were in full flight but Jackson's forces were losing momentum as cohesion between his units began to break down. The combination of the charge through the Wilderness terrain and the rapid flight of the Union corps had caused the assault to become disjointed, making it nearly impossible for individual units to remain in contact with other units or commanders. Not only were Confederate regiments mixed, but both Confederate and Union troops were finding it ex-

Lieutenant General Thomas Jonathan Jackson, CSA, (1824–63) earned the nickname 'Stonewall' at the First Battle of Bull Run.

tremely difficult to distinguish friend from foe. Incidents of troops accidentally firing upon friendly units added to the state of chaos and fear which prevailed.

The slowing of the Confederate attack frustrated Jackson as it appeared that his personal objective of reaching the United States Ford Road would elude him. He was sure that if he could gain possession of that road he could trap almost 50 per cent of the Union force on the southern side of the river. Confederate troops had indeed taken their enemy by surprise and had gained a strong advantage, but they stood in danger of losing it if the impetus of the attack were lost.

As Confederate officers struggled to reorganize their units to continue the assault, rumors began to circulate that Union forces were massing for a counterattack and cavalry charge along the road from Chancellorsville. Such rumors immediately caught Jackson's attention and taking his staff and couriers he set out to discover the true situation. In the darkness Jackson's group rode directly into a small contingent of Union soldiers who were themselves looking for the Union lines. That force loosed a volley of rifle

fire before they fled, killing several members of Jackson's staff and wounding the general himself in the right hand. Realizing the gravity of his error, Jackson ordered an immediate return to Confederate lines. As the horsemen sped toward the safety of their own lines, Confederate troops, tensed by the rumors of Union cavalry in the area, mistook Jackson and his staff for a Union force and opened fire. Two more of Jackson's party fell and he too was again wounded.

Within minutes General A P Hill and his staff appeared on the scene. They found Captain Wilbourn of the Signal Corps desperately attempting to drag Jackson to safety. As the officers clustered around Jackson Union artillery, focussing on the sound of rifle fire in that general area, opened fire blindly yet with great accuracy with shell and grape shot. General Hill was wounded and many of his staff killed. A surgeon arrived shortly thereafter and both Jackson and Hill were removed leaving General Rodes in

command. However, Rodes realized that the enormous responsibility was beyond his abilities and sent immediately for General J E B Stuart.

The Union forces of the right flank were in uncontrolled retreat yet the Confederate position was one of such chaos that further advance was impossible. Moreover, rumors were circulating among the troops, including one that both Jackson and Hill were dead. Stuart was doing his utmost to control the situation, but he could do little more than order the officers to reorganize their men in preparation for the following day's activities.

By the morning of 3 May Confederate officers had managed to restore some degree of order to their units and pursue the attack. Many of the Confederate troops had been more than 30 hours without proper food or rest, and although they had routed the right flank they were soon facing part of the Union army which was fresh and intact. The Union forces in that region had in fact begun to offer stiff resistance to the renewed attack when General Hooker intervened. Although his army had begun to stand against the surprise offensive, Hooker's confidence

had been shattered. He could not accept the fact that a force of such proportions had attacked through the Wilderness and began to doubt his intelligence sources. He became convinced that rather than being part of Lee's army the attackers were in fact another Confederate army entirely and that the Union forces were trapped between the second army and Lee.

Hooker's decisions have often been blamed on the fact that a stray artillery shell hit his headquarters that morning, knocking him unconscious and leaving him in a state of befuddlement. Whatever the reason, he ordered a general retreat of the entire Union army. His officers were astounded by the orders as they had restored the composure of their units and had prevented the Confederates from making any substantial gains in their renewed attacks on the right flank. With no small amount of consternation on the part of those officers the retreat was begun.

Elsewhere on the battlefield Lee had taken command of the entire army but he failed to isolate the retreating Union forces before they could cross the Rappahannock River. Arriving too late Lee

could do little more than apply pressure from the rear as he watched the Union army in its flight.

On 4 May Hooker decided to relieve some of that pressure by ordering Sedgwick to attack the lone Confederate division on Marye's Heights. By noon the attack had succeeded in breaking the Confederate defense, throwing the defenders back toward Lee and the bulk of his army. Word quickly reached Lee of Sedgwick's success. Frustrated in his attempts to catch and destroy a large portion of Hooker's retreating army, Lee shifted his entire army against Sedgwick. After only minor skirmishing between the two forces Sedgwick turned his corps and escaped across the river before Lee could bring the full weight of his army to bear.

For the first time during the war Lee was completely frustrated in his efforts. With Sedgwick's escape Lee again ordered a change of direction, heading once more for Chancellorsville to engage Hooker's main force. There was little actual hope of catching Hooker as the Confederate troops were thoroughly exhausted. The march and attacks of 2 and 3 May, coupled with Lee's massive changes in direction, had made further action impossible. Hooker successfully retreated and by the morning of 5 May the Army of Northern Virginia was in complete control of the battlefield at Chancellorsville.

*Left:* Following Hooker's orders, the Union army retreated, leaving the Confederates the victors.
*Right:* Major General Daniel E Sickles, USA.
*Below:* The Confederates attacked with such ferocity after their march through the wilderness that Hooker believed his force to be trapped between two enemy armies.

Although Lee and Jackson had managed to plan and execute a brilliant maneuver it was a somewhat hollow victory. It was true that the numerically superior Union army had been repulsed, but the defeat had been of the commander not the army. The Battle of Chancellorsville destroyed Hooker not the Army of the Potomac. It was obvious that the Union forces were regrouping after Jackson's initial assault and they would probably have stopped any further attacks from that direction. However Hooker could not believe that his grand strategy had been undone. His confidence was destroyed and he removed his army.

During the battle the Confederates lost 13,000 men as compared to 17,000 Union casualties. Worst of all for the Confederacy Stonewall Jackson died the following Sunday of complications and pneumonia. His loss was one which the Confederacy could not afford, and his death shocked both the North and South. Although it appeared that lack of leadership was the major factor in the Union's inability to gain a decisive Eastern victory, the death of General Thomas J Jackson, marked a turning point in that theater of war.

After the disastrous defeat at Chancellorsville, Lincoln was forced once again to search for a competent commander. As he considered the issue, he gave Hooker orders to maintain a loose contact with the Confederate army, keeping the Army of the Potomac between Lee and Washington. Physically the Union army had not suffered excessively from the preceding engagement. However, the morale of the troops and their officers had reached a critical low. In contrast the legend of

Confederate artillery was responsible for destroying Hooker's headquarters, leaving him stunned and confused.

Lee and the Army of Northern Virginia was increasing. In spite of being consistently outnumbered, as well as ill-equipped and short of supplies, the army and its generals continued to perform miracles on the battlefield.

Lee's primary concern was how to take fullest advantage of the situation. The defeat of the Union army at Chancellorsville had not been decisive. The ultimate destruction of the Army of the Potomac depended on a defeat on northern soil. Jefferson Davis was anxious for Lee to mount another invasion, not only to achieve that end, but in the hope that such an offensive would draw Union troops away from the West and the mounting threat to Vicksburg. In addition a northern campaign held the promise of the capture of military stores with which to reequip the Confederate armies. The effects of the blockade of Southern ports were being felt. Supplies and military equipment were being rapidly expended. The North, with its stockpiles, and the Army of the Potomac were the best source of Confederate resupply.

On 3 June the Army of Northern Virginia was just south of the Rappahannock river, beginning its march toward Culpepper, Virginia. On 9 June an insignificant cavalry action occurred at Brandy Station. During that engagement a Union cavalry force attacked and held their own against Jeb Stuart and the cream of the Confederate cavalry, demonstrating that they could be a match for Stuart and his troopers. Southern newspapers chose to turn on Stuart, questioning his abilities as a competent commander. The articles enraged Stuart as he considered both his name and honor to have been slandered. He set out to prove that he was still the master of the cavalry elite and that the Confederate cavalryman was without equal. As the campaign progressed Lee's

Major General J E B Stuart, CSA, led three of his brigades on a series of raids in western Maryland and Pennsylvania.

vague orders concerning the cavalry screening operation allowed Stuart outlets for his hostilities.

On 13 June General Ewell's Corps, which led the Confederate advance, reached Winchester, Virginia and after a minor engagement captured a large quantity of arms and ammunition, including 25 cannon.

Hooker attempted to move on a parallel course, trying desperately to keep track of the Confederate movements by sending out cavalry patrols. As Ewell was entering Winchester, Hooker received the intelligence that A P Hill's corps alone remained at Fredericksburg. He sent an immediate request to Washington that he be allowed to attack and destroy Hill's corps. Lincoln refused the request and after a bitter exchange reminded Hooker that his job was to maintain contact with the enemy and protect Washington.

Lee had ordered Stuart to cover the passes which were essential for the Confederate army's march through the Blue Ridge Mountains, to screen the army's movements and to harass the Union army as much as possible. Considering the generality of his orders, Stuart felt it to be an opportune time to refute the accusations against him. Leaving two of his brigades to carry out the screening operation, on 25 June Stuart and three brigades moved around Hooker's army with the aim of raiding and disrupting Union depots and lines of communication. Later he intended to head north and link up with Ewell's corps somewhere in Pennsylvania. Unconscious of Stuart's motives and aims, for eight crucial days Lee would be without the mobile eyes of his cavalry.

Ewell's corps moved into Pennsylvania and positioned itself between Carlisle and York, gathering supplies for itself

and the rest of the army. Ewell then split his forces into two columns, one capturing Carlisle and threatening Harrisburg while the other passed around Gettysburg, capturing York and continuing on toward Wrightsville. There the advance was halted as Union militia set fire to the bridge over the Susquehanna. The militia also managed to set fire to a large section of Wrightsville. The town might have been completely destroyed had not the advancing Confederate troops aided the residents in controlling and extinguishing the flames.

On 28 June Lee received the disturbing news that two days earlier the Army of the Potomac had crossed the Potomac River and had advanced on Frederick, Maryland. He also learned that after another confrontation Lincoln had replaced Hooker. The gap which Stuart's maneuver had caused in reconnaissance and intelligence gathering was beginning to make itself felt.

The new commander of the Army of the Potomac was Major General George G Meade. For the first time that army had a true military leader. His main concerns

Although victorious at Chancellorsville, the Confederates lost over 12,000 men, killed, wounded or captured.

were for the army and the defeat of his enemy, ignoring personal glory or gain. Meade was a quiet man whose appearance and bearing had earned him the nickname 'the most professional looking soldier' of the Union Army. Although often taken as

Hooker's army was ordered to maintain a position between the Confederate army and Washington.

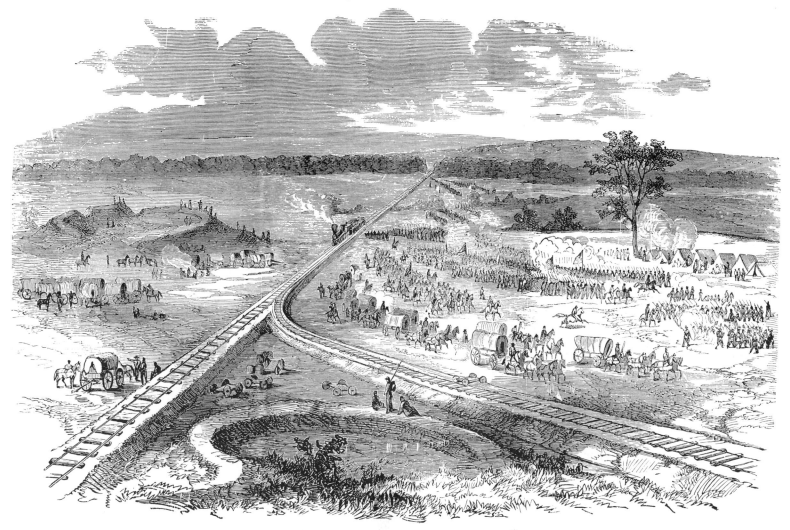

*Above:* The Union army tried to slow the
Confederate advance by setting fire to the railroad
bridge leading north across the Susquehanna.
*Right:* Major General George Gordon Meade,
(1815–72) became commander of the Army of
the Potomac three days before Gettysburg.

an insult to his abilities, it was a reflection
of his total commitment to his position as
a military man. A stern man he easily
became impatient with his subordinates
through his demand of perfection. Self-
discipline contributed to his ability for
clear thinking, and although his me-
thodical approach did not lend itself to
the rapid pace of the battlefield it contributed much to his ability to conduct
an active defensive action. He was a
fine administrator, staff officer and corps
commander, but many thought he lacked
the flair which would make him a good
field commander. Meade himself agreed
with that opinion. He was fully aware of
his own shortcomings and knowing them
would not allow himself to be drawn into
a situation over which he felt he had no
control. Lee recognized Meade's finer
qualities, and while Lee remained confident he realized that his new adversary
was not one to be underestimated.

On his appointment Meade moved to
block Lee between Baltimore and Washington. Deprived of Hooker's personal
intelligence force, Meade had little idea
of Lee's actual position. At the same time
Lee ordered all his generals to converge
on the Gettysburg area. Handicapped by
the loss of Stuart's reconnaissance Lee

Brigadier General John Buford led a Union scouting party which discovered the presence of a Confederate force in the area around Gettysburg.

A Union cavalry division, led by Brigadier General John Buford, was scouting along the road between Cashtown and Gettysburg. Buford felt certain that the brief incident of the previous day indicated that the Confederate army was concentrated in the immediate area. As a result, he sought support from Major General John F Reynolds, who assured Buford that he would be prepared to lend aid should subsequent action occur. With that assurance Buford positioned his four dismounted squadrons on McPherson's Ridge, half a brigade near the Mummasburg Road, and a full brigade behind with the support of a six-gun battery.

As Heth's division moved toward Gettysburg, Confederate skirmishers made contact with the Union forces on the ridge. Buford realized that he must buy time and for nearly two hours his dismounted troopers held the Confederates at bay. By nine-thirty Reynold's Corps was aware of the engagement and marching to support. Major General Abner Doubleday, who commanded the 1st Division of I Corps, had arrived at Marsh Creek soon after. It was rapidly becoming apparent that the encounter was magnifying as both armies were reacting with corps strength. Hill rushed forward with his division in an attempt to gain the upper hand by a flanking maneuver as Ewell's corps approached along the Carlisle Road.

With increased Confederate support the Union position was becoming precarious. Reynolds recklessly took personal charge of the situation in an effort to stabilize his corps. After calling for support from Major General Oliver Howard's XI Corps, Reynolds advanced to McPherson's Woods, and was killed minutes after his arrival. As ranking officer General Doubleday took command. However his indecisiveness caused the Union forces along the front to falter. In spite of the fact that Confederate troops had also decreased their momentum,

Buford reported back to Major General John Reynolds who ordered his men, about a third of the Union force, to march toward Gettysburg.

Union forces found themselves on the verge of collapse. Howard relinquished the command of his corps to his senior divisional commander, General Carl Schurz, and rode forward to relieve Doubleday.

The action was drawing an increased number of troops. The Union XI Corps was making a desperate bid to contain Ewell's approach from the north and to relieve the cavalry which had advanced earlier to meet that threat. It became obvious to General R E Rodes of Ewell's corps that the Union forces lacked a certain degree of cohesion and that an attack on the right flank of the XI Corps would break its defenses, allowing the Confederate division to attack from the rear. Following a Confederate artillery assault, Rodes launched an attack along the eastern edge of Oak Ridge. It did not

Reynolds was killed by a Confederate sharpshooter as he moved forward to arrange his battle line.

had decided to consolidate his army for its own protection. On 30 June a brigade of A P Hill's Corps moving along the Chambersburg Pike toward Gettysburg, in the hopes of locating the shoe depot rumored to be there, intercepted a Union cavalry division which Meade had sent to reconnoiter the area between Gettysburg and Hanover. Both commanders were appraised of the brief encounter yet had so little substantial information that neither truly anticipated a major action. However as a precaution Lee called Longstreet's corps from Chambersburg and Ewell's corps from York, ordering them to rendezvous at Cashtown. In turn Meade continued to develop positions along Big Pipe Creek, a site which would offer an advantageous defense should Lee make a drive toward Baltimore or Washington.

The same day Meade sent his III Corps to Emmitsburg, just south of the Pennsylvania border and the I and II Corps toward Gettysburg. He and his headquarters staff were a full day's ride behind the advance, which caused Meade no alarm as he considered it unlikely that any further contact would be made for days.

At eight o'clock on the morning of 1 July Lee decided to send the lead divisions of Hill's corps, under the command of Major General Henry Heth down the Chambersburg Pike. The objective remained the Union storage depot, but they were also ordered to reconnoiter and ascertain the Union strength in the vicinity. Stuart's absence from the scene has often been cited as the reason for Lee's decision to use infantry for such a mission, yet Lee had the cavalry brigades which Stuart had left behind and could have deployed them more wisely than he did. In truth it was the absence of Stuart, who had always seen to such matters, which prompted Lee's decision.

Lee's 'Old Warhorse,' Major General James Longstreet, CSA, (1821–1904) did not believe Lee should take the offensive at Gettysburg.

meet with the success he had anticipated and two of his divisions were virtually destroyed by the Union resistance.

At that same time Hill was increasing the action against the Union I Corps, Major General William Dorsey Pender's Division was brought in. The successful turning of I Corps' right flank was more than the Union troops could tolerate. They relinquished their position on Seminary Ridge, retreating to the defensible position of Cemetery Ridge, allowing Gettysburg to fall into the hands of the Confederates.

On its northern flank XI Corps had been thrown into complete confusion by the renewed attack of Early's Division as it approached from the northeast. With the Union forces in a state of chaos, retreating on several fronts, it seemed that the Confederates would carry the day. Lee had arrived on the battlefield and was witness to the success of the attack against the I Corps. He sent a message to General Ewell to attack Cemetery Hill 'if practicable.' In doing so Lee had again made the mistake of failing to give his subordinates detailed orders, believing that Ewell would react as Stonewall

Jackson would have and carry on toward the objective. Such orders merely confused Ewell. That confusion, coupled with the losses he had sustained, the chaos of the battle and the inflammation of his leg amputated after the Second Battle of Manassas, caused Ewell to delay his attack while he awaited the arrival of the remaining units of his corps.

When the reinforcements arrived he sent a small reconnaissance force forward to determine if Culp Hill, which overlooked Cemetery Hill, was occupied. By the time he took action it was and he gave up the idea of assaulting the position until the following day. If Ewell had pursued his attack against the disorganized units which had mounted Culp Hill the Battle of Gettysburg might well have come to a swift conclusion that evening.

During that first day General Meade, still some distance away at Taneytown, received reports of the developing battle. He was also shocked and distressed by the news that his long-time friend General Reynolds had been killed. His dismay did not prohibit his prompt decision to send General Winfield Scott Hancock to assume command of the Gettysburg forces. Hancock was regarded as a courageous, sensible officer and to Meade's thinking the man most able to fill the required role. General Howard took exception to being

replaced by an officer of junior rank when Hancock arrived to inform him of the replacement. After a brief interchange, during which Hancock quite simply restated Meade's orders, Howard withdrew graciously.

Well-known to the troops, Hancock restored the flagging confidence of the Union forces. He swiftly established a well-ordered defense around Cemetery Hill, and the Confederate attackers met such rigid resistance that Lee refrained from further assaults in that area.

The action of 1 July had caused almost 10,000 Union casualties as compared to 7000 Confederates. Lee enjoyed a superiority of more than 10,000 troops, yet the failure of his generals, particularly Ewell, to pursue their initiative would cause that advantage to vanish with the arrival of Meade's remaining forces.

By the morning of 2 July, it was evident that Ewell's hesitation in the attack on the right flank and his failure to take Cemetery Hill had cost the Army of Northern Virginia an early victory. Lee's strategy would have to be revised to combat an enemy which held a strong defensible position on the hills and ridges south of Gettysburg. Lee lacked only one infantry division out of his full force on the battlefield, while Meade had slightly less than 75 per cent of his army present. The element of time definitely favored the Union general. If Meade could contain Lee's efforts until early afternoon when the remainder of the Army of the Potomac would arrive, he would have not only the defensible positions but sheer numbers in his favor. There were those in Meade's staff who questioned the influence of those additional troops as they would arrive after a forced march of more than 30 miles and would surely reach the battlefield exhausted. Yet Meade depended on the added strength of those units as both fundamental and psychological factors in his strategy.

Early that morning Lee held conferences with both Longstreet and Ewell. He had decided that the weakest points of the Union army were its flanks. Ewell was to push his corps from the north on the Union right flank while Longstreet's corps would take action on the southern left flank. The attacks were to be made almost simultaneously, with Ewell attempting to distract as many Union troops as possible, suggesting that his was the main assault. Longstreet would then launch his attack threatening the Union army's rear.

Under the threat of being cut off from his supply and communication lines Lee believed that Meade would be forced to abandon his defensive positions and re-

*Right:* On 2 July Longstreet's Corps marched the full length of the battlefield in the hope of surprising the Union defense.
*Above right:* During the many attacks made on Cemetery Ridge, the opposing armies came close enough to engage in hand-to-hand combat.

Four Union Generals present at Gettysburg. Seated, Major General Winfield Scott Hancock, Major General David Birney, Brigadier General Francis Barlow and Brigadier General John Gibbon.

treat along the Baltimore Pike. A P Hill's Corps would not be actively involved in the battle, but was there to employ their artillery, act as a reserve and keep the Union center stationary.

Lee's strategy met with stiff opposition. Ewell was skeptical about his role as he felt that he had neither the troops nor the advantage of position for the type of offensive Lee demanded. Longstreet was also in opposition, stating that the Confederate position was as strong defensively as the Union's and questioning the wisdom of taking the offensive. He thought they should provoke Meade to take the initiative. Lee paid little attention to Longstreet's plea. A serious split developed between Lee and Longstreet during their conference which would affect not only Longstreet's performance but the ultimate outcome of the battle.

Although the strategy called for the offense to begin that morning of 2 July, it was late afternoon before Longstreet had positioned his troops at a point from which they could launch their attack. At the same time Meade had ordered his forces to disperse along Cemetery Ridge. Major

General Daniel Sickles, commander of the Union III Corps, was assigned to the far left flank where he was to anchor his defenses on the hill known as the Little Round Top. Upon surveying the area he decided that he would have a better position some three-quarters of a mile ahead of his assigned position. Without consulting Meade, Sickles advanced his entire corps and placed it with its right flank bordered by a peach orchard. His left flank faded back at an oblique angle to the vicinity known as Devil's Den. The result was that the Little Round Top and Hancock's left flank lay fully exposed.

Upon discovering Sickles' maneuver, Meade was furious. Sickles attempted to vindicate his decision by claiming that his orders had not been specific. In the face of Meade's anger, Sickles offered to withdraw to his former position. Knowing that the Confederate forces were rapidly approaching, Meade replied 'I wish to God you might, but the enemy won't let you.' Sickles' scouts confirmed that Longstreet's column was advancing and it was too late to withdraw.

Longstreet was still unhappy with Lee's strategy. Although he sent three divisions forward, Anderson's, McLaws', and Hood's, the attack did not begin until four o'clock in the afternoon and the co-

ordination between the divisions was poorly managed. Anderson and McLaws struck against Sickles' floundering units while Hood swept across the Devil's Den toward the Little Round Top.

At that point Major General G K Warren, inspecting the Union defenses in that area, discovered that Sickles had left the Little Round Top totally unmanned. Warren realized that if the Little Round Top was lost not only would Union supply lines be endangered but the entire rear of the army would be exposed. He set up a hasty defense with the few men who had accompanied his tour, knowing that such a defense could not hold for more than a few minutes once Hood's Division arrived on the scene. Warren then galloped away to gather as many troops as he could to defend the hill.

Major General George Sykes' V Corps was moving forward in support of Sickles at the Peach Orchard as Warren approached. Intercepting that force, Warren diverted some of them, barely in time, for the defense of the Little Round Top. The fighting which ensued was some of the bloodiest of the entire battle, yet the Union defenders managed to hold.

Further north McLaws and Anderson were forcing Sickles' troops back from the Peach Orchard and neighboring Wheat-

*Left:* Confederate sharpshooters managed to move into 'Devil's Den,' but not always successfully.
*Above:* The hilly terrain of Cemetery Ridge gave a distinct advantage to the Union troops who held the high ground.

field. Although Sickles had been reinforced by elements of both Sykes' and Hancock's corps, the Confederates could not be held back. It was apparent that Sickles' position was lost. However it was also apparent that if the Confederate forces managed to capture that lower part of Cemetery Ridge the Union army would be put in such a precarious position that Meade would be forced to call a retreat.

The First Minnesota Infantry Regiment, a veteran unit whose ranks had been reduced to battalion strength, charged against overwhelming odds to fill the gap and prevent the Confederate troops from surging forward. Within minutes the unit suffered more than 80 per cent casualties, but they succeeded in halting the Confederate advance. Meade then took a calculated risk and deployed troops from his right flank to bolster the left. The successful charge of the First Minnesota and the addition of reinforcements cut the momentum of Longstreet's attack.

Ewell's simultaneous assault to pin down the Union right flank and prohibit such redeployment to the left had failed to materialize. By sundown Ewell was only just beginning to make an uncoordinated advance against Culp's and Cemetery Hills. Although one Confeder-

Various aspects of the battle of Gettysburg as painted by Paul Philippoteaux in 1884, including a field hospital (*top right*).

ate brigade managed to gain ground they had accomplished little toward a victory. Cooperation between the two offenses had been virtually nonexistent, leaving Lee to face another day of battle.

Although 2 July had seen heavy losses on both sides, with a staggering 50 per cent casualty rate on the Union's left flank alone, Meade's army had maintained a solid front. The Union army had lost ground but it remained in a favorable position.

Meade held a council of war that night and after listening to the opinions of his officers decided that his army would maintain its position for one more day. Earlier in the day Meade had instructed his staff to conceive a plan for extracting the army from its position at Gettysburg. However the army had proven itself capable in spite of the difficult situation caused by Sickles. Whether it was the fact that they were fighting on Northern soil, many for their own state of Pennsylvania, or the fact that they were simply tired of running, the morale of the soldiers of the Army of the Potomac was the highest it had been for some time.

The primary concern was to discover where the next Confederate offense would strike. Meade felt that his flanks had been secured which left only the center of his

*Above:* In a council of war, held the night of 2 July, Meade agreed to hold the Union position for one more day, rather than retreat.
*Above right:* Following customary practice, Meade used this farmhouse as headquarters.
*Left:* Major General George Pickett, CSA, ordered his men to charge in a maneuver that was sadly outdated and a disaster for the Confederates.

*Left:* As Pickett's Division made its final assault, General Hancock ordered his artillery to move up. Moments later he was wounded.

line to be considered as a possible weakness. To counter that he moved men and artillery in preparation for a probable attack on that sector.

That same night Lee, too, held a council of war. It was painfully evident that his key corps commanders had failed to take advantage of situations during the previous two days. It was imperative to Lee to find a swift means to end the battle. Although events had not gone according to his desires, Lee remained confident that his soldiers could accomplish the seeming impossible as they had done so often in the past. He believed that the Union morale would soon crumble. He also surmised that as Meade had syphoned his forces to bolster his flanks, the center had been weakened. It was against that center that Lee would launch his main assault while Ewell continued to attack the right flank.

Again Lee faced opposition from Longstreet who again proposed that the Confederate army take an active defensive posture and wait for the Union forces to counterattack. In that way Confederate troops could inflict heavy Union casualties, suffering a minimum themselves. Longstreet was also of the opinion that Lee's plans for a frontal assault were suicidal and he had no stomach for sending his men to the slaughter which he was convinced awaited them.

As the battle was renewed on 3 July, Ewell's troops resumed their attack on the Union right flank. They were greeted with a punishing barrage, laid down by the artillery which had been brought forward to strengthen the defenses. At eight o'clock in the morning a full-scale assault was launched against Culp's Hill and the vital Baltimore Pike. For more than three hours the Confederate soldiers threw themselves against the position only to be caught in a Union crossfire. It was clear that the tide was against Ewell's forces and after sustaining heavy losses they withdrew.

The Confederate dead were so numerous that their bodies covered the field. After the battle was ended, an inspection of that area revealed that the foliage had been stripped by rifle and artillery fire, and several trees which had been left standing had more than 200 bullets embedded in them.

Early in the afternoon the 140 guns of the Confederate batteries along the two-mile front began a bombardment of the Union center lines. They were answered by some 80 Union guns in one of the most massive artillery engagements of the war. To a large degree the Confederate artillery overshot the ridge, but after two hours Brigadier General Henry Hunt's Union batteries began to withdraw to conserve their ammunition for use against the impending attack. Colonel E P Alex-

Since action photographs were not possible in 1863, the best idea of the battle is given by on-the-spot sketches of artists like A R Waud.

ander, director of the Confederate bombardment, sent a message to Major General George E Pickett, whose divisions had been selected to lead the 15,000 man charge, to begin the assault as the Union guns were retreating and the Confederate artillery were almost out of ammunition.

Pickett rode directly to Longstreet to request permission to attack. Longstreet stared straight ahead and nodded, believing he was sending his men to certain death. The long gray lines moved out of their defenses and marched toward the Federal line. On the Union side officers

The Union losses at Gettysburg were only 23,000 and less than 3000 dead compared to the Confederate losses of over 30,000.

steadied their men, giving orders that they were not to fire until the Confederate soldiers were well within range.

At the moment when Confederate artillery could not offer support, as their own troops were too close to the enemy, Hunt unleashed the Union artillery against the advancing infantry, and Pickett's Charge began. Of the 15,000 who marched forward only a few hundred reached the Union lines. Some 9000 lay dead or wounded in the no man's land between Seminary and Cemetery Ridges. The few thousand survivors staggered back, broken and dejected from their suicidal mission. General Lee met his returning soldiers, moving among them to praise them for their bravery, appalled by the miscalculation of his strategy. The man who had been sickened by the slaughter of Union troops at Fredericksburg was himself the architect of such an

assault. He told his men that he and not they had lost the fight and humbly asked them for their continued support.

On the afternoon of 3 July Stuart finally located the battle and was engaged by Union cavalry several miles east of Gettysburg. Several days earlier he had discovered the army's position through a newspaper article found during a raid and had moved immediately to rendezvous with Lee. In the engagement outside Gettysburg four Michigan regiments, led by a stubborn young brigade commander, George Armstrong Custer, kept Stuart's forces well occupied. Stuart finally broke off, again humiliated by his lack of success, and went on in search of Lee. He had wandered over miles of Pennsylvania countryside with little to show for his efforts but a further loss of esteem.

On the evening of 3 July Lee pulled the corps of Ewell and Longstreet back into line with Hill's corps on Seminary Ridge to consolidate his forces and await a Union counterattack which never came. The following day, in torrential rain, they withdrew.

It was Sunday, 5 July, before Meade fully realized that Lee was in retreat. He sent a brigade of cavalry and Sedgwick's IV Corps in passive pursuit. Finally on 7 July Meade left Gettysburg. Ten days after the battle, Lee crossed the Potomac River virtually unmolested.

Meade was criticized by many, including the President, for his failure to follow up the Gettysburg victory. Fighting one of the greatest land battles in the country's history had strained the capacities of his troops to their limits. Meade felt it was more important to bury the dead, tend to the wounded, and recuperate from the activities of the previous weeks than go off in perhaps vain pursuit of the enemy.

The Union had suffered more than 23,000

In the final assault on Seminary Ridge the Confederates, led by Brigadier General Lewis Armistead, breached the Union defenses, but were beaten back.

casualties compared to over 30,000 for the Confederacy. Although those figures are disputed, it has been accepted that there was a combined total of more than 50,000 killed, wounded, or missing. These figures included ten generals killed and many more were wounded. The battle had severely crippled both armies, but Lee had suffered most. He would never again be able to mount a major offensive.

The new year had brought many changes in the western campaign. The war in the West was centered around the Mississippi River and had been moving toward one objective. Vicksburg had to fall. To the South Vicksburg was the final link between the Western states and the rest of the Confederacy. If Vicksburg were lost it would give the North both a strategic and moral victory. Strategically the fall of Vicksburg would give the Union supremacy over the Mississippi River. Morally, it would greatly affect the Southern people, as Jefferson Davis had sworn that Vicksburg would never be taken.

Lincoln had begun to put pressure on the Mississippi River campaign. Discord

On 4 July, Lee retreated, leaving the Confederate dead behind on the battlefield to be buried by Meade's forces.

was evident in the western farmers, who needed the river as an avenue for transporting their goods to market. Those states might break with the Union or at least bring pressure to bear to end the war and capitulate to the Confederate demands. If the farmers should advocate the peace movement the war must end and the nation would remain divided.

In late December and into early January, Grant's earlier attempt to capture Vicksburg had been repulsed. There was no major military defeat involved, merely misconception and miscalculation on the part of the Union command. From the end of January until early April the Union army approached the problem of capturing Vicksburg from several dif-

ferent angles. One plan was devised to bypass Vicksburg by cutting a canal through the narrow finger of land on the western Mississippi shore opposite the city garrison. The idea was strongly supported by President Lincoln and excavation for the canal was begun.

Sherman's XV Corps was in charge of the operation which proceeded fairly well until March when the rising Mississippi flooded the entire area. The unfinished canal was destroyed and equipment lost.

At the same time another attempt was made to send a naval force down the tributaries of the Yazoo River to capture the Confederate dockyards at Yazoo City. That attempt proved unsuccessful. Although the flotilla was accompanied by an overland force, Confederates in the area managed to harass, block, and finally repulse the Union gunboats by mid-March.

With the failure of those two efforts Grant decided to adopt a new strategy. Thus far all operations against the city had come from the north. Owing to the natural lay of the land the northern flank was without a doubt the strongest, lending an added advantage to the Confederate defenders. Also the garrison received the majority of its supplies and reinforcements from the southeast, primarily via Jackson, Mississippi. In the course of any northern assault which the Union might mount the city was constantly open to supplies and reinforcements.

Grant considered those points and decided that the way to the capture of Vicksburg lay not in direct attack but in the isolation of the city. He formulated a new strategy based on that hypothesis. In mid April Grant ordered seven gunboats, a ram, and several cargo steamers to move south on the river past Vicksburg under cover of darkness. Much to everyone's surprise the flotilla accomplished its task with a minimum of damage. By 20 April Grant and a land force were on the move. They marched along the Louisiana bank of the river, capturing the river town of New Carthage then proceeding on toward Bruinsburg.

As the Union troops progressed, ships continued to run the gauntlet of guns at Vicksburg to carry supplies to Grant's forces. Grant now believed that success would come through keeping his forces independent of fixed lines of supply. He had learned during his earlier campaign that the land around Vicksburg could support his army without the necessity of resupply. His army could live off the land and by travelling light Grant believed that his objectives could be more swiftly and easily gained.

By 30 April Grant had succeeded in capturing Bruinsburg and was ferrying troops across the Mississippi to the eastern shore. The maneuver took the Confederate command completely by surprise. They had never anticipated an attack from that direction and were uncertain of Grant's intentions. Their indecision resulted in Grant taking all the initiative.

On 1 May Grant sent part of his XIII Corps to capture Port Gibson. By 7 May Sherman's XV Corps had crossed the river at Grand Gulf, and Grant had succeeded in moving the majority of his army

across the river. Confederate forces in the area found that they were constantly being outflanked as they struggled to position themselves between the Union army and the obvious objective of Vicksburg. Confounding his enemy Grant moved instead toward Jackson, the capital of Mississippi.

General Joseph E Johnston, acting

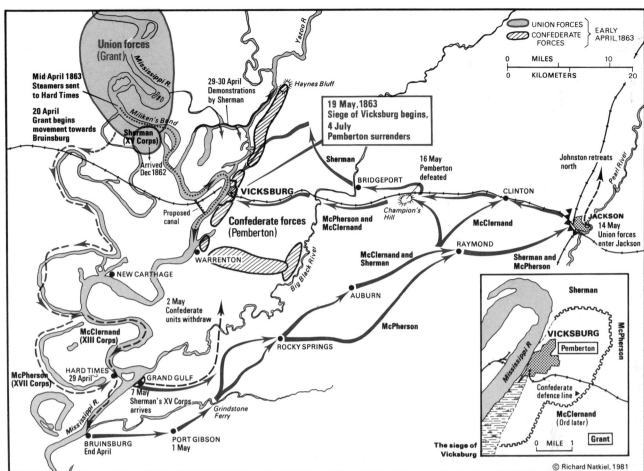

*Above left:* A rare photograph of Vicksburg taken in 1863 during the siege.
*Below:* The Union forces tried to cut a canal through a spit of land opposite Vicksburg in an effort to allow Federal gunboats to pass down the Mississippi unmolested.
*Right:* The canal was discontinued after flooding in the spring.

Major General Ulysses S Grant, USA, (1822–85)
proved by his victories in the West to be the
general the Union (and Lincoln) needed.

Lieutenant General John Clifford Pemberton
commanded the Confederate defense of the fortress
of Vicksburg.

commander of the Confederate forces in
the West, was caught off guard. With
only two brigades at his immediate disposal he chose to retreat north to meet
reinforcements which were to arrive from
the East. Combined with the troops of
Lieutenant General John C Pemberton,
who commanded the defenses of Port Hudson and the Vicksburg garrison, Johnston
would have an army which numbered
more than 50,000. Johnston felt confident
that he could stop Grant and possibly
defeat him quickly in one battle.

Johnston was unaware that Pemberton
was under strict orders from Jefferson
Davis not to leave Port Hudson or Vicksburg unguarded at any time for any
reason. In compliance with those orders,
Pemberton left more than 10,000 men
behind as defense. Instead of joining
Johnston he marched to sever Grant's

lines of supply and communication, which
he believed ran along the route that
Grant had recently taken. Pemberton's
move played directly into Grant's hands.
The link between the Confederate forces
was broken and Pemberton wasted valuable time and energy trying to cut supply
lines which simply did not exist.

Grant's forces entered Jackson on 14
May destroying both its rail junction
and those military stores which he could
not use himself. Two days later he engaged Pemberton's forces at Champion's
Hill. After five hours of heated battle the
Confederate lines collapsed and fled back
toward the 'safety' of Vicksburg.

Pemberton had made a fatal tactical
error. Johnston's forces were waiting to
the northeast, yet Pemberton retreated
away from them. Had he made his way
toward Johnston, Grant would have been
trapped between a large field army and
the fortification at Vicksburg. To save
the remainder of his army Pemberton left
behind a force of 1700 men and 18 field

pieces as a rear guard. They were captured
on 17 May after a brief skirmish at the Big
Black River.

By 19 May Grant's army stood outside
Vicksburg. He felt certain that Pemberton and his army were completely de-
moralized, which in fact they were, but the
garrison force which had been left behind
was fresh and compensated for the weari-
ness of the other troops. The first Union
assault was consequently repulsed. The
staunch defensive resistance surprised
Grant and he reassembled his forces for
another attack. He wanted the city taken
as quickly as possible as he knew that
Johnston's forces were gathering less
than 50 miles away. Though smaller than
his own, Grant did not want it to arrive
in time to aid the garrison.

At ten o'clock in the morning on 21 May
Union artillery began the bombardment
of the Vicksburg fortifications. Grant had
placed Sherman's XV Corps on the northern flank, McPherson's XVII Corps to the
east, and McClernand's XIII Corps to the
southeast. With a combined attack by all
three corps Grant counted on a swift
victory. The XIII Corps, which had made
some headway against the defenses, requested reinforcements. Grant had positioned himself to view the attacks of
Sherman's and McPherson's Corps and
refused the request, adding his limited
reserves to the efforts of those two corps.
The XIII Corps could not hold its position
without reinforcements and the assault
crumbled. The withdrawal caused the
entire attack to lose momentum and the
Union forces were forced to abandon the
assault.

Grant hastily reviewed the situation
and decided that rather than expend his
manpower in unproductive attacks on
the fortifications he would lay siege to
the city. His earlier efforts in destroying
all avenues of resupply and reinforcement

*Right:* The early attacks on Vicksburg were a
series of skirmishes and were successfully repelled
by the Confederates.
*Above:* The garrison at Vicksburg built a series of
strong defenses while Grant's army marched to
Jackson, Mississippi.

to the city would be put to full use.
Isolated, it would only be a matter of time
before the city and garrison fell. Several
members of Grant's staff were of the
opinion that Vicksburg would be able to
withstand a conventional siege. Sherman
pointed out that they had already achieved
a great victory even if they were unable to
capture the city. Grant's army had in fact
captured 89 field pieces, taken prisoner
almost 6000 enemy soldiers, destroyed
the military stores in Jackson, and completely disrupted all Confederate operations in the area. However Vicksburg had

*Below:* Grant had Vicksburg surrounded by three
armies, including Sherman's corps whose defenses
were sketched by F B Schell.

After the siege began, ammunition and supplies were brought in by scouts. Rations became scarce very early on.

been Grant's ultimate objective and he had no intention of being denied that victory.

It soon became obvious that the reinforcements for which Johnston had been waiting were not forthcoming. They had been diverted to Lee's army in the East to lend their weight to the invasion which he was mounting against the Northern states. That reduced the threat which had concerned Grant and gave him added confidence in his ability to force Vicksburg into submission through siege.

With success so close at hand Grant had no desire to waste time and lives on a mismanaged siege. Grant searched his command for officers with more advanced training as engineers. A two-day truce, meant to allow both armies to see to their dead and wounded, gave Grant a short respite with time to search for able engineers. Two officers, Captain F E Prime and Captain Cyrus B Comstock, were selected to head the engineering unit. During the truce they worked with the burial details, taking advantage of the opportunity to inspect the Confederate fortifications and

defense system. Their Confederate counterpart, Colonel H S Lockett, was deprived of a similar opportunity to study the Union forces by General Sherman who went to apparently great lengths to engage the colonel in persistent conversation. The efforts of Captains Prime and Comstock gave Grant a great advantage over the following weeks.

Throughout May and June both armies turned to trench warfare. During the night soldiers would advance and dig new trenches, while during the day they fought to retain them. They also resorted to mining, digging trenches as near to the enemy's as possible. At a pre-determined point a shaft would be dug from one trench under the trenches of the enemy. A large quantity of explosives was then placed at the end of the shaft. When detonated the explosion would rip a hole in the enemy's trench defenses through which the attackers would rush. The procedure would then begin again. To counter such Union efforts Confederate troops filled wagons with dirt, covered with a canvas and nicknamed 'sausages' by Colonel Lockett, which were then

*Right:* Trench warfare and mining were both used during the siege of Vicksburg.

Engineers under the command of Major General James McPherson managed to scout through the Confederate defenses while seconded to the burial details.

used to block the gaps made by the Union mining.

Massive Union artillery barrages were also used to destroy the defensive fortification. Confederate engineers recorded that as quickly as their men could shovel earth for the defense works Union artillery would send it flying through the air. Lockett himself barely escaped death on several occasions while inspecting the defenses.

By the end of June miles of trenches surrounded Vicksburg on its landward sides. More than 200 Union artillery pieces had been emplaced. The siege had become a curiosity. As Northern newspapers related the events at Vicksburg, politicians, friends, and families of the soldiers, as well as general 'do-gooders' flocked to the site. At times the Union camps took on a carnival atmosphere. This was not the case for the Confederate defenders. Supplies of food and fresh water dwindled. By mid-June the defenders, both military and civilian, were on strict rations. Mule stew, cane shoots and rodents were among the basic fare. Coffee and flour were replaced by any reasonable imitation.

Lacking even the most basic food stuffs the defenders were finding it difficult to continue the battle. Reviewing his troops Pemberton realized that although they were willing to fight on, many were simply not in any physical condition to do so. By the end of June many Confederate soldiers lived, ate, slept, fought and died at their positions, held there not only by the battle but by a lack of energy as well.

Such heroic spirits could only prolong the inevitable as ammunition supplies were diminished with each passing day.

On the night of 2 July Pemberton held a meeting with his staff to discuss the desperate situation. It was obvious Johnston's army would not be coming to their aid, and Grant's army was growing ever stronger. Pemberton and several officers felt that the importance of Vicksburg made it imperative that they continue the defense, but Pemberton also realized that he was responsible for the civilian population and their welfare. Pemberton put it to a vote and majority opinion dictated that peace should be made.

On 3 July Pemberton sent one of his officers, General John S Bowen to ask for an armistice. Grant gave his famous reply of 'unconditional surrender' as the only terms available for discussion. Pemberton was initially furious at such a demand, yet he saw little alternative. By ten o'clock that night the terms of surrender had been drawn up. Vicksburg had fallen. On 4 July Union troops accepted the formal surrender and entered Vicksburg ending their long and arduous campaign.

The defenses of Vicksburg yielded more than 170 artillery pieces and 60,000 small arms, and when Port Hudson fell five days later, the Mississippi was once again opened to shipping and river traffic. The tide of war in the West had shifted against the Confederacy.

The Battle of Vicksburg revealed the capable and imaginative qualities of Ulysses S Grant. His theory that the defeat of an enemy was based upon the elimination of that enemy's resources had proved effective. Yet his respect for his adversary meant that he would not add disgrace to defeat. Grant's ability to perceive a situation and develop an inno-

At the beginning of June, Vicksburg was surrounded by an elaborate system of Union trenches.

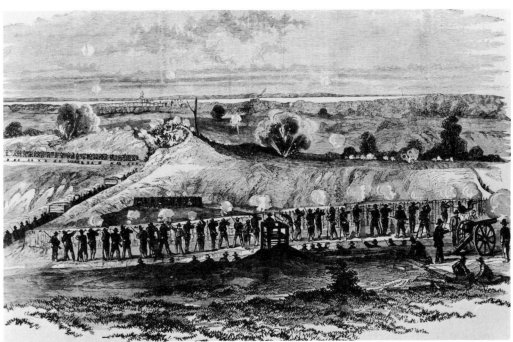

Pemberton surrendered the town and garrison to Grant on 4 July 1863. The length of the Mississippi River was in Union hands.

toward the Union army in the hope of engaging it at a point advantageous to the Confederates. The Union intelligence sources informed Rosecrans almost immediately of Bragg's withdrawal from the city. The Union general took the information as an indication that Bragg was in retreat.

Rosecrans' reaction was to divide his army into three separate forces so they might cross the mountains more easily and rapidly in pursuit of Bragg. In doing

vative strategy would bring him to the forefront as the general most needed by the Union.

The capitulation of Vicksburg enabled Grant to concentrate on eastern Tennessee, although one part of the army was sent down the Mississippi to take part in a drive into Texas. Other divisions of his army moved toward Arkansas.

The Mississippi River was under Union control and the next strategy was to split the South in half once again by cutting through Tennessee and across Georgia to the Atlantic Coast. If this division of the Confederacy could be accomplished it would effectively destroy the vital rail lines and place the munitions and manufacturing of the South open to Union assault.

During July, the Union army and navy made a concentrated effort against the South Carolina coast in an attempt to capture Fort Wagner and Fort Sumter. Confederate resistance was strong and although Fort Wagner was finally taken in September, Sumter continued to hold out. The blockade of the Atlantic and Gulf Coasts, coupled with Union domination of the Mississippi River had put a stranglehold on the Confederacy. It remained for the Union to destroy the core of the Confederate resistance which stretched from Richmond to Alabama. The main industrial resources, on which the Confederacy was dependent since its isolation from European supplies, were located in that area. The recent Union

success held the promise of victory if that important region could be taken.

Lincoln encouraged the offensive in Tennessee. Knoxville was an important link for major east–west rail lines and its capture would constitute a major blow to the Confederacy. Also, a Union move into that region would give heart to those who had remained loyal to the Union cause. It had been two years since Lincoln had attempted to assist that region. For several months General Burnside had been reorganizing and training his newly formed Army of the Ohio. In mid-August he took Knoxville virtually uncontested. Within a week he had also defeated a Confederate force and captured the Cumberland Gap. These victories gave the Union complete control of most of eastern Tennessee. However, the Confederate forces stationed in Knoxville had been withdrawn to defend Chattanooga and it appeared they meant to make a stand against the Union offensive. A Southern victory at Chattanooga would more than compensate for the loss of Knoxville.

By mid-August General Rosecrans' Army of the Cumberland was marching toward the Tennessee River and Chattanooga. He had crossed the river on 4 September and was preparing the next phase of his operation. He decided to swing behind the Confederate forces and sever their lines of communication and supply. The garrison would then be forced to attack or starve.

General Bragg, commander of the Confederate forces in that area, had intelligence that Rosecrans was moving some distance south of Chattanooga. He decided to evacuate the city and advance so Rosecrans spread his army danger-ously thin with more than 40 miles between the left and right flanks. There were no major roads over which the sections could march to reunite. If any one of the Union corps were attacked it could easily be defeated before reinforcements could arrive.

Bragg's Army of Tennessee had re-located near Lafayette, Georgia and had increased considerably in size since it had fought Rosecrans at Murfreesboro. Bragg had also consolidated the forces which had been at Knoxville. Should he en-counter any one corps of Rosecrans' divided army the Confederates would have had a superiority of three to one. Bragg's main problem was that he knew very little about the state of the Union advance. Believing that Rosecrans had divided his army into only two columns Bragg decided to strike against the lead division of what was actually the Union center corps. After defeating that force he intended to turn and engage the remainder of the Union forces.

Bragg's strategy might have been a sound, straightforward military opera-tion, but his plans never materialized. The Confederate command was suffering from a lack of confidence in its commanding general. Mutual distrust was so great

*Below:* Longstreet's Corps was sent west to reinforce the Confederate Army of Tennessee under General Braxton Bragg, just in time for the battle of Chickamauga.

Leonidas Polk, Lieutenant General of the
Confederate army and Bishop of the Episcopal
Church commanded the right wing of the Army
of Tennessee.

that the Army of Tennessee had virtually
ground to a halt. The stagnant state of
Bragg's army gave Rosecrans the time he
needed to correct his errors and recon-
solidate his army.

Time was all-important. It would take
Rosecrans two days to regroup, while
Bragg felt that the longer he waited the
stronger his own army would become.
Troops were being siphoned from Longstreet's Corps of the Army of Northern
Virginia to reinforce his army. However,
the capture of Knoxville had severed the
rail link between Richmond and Bragg's
main army, forcing the reinforcements to
travel through the Carolinas and Georgia.
The Confederate rail system, which was
poor at the best of times, was overburden-
ed by that troop movement. Bragg had
no choice except to sit and wait if he
wished to use the troops from the Army of
Virginia in his attack.

By 18 September, at least three brigades
of Longstreet's Corps would have arrived,
and Bragg decided to wait before launching his attack. On that morning Bragg
sent his forces to cross the Chickamauga
Creek with the objective of enveloping
the Union flank. The troops arrived at the
creek only to discover that Union forces
had been positioned to defend the main
bridges and fording sites.

By evening a mere handful of the Confederate troops had been successful in
reaching the western banks of the Chickamauga, but under cover of darkness more
than 75 per cent of the Confederate forces
managed to cross the creek. It was obvious where the main Confederate offensive was being directed and Rosecrans
sent General George Thomas' XIV Corps to
support the left flank.

Confederate commanders were surprised by the number of Union troops they
encountered in the early daylight hours of
19 September, and neither army was
familiar with the densely wooded terrain
around Chickamauga. As the fighting

began both forces lacked proper coordination. By the afternoon the Union position
had been strengthened by the arrival of
III Corps, but the advantage was lost as
increasing numbers of Confederate troops
crossed the creek. By the end of the day
there was not one unit of either army
which had not seen action.

That evening two more brigades from
Longstreet's Corps and the general himself arrived. Longstreet expected to be
met by Bragg and given an assessment of
the situation. He waited but no member
of Bragg's staff appeared. Longstreet
feared the worst, that Bragg had been
killed or was wounded, and he set out in
search of the commander of the Army of
Tennessee. At one point during the search
Longstreet encountered a group of soldiers
and demanded to know their unit. The
soldiers appeared to be as bewildered and
confused by the darkness as Longstreet
and his staff. They answered the general
then stated that they too were lost and
asked for directions. Upon hearing the
troops respond with the numerical desig-
nation of their units Longstreet realized
that they were not Confederate soldiers,
whose habit it was to call their units by
their commanding officer's name. Likewise the Union soldiers were unaware
that they were responding to a Confederate officer. The chance encounter was
more than Longstreet could endure. He
decided that the safest course of action
would be to fade away into the darkness
and search for Bragg's headquarters in
the morning.

Longstreet eventually located Bragg
early on the morning of 20 September in
the process of reorganizing and preparing
for the day's attack. Bragg had decided to
split his forces. Half, under Lieutenant
General Leonidas Polk, had orders to
continue the assault on the Union left
flank. Longstreet was given command of
the remaining forces with the purpose of
following-up any advantages presented
by Polk's attack.

As the Confederate attack began it was
discovered that the Union forces had
retreated during the night to a more
defensible position. In doing so they had
not only shortened their lines but had
strengthened their position at the exact
location of the renewed Confederate offensive. The attack was easily blunted.
Polk's troops threw themselves vainly
against the Union defense and as casualties mounted he was forced to fall back.
Longstreet took up the assault. As his
forces moved forward they found a large
gap in the Union lines of defense. Through
a misinterpretation of orders an entire
Union division had shifted from the right
flank to reinforce the left. The error had
been overlooked and as Confederate forces
took advantage of the error, pouring
through the gap, the Union right flank
crumbled.

Bragg's attempt to envelop the Union
left flank had failed miserably, but the

secondary attack on the right flank had
succeeded beyond his expectations. Longstreet recognized that the Union army's
morale was deteriorating rapidly and
decided to swing to his right and continue
to press his assault. With Longstreet
sweeping toward the rear Union troops
formed a defense along a ridge just south
of Snodgrass House. The desperation of
the Union forces gave a taste of victory to
their Confederate attackers, but the 1st
Division of the Union reserve corps
arrived just in time and kept the Confederates at bay. Sensing the imminent
victory, Longstreet sent an urgent message to General Bragg that with the aid
of reinforcements the battle could be won.
The problem which had continually
plagued the Army of Tennessee surfaced
once again as Bragg balked at the suggestion. True to character he refused to
listen to the opinions, how ever well-
informed, of his subordinates, insisting
that the original strategy was sound and
that he would continue to keep the right
and left flank attacks separate.

Rosecrans troops had been driven from
the field by Longstreet's initial attack and
what remained were those forces under
the command of Major General George
H Thomas. A man of patient, stubborn
character, Thomas decided that the as-
sorted remains of the original three corps
would retreat no further. Every foot of
ground was bitterly contested, but by
nightfall the Confederate forces had managed to push Thomas' units back almost
half the distance from the battlefield to
Chattanooga. Thomas found a site which
offered a suitable defense and there, for
almost 24 hours he waited, for a renewed
Confederate offense.

The Battle of Chickamauga ended with
the Army of Tennessee in possession of the
field. They had sustained 18,000 casualties
to Union losses of 16,000, though the
Confederate forces had captured several
thousand small arms and 50 pieces of
artillery. The victory ignited a spark of
hope within the Southern states. Perhaps
the fortunes of war were again changing
and the defeats at Vicksburg and Gettysburg were but temporary setbacks from
which the Confederacy would soon recover.

As at Murfreesboro the previous year,
Bragg was victorious but failed to pursue
his advantage. The Union army was
obviously moving toward Chattanooga,
so Bragg allowed Rosecrans to retreat to
the city where Confederate forces would
then lay siege. Such a plan would have
been totally unnecessary if Bragg had
quickly pursued the disorganized Union
retreat.

Chattanooga lay on the banks of the
Tennessee River, surrounded by mountains. A few poor roads ran into the city. Assuming that the Union army's only avenue
of resupply would be the river, Bragg intended to besiege and starve the Union
army into submission rather than fight

another battle. To that end he positioned his forces primarily on the south side of the city. The most commanding position was Lookout Mountain to the southwest which had an advantageous view of the river at Moccasin Bend. Holding that height would make it impossible for the Union to move supplies along the river or the roads north of it. He also distributed troops along Missionary Ridge which ran along the southeastern edge of the city. His deployments complete, Bragg waited for Rosecrans to make the next move.

Possessing those two high points, with Chattanooga in the valley between them, made Bragg confident in his siege operation. The principal flaw in his plans was an apparent lack of consideration for the conditions of other areas of the war, and if those conditions would allow him to hold a successful siege. Grant's victory at Vicksburg had freed a large number of Union troops from the Mississippi River area for redeployment elsewhere. Also, should the defense of Richmond require it, Longstreet's Corps would be stripped from Bragg's army and return to the Army of Northern Virginia.

Finally, Bragg did not propose an active siege such as the one Grant had employed at Vicksburg. He failed to fully encircle Chattanooga. A complete encirclement would have forced the Union army to either surrender or attempt to break out.

As the siege commenced Bragg was again at odds with his staff and generals. Some officers had almost reached the point of open revolt, and a growing dissent burdened the army. In the light of the feelings of Bragg's officers, his ability to conduct a successful siege was questionable and perhaps resulted in his 'wait and see' attitude.

The issue became so pronounced that the Confederate President, Jefferson Davis, appeared on the scene to resolve the differences between his commander and his generals. However the rift was so deep and Davis' loyalty and friendship for Bragg so strong that nothing was accomplished. Davis refused to believe that his generals would allow their personal feelings to jeopardize the army, and the cause.

While the Army of Tennessee struggled with its personal difficulties, the Union was working desperately to reinforce Rosecrans. 'Fightin' Joe' Hooker was sent from Virginia with units from the Army of the Potomac's XI and XII Corps. General Sherman was on the march from the Mississippi River with a large force from the Army of the Tennessee. Less than a month after the Battle of Chickamauga, Grant was given the command over all Union forces in the West. He replaced Rosecrans as commander of the Army of the Cumberland with General Thomas.

Bragg's only aggressive action was to send General Joe Wheeler's cavalry on a raid into Tennessee to destroy lines of communication and supply destined for the besieged troops at Chattanooga. The fact that is was an isolated action without further coordinated efforts meant that the approaching Union support was merely delayed not halted altogether.

On 23 October Grant arrived at Chattanooga. Thomas' staff immediately presented him with a plan which would open new supply lines to the west, across Raccoon Mountain and the river, to roads north of Chattanooga. At the same time, Hooker's forces arrived via the northern bank of the Tennessee River, northwest of the city. Hooker's role in the intended plan was to move towards Brown's Ferry where a pontoon bridge across the river would be constructed. Once Hooker had secured the area he would guard the intended supply route and the bridge site. Grant gave his approval and the plans were put into action. Within the five days

Late in summer the Confederate navy made a concerted effort to break the Federal blockade on the eastern seaboard.

The resistance of the Confederate army outside Chattanooga refuted the rumor that they were in retreat.

The Federal superiority at Lookout Mountain was tested by the terrain. The battle was fought in a heavy mist and the Confederate position worsened as darkness fell.

the supply problem had been solved. Grant waited only for the arrival of Sherman's reinforcements to swing the balance of power in favor of the Union before attempting to break the siege and attack Bragg's army.

Bragg, receiving reports of the Union build up and the reopening of a new supply line, reevaluated his previous plans. He decided to divide his army once again, sending Longstreet to eastern Tennessee to lay siege to Burnside's forces at Knoxville. His reasoning for such an action at such a time has often been questioned. It merely frightened the civilian population of the area and gave Grant an increased belief in his ability to defeat Bragg once Sherman arrived.

In mid-November Sherman's forces reached Chattanooga. Grant had decided to ignore the area around Lookout Mountain, concentrating his main efforts against Missionary Ridge. Sherman's role involved an extensive march from the far western flank, across Hooker's pontoon bridge, to the Union far left flank, where he would recross the river, and finally launch his assault against the northern edge of Missionary Ridge. Sherman's assault was to be a surprise attack, and as Lookout Mountain commanded a view of most of the valley, Sherman was

forced to follow the northern bank of the river which provided the concealment of forests and hills.

Sherman's attack was scheduled to begin on 21 November, but heavy rains and the rupturing of the pontoon bridge forced him to leave one division behind with Hooker. The decrease in his troop strength would mean a delay of two or three days in the execution of his maneuver. Although Grant's original plans had included neither Hooker nor Lookout Mountain, it became evident that with the addition of Sherman's division, Hooker should be able to bring pressure to bear against the Confederate left flank in its position on the height.

Sherman was approaching his destination when Grant received the intelligence that Bragg was withdrawing. In disbelief he decided to test the validity of such information by launching an assault against the center of Bragg's position on Missionary Ridge. On 23 November Union troops advanced and engaged the Confederates in the Battle of Orchard Knob. It was only a Confederate outpost, but the stiff resistance told Grant that Bragg could not be retreating. Finally the Union forces overpowered the Confederate resistance, the position was taken.

On 24 November Hooker's forces attacked Lookout Mountain in an engagement dubbed 'The Battle above the Clouds.' Lookout Mountain rose some 1500 feet above the town of Chattanooga, and although the battle was staged below

the peak and not actually in the clouds, the heavy mist which prevailed gave the battle its title. The outcome of the encounter was inevitable as Hooker had a superiority of six to one. Confederate defenders made a desperate stand at Craven's House, but as darkness approached their position became ever more difficult and they withdrew to join the main bulk of the army on Missionary Ridge.

While Hooker assaulted Lookout Mountain, Sherman crossed the river in the final leg of his maneuver and attacked what he thought to be the northern slopes of Missionary Ridge. He actually succeeded in capturing the hill known as Battery Heights just north of the ridge. His attack had surprised the enemy but Sherman realized that his error had cost him that element in the actual attack, and that on the following day the Confederate defenders would be amply prepared.

On the morning of 25 November, Sherman launched his six divisions at the ridge against General Patrick Cleburne's lone Confederate division. The action was so fierce and the Confederates so determined that in places where the ridge was too steep to bring cannon fire to bear they threw boulders and cannon balls down on their attackers. Sherman's forces were repulsed and Cleburne's troops held their position.

As Sherman's division began to falter, Grant wondered what had become of Hooker. He had been scheduled to launch an attack against the Confederate left flank to disorganize their command and prevent them from moving troops to the right flank. Unable to wait any longer for Hooker, Grant ordered General Thomas' forces, who faced the center of Missionary Ridge, to advance. The wisdom of such an attack was questioned but the closer Thomas' troops drew to the Confederate defenses the less they were harassed by enemy fire. It soon became apparent that Bragg's army was in full retreat. Within an hour of Thomas' attack the Confederate forces had abandoned the battle. Grant attempted to exploit the situation by pursuing the Confederate army, but throughout the day of 26 November Cleburne's troops fought a fanatical rear guard defense which allowed the army to retreat intact.

The unexpected retreat has often been blamed on the excellent view which the Confederate troops on Missionary Ridge had of the valley. Before them they could see the massing of a large Union army, while they knew that there was activity on both flanks of the ridge. Feeling that retreat, like discretion, was the better part of valor they abandoned their positions rather than face another battle. The Army of Tennessee had not lost its will to fight, for it would fight against great odds in the future. It was simply that the soldiers saw no profit in continuing such a battle and their generals, at odds with Bragg, merely followed through with the retreat.

Bragg's victory at Chickamauga had quickly been negated by the events at Chattanooga. Union forces were victorious on all major fronts. Grant's 60,000 troops had suffered approximately 10 per cent casualties, while the Confederate losses numbered some 7000, of which 4000 were either captured or deserted. It was glaringly evident to Jefferson Davis that in spite of his fondness for Bragg, he had to be replaced, and General Joseph E Johnston assumed command of the Army of Tennessee.

Grant had broken the alleged siege at Chattanooga and his attention turned to Knoxville and Longstreet's siege against Burnside's Army of the Ohio. Informed that Grant's forces were on the move to reinforce the Knoxville garrison, Longstreet made a valiant effort to capture the city but was repulsed. With that failure he drew toward the border of North Carolina to take up winter quarters.

The year of 1863 drew to a close with the balance weighing heavily in favor of the Union. The complete subjugation of the South seemed imminent. No longer could the Confederacy take the war into the North. They would be forced to take a defensive stance, hoping that the Union would grow weary of war or that some miracle would occur to bring new hope for the future.

Federal supply trains were under constant threat from Confederate guerrilla bands.

The Battle of the Wilderness was fought over the same ground as the battle of Chancellorsville the previous year.

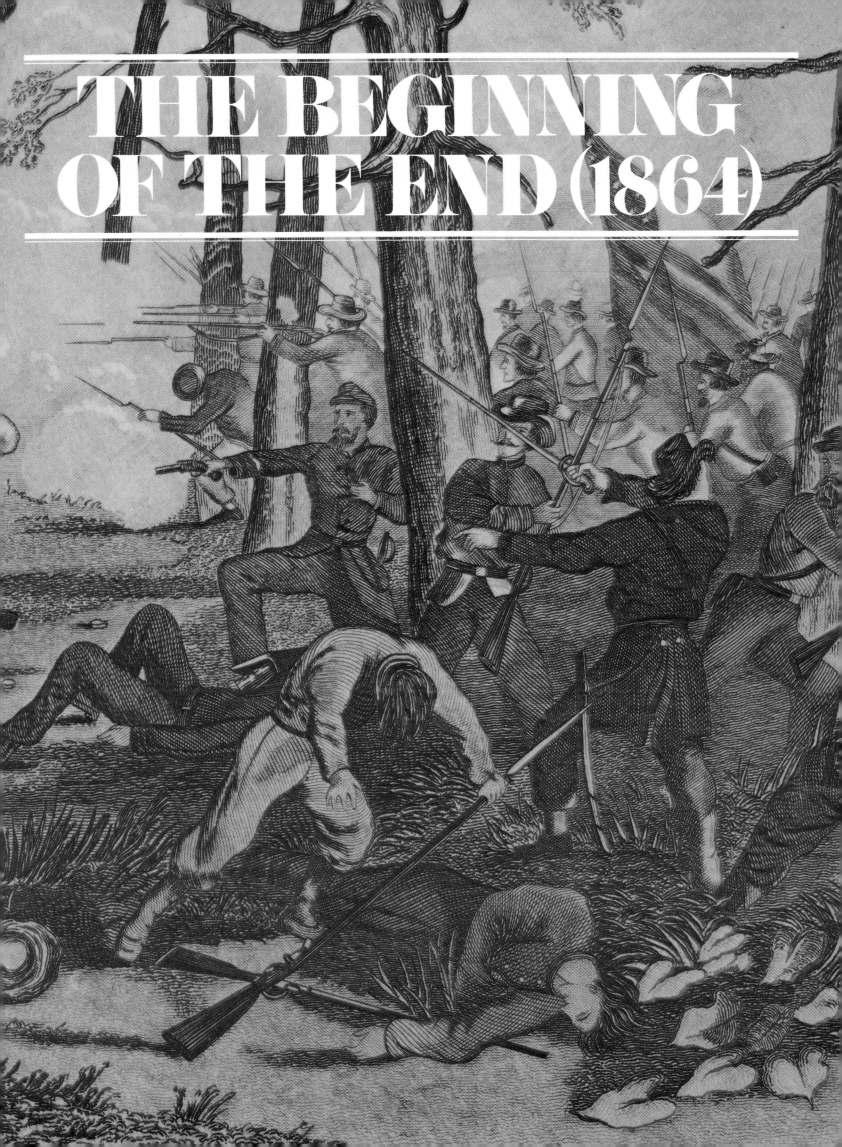

# THE BEGINNING
# OF THE END (1864)

The year 1864 began with a Union advantage and Northern hopes of quelling the Southern 'rebellion' were optimistic. There were those who believed that a strong effort by the Union armies during the spring and summer would break the Confederacy completely. Ulysses S Grant was the hero of the moment. He had become the favorite of the people, and of Lincoln and the Congress as well. Many felt that at last they had found the man to lead the Union armies to victory and put an end to the seemingly endless conflict.

Grant was not so optimistic. Since Shiloh he had known that his adversary's will to fight was strong, and even though everything seemed to be against it the South would not give up by summer, Grant knew that the task of defeating his enemy would be neither swift nor simple, and at least one, perhaps two, more years of fighting lay ahead.

In the early months of 1864 the federal government revived the rank of Lieutenant General for Grant. He was also given command of all the armies of the United States. The rank of Lieutenant General had only been given twice before in American history, and Winfield Scott had only been 'breveted.' Thus, Lieutenant General Grant ranked with only one other American officer, George Washington.

By association Grant was elevated to a position of public acclaim and recognition which actually embarrassed him. So many others had sought to use their positions and the war to realize ambitions which would probably have been unattainable during peacetime, but Grant had no desire for that life. He was a man practicing the trade which he had been taught. He knew the cruelty, destruction and degradation of his profession at first hand and wanted only to end the war as swiftly as possible.

Although Grant was extremely popular, few people knew anything about him except what they read in papers or heard in gossip. The idealization of Grant was in direct contrast to his actual appearance and personality. On his arrival in Washington on 8 March 1864 to formally accept his new rank and position no one recognized Grant and his son as they left the train station. The sophistication of the capital could tear men away from duty or drive them to it. In Grant's case, after only a few days in Washington he knew that he had to rejoin his army. Once the initial excitement over his appointment had subsided, Grant applied himself to the task at hand. He was a soldier and knew that if the war was to be won certain changes had to be made immediately. The first item on his agenda was a reorganization of the entire military establishment,

*Above:* Grant was given command of all the armies of the United States, with the rank of Lieutenant General in 1864.
*Above right:* Henry Halleck was appointed to be Grant's Chief of Staff.
*Left:* Major General William Tecumseh Sherman, USV, (1820–91) replaced Grant as commander of the Union army in the West.

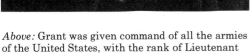

*Above:* Meade still commanded the Army of the Potomac, although Grant joined this force in the field.

from the staff down to the corps and regiments. His appointment was made in March, which meant that his reorganization program would have to be completed within two months before the weather broke and the summer campaigns began.

Acting in his capacity as General in Chief, Grant retained his former commander General Halleck as a liaison officer in Washington. Grant understood that Halleck's potential lay, as Lincoln had once said, not in his military value but as a 'first rate clerk.' Halleck's duties would free Grant from the administrative affairs which would have entangled him if he had been required to remain in the capital.

He gave Sherman the command of the West, including Grant's former position as commander of the Military Division of Mississippi. He then appointed Major General James McPherson as commander of Sherman's army. Grant wanted to replace the men in key positions with men of his own philosophy, but he also felt it was important to relieve some of the individuals whose ineffectiveness in command was, in Grant's opinion, like 'committing little better than murder.' He tried to remove men who had received command through political influence, but he soon discovered that he was virtually powerless to change certain appointments. Lincoln was sympathetic but 1864 was an election year. It would have been political suicide to campaign without the support of the political power such men could wield in certain parts of the country. If Grant could not remove those 'ineffective' commanders he decided that he 'would damn well use them.' He reassigned those generals from second line, 'safe' duty to the front so that they could accomplish something more than the consumption of food and the digging of latrines. It would not have greatly dis-

pleased Grant if those particular generals betrayed their own faults and inabilities in the execution of their new assignments.

With Sherman in command of the West and Halleck spearheading the administrative efforts in Washington, Grant assigned himself to the field, attached to Meade's Army of the Potomac, which was immediately dubbed 'Grant's Army.' Meade, being the true soldier that he was, took no offense at the change, in spite of the fact that he had been the general who commanded the army in its darkest days and had achieved the victory at Gettysburg. Grant never intended to remove Meade or usurp his authority as army commander, but as General in Chief of the armies he felt that he could only operate from the front lines. The ultimate foe was Lee and the Army of Northern Virginia and Grant felt his place was definitely directly opposite Lee with the Army of the Potomac.

Major General Alfred Pleasanton was replaced as commander of the Union Cavalry Corps by Major General Phillip H Sheridan. Sheridan had been recognized as a dogged fighter and campaigner who was not afraid to take a calculated risk and who could often inspire his men to accomplish the seemingly impossible. Grant recognized that Sheridan could supply the much needed spark to the Union cavalry and enable it to adequately rival Stuart and his Southern troopers. Sheridan might take the initiative away from Lee's legendary horsemen.

Grant's prime objective was to coordinate a strategy which would involve all the Union armies, moving continuously against objectives in the South. He had often referred to the Union war efforts as

On 6 May Hancock's II Corps struck the Confederate right flank and began to rout the troops of AP Hill's corps. The battle appeared lost when Longstreet's corps arrived on the battlefield. Forming on the run they threw themselves recklessly against Hancock's men and through sheer nerve and courage drove the Union attack back to its starting point. Longstreet saw that the advantage had swung in his favor and decided to continue his attack and organize a counteroffensive against the Union left flank.

That counteroffensive had all the earmarks of reenacting Jackson's famous flank attack of the previous year, if it could succeed. It did not. As the assault began a Confederate unit accidentally fired on Longstreet and his staff, severely wounding the general in the throat. Disaster seemed to be repeating itself. Lee, making his way to the front, saw Longstreet lying wounded not far from the place where Jackson had been mortally wounded a

nothing more than a mass of troops striking at different points at different times, limited in scope and purpose by the shortsightedness of their commanders. With Sherman in the West and Grant in the East there could only be one ultimate objective, the destruction of the enemy. Coordination was the factor which would play a decisive role in the new strategy. Grant did not intend to allow the South to relax its vigilance or shift its troops from one front to another. He knew that if he kept the pressure strong enough, long enough, the weight of that pressure would soon be too much for the Confederacy to tolerate.

The over all strategy was fundamental. The Mississippi region had been secured and Sherman was ordered to strike against the heartland of the South, toward Atlanta and the coast, and destroy the industrial and munitions factories located there. Grant, leading the Army of the Potomac, would strike through Virginia with the ultimate goals of eliminating Lee's army and seizing Richmond.

On 4 May 1864 Grant launched his spring campaign. Although hoping to catch Lee's army in a position where it might be easily destroyed, Grant was aware that a more realistic outlook for the campaign would probably be that of attrition, wearing Lee down little by little without the Union army suffering defeat through error or miscalculation. Grant made his intentions clear. The Army of the Potomac was to move against Lee with such ferocity that the Confederate commander would be harassed to the limits of his endurance.

Sending General Franz Sigel through the Shenandoah Valley and General Benjamin Butler's Army of the James toward Richmond via the southern bank of the James River, in an attempt to isolate Lee from the heart of the Confederacy, Grant drove the Army of the Potomac across the

*Right:* II Corps under the command of Major General Hancock encamped on the Brock Road between the Wilderness Tavern and Spotsylvania Court House.
*Above:* By June 1864, the Union Army of the James was building fortifications around the perimeters of Richmond and Petersburg.

Rapidan River at Germanna's Ford. He was on a course for the Wilderness where less than one year earlier the Army of the Potomac had been defeated at the Battle of Chancellorsville.

Lee, aware of Grant's movements, viewed the situation as extremely favorable. His army still had room to maneuver and a chance to catch Grant's army on the flank as they marched. Although the opportunity was to Lee's advantage, he did not feel comfortable opposing the new commander of the Union forces. Unlike the previous Union commanders whom Lee had known personally, which had enabled him to assess and exploit their weaknesses, Grant was an unknown quantity, known only through reputation and hearsay. His strategy and tactics in the West convinced Lee that Grant should be taken seriously.

Nevertheless Lee marched his army forward to engage Grant's flank as the Union army advanced toward the Wilderness. Grant, who had been keeping watch for such an action, turned to meet the challenge. On 5 May just west of the Wilderness Tavern, near the point where Jackson had initiated his flank attack against Hooker's army, the Army of the Potomac and the Army of Northern Virginia met. The advantage lay with Grant in the early stages as Lee's forces had marched a great distance and were sent piecemeal into the battle. As the troops of both armies continued to arrive, the Battle of the Wilderness grew with neither side able to gain a decisive advantage. By afternoon both armies were stretched along a five-mile front.

year before, and nearly lost the will to continue the battle. However, the confusion overtaking Longstreet's corps forced Lee to act and he ordered a halt to the counterattack and a reorganization of the units.

Hancock's men had managed to prepare defensive breastworks, but the furor of the Confederates was so great that Longstreet's corps easily captured those defenses. Victory seemed imminent until a brush fire spread between the Union and the Confederate forces, halting the advance and causing the Confederate troops to lose their momentum. By the time the fire was under control Grant had deployed a successful counterattack against the Confederates still at the breastworks, and the Confederate troops were driven back.

Grant reported more than 17,000 casualties from his army of 100,000, and Lee lost 8000 of his 60,000 man force. The Battle of the Wilderness had for the most part been fought over the same ground as the Battle of Chancellorsville. The bones of those who had not been found by burial parties after that battle still lay on the ground and the fire which had blazed through the thickets had caused hundreds of men who were wounded or unable to escape the flames to burn to death. Their screams were heard even at the farthest edges of the front. One Confederate soldier described the battle as 'true hell on earth.'

The Battle of the Wilderness was a stalemate. Lee's army had emerged bloodied but not defeated. Lee counted himself fortunate, except for the wounding of Longstreet, whom he considered irreplaceable, and planned to rest his troops while the Union army retreated.

On 7 May Grant gave orders for the army to proceed south through the night. That move took Lee completely by surprise. He had no idea what Grant's intentions were but he knew instinctively that his opponent had indeed come to fight.

The Confederate officer corps, which was the pride of the Army of Northern Virginia, had been severely depleted by losses at Chancelorsville, Gettysburg and finally at the Wilderness. Longstreet's wounds would incapacitate him for months. A P Hill had become ill through the wearing effects of the war. Lee found that the burdens of battle had become more taxing as he was forced to personally serve in the field. That role was not to Lee's liking, but as his most able generals were taken from him he had to accept that aspect of his command.

In the middle of the afternoon of 7 May Stuart's cavalry engaged in a sharp action with Union troopers several miles north of Spotsylvania Courthouse. Shortly after breaking off the Confederate cavalry unit sighted what they considered to be Grant's headquarters breaking camp and heading south. That was sufficient evidence for Lee. Obviously Grant had no intention of 'turning-tail' and was de-

*Above:* At this time the Confederate forces were also defending the Valley of Virginia.

monstrating his resolution to continue south. Keeping the Army of the Potomac between Richmond and the Army of Northern Virginia, and denying Lee the mutual protection of his own capital, Grant was again preparing for battle. In retaliation Lee instructed Major General Richard H Anderson, who had replaced the wounded Longstreet as commander of the I Corps, to 'march with due haste' to Spotsylvania. Lee would follow with the remainder of the army as quickly as possible. Lee's orders to Anderson were to march no later than three o'clock on the morning of 8 May, but Anderson, who was extremely conscientious, felt that it would be prudent to commence the maneuver as early as possible and set out four hours earlier at eleven o'clock on the night of 7 May.

As Anderson marched the Confederate cavalry under Stuart was engaged, on an increasing scale, with the Union cavalry and the lead elements of Grant's army as it too marched toward the crossroad. Stuart, like Grant, knew that if that section were taken by the Union forces Lee would be effectively blocked from the Confederate capital. Although Stuart's troopers were giving a fine account of themselves, the situation was becoming critical. In desperation Stuart sent word back along the Confederate proposed line of march to seek aid for his beleaguered troopers. Anderson's forces, who had marched throughout the night were only three miles from Spotsylvania, preparing for breakfast, when Stuart's message

*Above left:* Unknown to each other, the Union and Confederate armies were racing toward a confrontation at Spotsylvania.
*Left:* The battles around Spotsylvania lasted for almost two weeks involving some of the most bitter fighting of the war, with combats taking place every day.

arrived. Anderson immediately acknowledged the desperate nature of the situation and ordered his troops to march toward the sound of gunfire.

Shortly after eight in the morning on 8 May the lead division of I Corps, commanded by Brigadier General J B Kershaw, relieved the harassed Confederate cavalry division of Fitzhugh Lee. They drove back the Union assault which would surely have carried the position had not those reinforcements arrived. The Confederate troopers were near the point of exhaustion from the uninterrupted assaults and could have been easily routed.

Sheridan was quick to grasp that he was no longer fighting Stuart's wearied men and that fresh troops were being added to the Confederate defenses. Sheridan ordered his troopers to withdraw and he began probing along the Confederate lines to test and evaluate the strength of the enemy's forces. General G K Warren's V Corps, a single division of which had been supporting Sheridan's troops, was now completely on line and participating in the battle. Anderson's precipitate action saved Lee from a situation which could have meant the end for his army, Richmond and the Confederate cause.

The Confederate troops skirmished intermittently throughout 8 May as they built trenches and fortifications to improve their position at the crossroads. Generally it took an army three days to construct front line fortifications and field works, yet those troops managed to accomplish in 24 hours what should have taken 72. General Meade and his staff were astonished by the Confederate soldiers' ingenuity and speed and it became obvious that the Confederate troops could be dislodged only by a major confrontation.

The following day, 9 May saw little action between the two armies, though a Confederate marksman sighted and killed Major General John Sedgwick, com-

mander of the Union VI Corps. Grant permitted General Sheridan to take his cavalry corps and break away from the mass of the army with the purpose of raiding Lee's lines of communication and the Confederate rear area. Lee's own cavalry had been granted sufficient rest and Stuart was able to counter Sheridan's move and overtake the larger Union cavalry force on 11 May at a site known as Yellow Tavern, just north of Richmond. During the ensuing battle Jeb Stuart was killed, a fact which many said was as fierce a blow to the Confederacy as Jackson's death one year earlier. The outcome of the engagement was a minimal Union advantage but the loss of Jeb Stuart was more devastating than any Confederate defeat might have been.

With the cavalry forces away from the main concentration of both armies, Grant and Lee had condemned themselve to fighting blind. Troops were thrown against positions along the length of the front line, searching for a weak point through which to make a breach in the enemy's lines.

By the evening of the 9th Lee's forces had taken their positions at Spotsylvania. A salient dubbed the 'Mule Shoe,' which was more than one and a half miles wide at its base, had emerged from the original Confederate lines. Most of the Confederate commanders had doubts as to the ability of the fortifications on the salient to withstand the pressure if the Union

Major General J E B Stuart, commander of Lee's Cavalry Corps was killed in a skirmish at Yellow Tavern.

By 8 May the Union V Corps under the command of Major General Gouverneur Warren was encamped two miles north of Spotsylvania Courthouse.

forces were to attack it in great numbers. Critics pointed out that if the Mule Shoe was broken, the Union forces would have little difficulty in either surging into the rear of the Confederate army or in splitting it into two sections which would be unable to support one another.

However Ewell and several of the army's senior engineers had great faith in the construction of the fortifications which comprised the Mule Shoe. They were convinced that as long as a good number of artillery pieces were assigned to its defense, the salient would be secure. Ewell also pointed out that the salient would be crucial to the outcome of the battle. Such an area would without a doubt draw a major Union attack in the hope of pinching off the salient, surrounding it, then of course driving through to the Confederate rear. No general would ignore such an opportunity. As a result, Ewell was convinced that if Lee supported him and his troops in the Mule Shoe, Grant would throw his army against it and be destroyed in the process.

On the evening of 10 May Grant launched the anticipated attack against the salient. Throughout the day he probed to find a weakness, but the Confederate resistance was so strong that little was gained by the Union attacks. One brigade, under Brigadier General Upton, managed to surprise a section of the Confederate line. Some gains were made when Confederate troops under Generals Johnson and Gordon counterattacked, driving the Union forces back. That particular incident though not actually successful, impressed Grant and he decided that if the attack were renewed on a far grander scale it might indeed prove to be the weakness for which he had been searching

to dislodge the Confederates from their positions.

On 11 May Grant maneuvered 75 per cent of his army into positions around the salient. That massive movement did not go undetected by the Confederate line commanders and they relayed the information to their commanding general. Lee once again misinterpreted and underestimated Grant. Lee believed that only two courses of action were open to his adversary; either to fall back toward Fredericksburg and regroup, or be bold once again as he had been at the Wilderness and sidestep Lee's position to move around the Confederate right flank. Lee did not realize that Grant was only maneuvering for a full-scale assault, and gave orders to his commanders to be prepared to move the army on a moment's notice. Lee's gravest error was pulling two battalions of artillery from a position, which had protected the salient, and placing them at a point which would enable rapid movement and deployment to the new battlefield to which Lee felt Grant was going to draw him.

Before dawn on 12 May, Lee's error in judgment was felt in earnest as Union artillery fired on the Confederate positions. The few Confederate pickets skirmished with Union troops of Hancock's corps as they became barely visible in the early morning fog. Hancock's II Corps, which had been drawn up in a classical Napoleonic mass column, smashed through Johnson's division which they outnumbered by more than ten to one and drove rapidly through the Mule Shoe to the second line of defense held by General Gordon's division. Hancock's initial success was hampered as his troops were disorganized not only by the attack but by the large number of Confederate prisoners taken. Also, the confining space of the salient had funneled the Union troops into an area of less than one square

mile, hindering their ability to capitalize on the initial success.

As the Union assault floundered, Gordon organized his and Rodes' divisions into a second line of resistance, managing to blunt any further advancement by Hancock's corps. By mid-morning the situation had developed into a stalemate with both sides fighting fiercely to merely maintain status quo. A Confederate officer who had seen fighting at both Gaines' Mill and Gettysburg wrote that the fighting at the salient was more intense than any he had previously seen.

Grant sensed that there was a strong possibility that the Army of Northern Virginia would be crushed if he brought up his reserves. Lee, sensing the same, tried to take back some of the initiative by ordering a counterattack along the west face of the salient. The fighting which followed, was dubbed the 'Bloody Angle.' The carnage and destruction of that engagement rivaled that of the fiercest battles of the Civil War. Both armies appeared to be fighting for their very lives.

The battle raged and as an ever increasing number of casualties were taken, a torrential downpour began. One young Confederate trooper claimed that God Almighty was trying to wash the ground clean of the blood that they had spilled on those few acres.

For six more days Grant hammered at Lee but without success and by 18 May both sides were completely exhausted. The following day Ewell pulled his crippled corps from the trenches trying desperately to ascertain if Grant had given up the fight or had decided once again to side-step the Confederates and move against Richmond. Ewell's II Corps ran directly into Grant's heavy artillery, which had been recently called forward from the reserves near Washington. After a confused skirmish the Confederate forces retired.

With that skirmish the Battle of Spotsylvania ended. While an exact count of casualties varies according to the source, the number is generally conceded to be approximately 10,000 combined, it was the number of losses sustained in so small an area which made them seem phenomenal.

Grant swung his army wide, slipping around Lee's army and continued on a course for the James River and Richmond. Union losses had been severe, but Grant knew that he had more than enough reserves to offset his losses. Lee clearly did not have enough troops to continue in the style of campaign that was being waged. Attrition was showing its effects on the Confederate army as well as on Lee himself. Ewell's corps had been reduced to little more than a strong division and Lee was fully conscious that all he could do was desperately fight defensive battles, hiding behind entrenchments in an effort to block Grant's movements toward the Confederate capital.

Grant spent the remainder of May probing the strengths of the Confederate army in an effort to turn Lee's flank or catch the Confederate command off guard. On 3 June Lee and Grant met near Mechanicsville at the Battle of Cold Harbor. Once again Grant chose to meet his enemy directly, ordering a massive frontal assault on the Confederate position which was repulsed with a large number of Union casualties. The fighting in that area continued until 12 June without definite resolution.

Elsewhere the Union armies were experiencing a similar lack of success. Sigel's defeat in the Shenandoah Valley and Butler's mismanagement of the operation below Richmond gave Grant no support. The pressure remained on the Army of the Potomac to continue its attacks on the ever weakening Army of Northern Virginia.

After Cold Harbor Grant decided to shift his army. He resolved to move to the

*Right:* The horrors of the fighting at the 'Bloody Angle' were increased by the heavy spring rain.
*Below:* In July 1864, a Confederate force commanded by Jubal Early came within five miles of Washington in an attempt to draw Grant's army away from Lee to the defense of the capitol.

N. B. FORREST.

Nathan Bedford Forrest commanded a Confederate cavalry detachment in a series of raids in the West.

south bank of the James River, slip below Richmond, and then isolate the Confederate capital by besieging Petersburg. Again Grant detached Sheridan's cavalry corps to divert Lee's attention and give the Union army time in which to gain its objective. Sheridan was ordered to meet General David Hunter, General Sigel's replacement, who had taken command of the Shenandoah campaign and captured Staunton, Virginia.

To counter that action Lee detached Major General Jubal Early's corps and two divisions of cavalry. That cavalry, under the command of General Wade Hampton, successfully drove Sheridan's forces back at the Battle of Trevilian Station, and Early's corps defeated Hunter near Lynchburg, forcing the Union forces back across the Blue Ridge Mountains.

At that point Early startled even Lee with his next maneuver. He knew that time had to be bought for Lee and the Army of Northern Virginia, and that he somehow had to disrupt the flow of Union reinforcements that Grant so distinctly relied upon in his battle of attrition strategy. Only one thing could stop that flow and be considered of significant importance to pull those troops away. That was a threat to the Union capital.

By 11 July Early had marched his corps out of the Shenandoah Valley and was within five miles of the White House. Panic reigned in Washington and Grant was forced to detach a corps from his army to reinforce the Washington garrison.

Early, a realist, knew that his small force could not hope to capture Washington, but his troops gave a good account of themselves in a skirmish at Fort Stevens on 12 July. The North was completely convinced that it was Early's intention to capture the capital. Lincoln himself stood on the ramparts of Fort Stevens to watch the battle. As Northern forces and reinforcements consolidated, Early

realized that his hoax could not continue without endangering the very existence of his men, and he withdrew across the Potomac River.

Early's diversion was one of the most astounding of the Civil War. In boldness and imagination it was comparable to Jackson's Valley Campaign of 1862. He had succeeded not only in saving Lynchburg but had cleared the Shenandoah Valley of all Union troops and caused Grant to allot a percentage of his forces from the sieges of Richmond and Petersburg to the defense of Washington.

At the same time, in the West, Sherman was moving from Chattanooga. He planned a strike at Atlanta and the heart of Georgia, the crossroad of the Confederacy around which industry and the railroad had grown. Sherman, who had succeeded Grant, had more than 100,000 men under his command divided into three armies. The first was Major General George Thomas' Army of the Cumberland; the second, Major General John Schofield's Army of the Ohio; and the third, Major General James B McPherson's Army of the Tennessee. Sherman had no less than 20 infantry divisions, four cavalry divisions, and more than 250 field artillery pieces with which to accomplish his drive into the South

Opposing him initially was the ill-fated Braxton Bragg, whose Army of Tennessee had been soundly defeated by Grant at Chattanooga and driven back into Georgia. That Confederate army, under Bragg's influence, had been stricken by a severe defeatist attitude. Its soldiers claimed that their officers' ranks could be told not by their braid insignia but by the number of bullet holes they received in the seats of their pants during their retreat. Desertion in the ranks was officially listed in the hundreds, but more realistic figures indicated that thousands of soldiers were absent without leave.

The Army of Tennessee's effectiveness was almost nil, except for one or two divisions such as Major General Patrick Cleburne's Division which had acquitted itself well at Chickamauga and Chattanooga and whose fighting spirit did not yet appear broken. But even that division was not without its percentage of deserters. The high desertion rate was not only a result of low morale, but was also due to the army's deficiencies in the food, clothing and ammunition necessary to conduct itself as a viable fighting force. After long debate, Lee convinced a very begrudging Jefferson Davis to institute an investigation into the Army of Tennessee's plight and to replace Bragg with General Joseph E Johnston.

Davis, a lifelong friend of Bragg's, fought against his replacement but the evidence was overwhelming. A change had to be made or Bragg's army would cease to function completely and the Union troops would literally walk across the South to victory. Johnston was given

command of the army but Davis tried to make it appear as though Bragg was being promoted to a new position rather than being relieved of command. He appointed Bragg as 'Special Military Advisor' to the Confederate President in an effort to eliminate any embarrassment his friend might suffer.

Johnston was appalled at both the physical and emotional condition of the army. In one of his first actions, designed to combat the problem of desertion, Johnston called for amnesty for all deserters who voluntarily returned to their former regiments. He also promised the men an active furlough system. The objective of that system was not only to allow the men a chance to go home and visit their families, but to alleviate the problems involved in supplying and feeding the army in the immediate future. Furloughed men would be better fed at home and probably sufficiently reclothed by their families.

Johnston's next aim was to reestablish confidence in the army. He insisted on discipline and drill and held mock battles during the winter and early spring to increase the efficiency of both the men and junior officers. He was realistic in his approach to the type of fighting the troops would be engaging in and spent a great deal of time drilling the men in the procedures of digging field entrenchments to enable them adequately to defend themselves against the larger Union forces.

By spring 1864 the Army of Tennessee had been put back on its feet and enjoyed an excellent state of morale. However, the whole affair continued to annoy Jefferson Davis. His friend had lost his command to Johnston and Davis constantly harassed Johnston in the hope he would fail as Bragg had done the previous year. Johnston withstood the pressure.

Johnston's strategy was to goad the Union army into relinquishing its ambitions by making the cost of victory intolerable. Johnston intended to bleed Sherman every step of the way, giving not an inch of ground cheaply to the Union invaders.

In one bid to stem Sherman's advance General Nathan B Forest was ordered to conduct operations in Kentucky, Tennessee, and along the Mississippi River to disrupt and imbalance the Union through the necessity of transferring troops to repulse him. During the month of March Forrest raided as far north as Paducah, Kentucky and on his return operations captured Fort Pillow. The 'Fort Pillow Incident' was one of the truly dark moments of the Civil War which many tend to gloss over or ignore. The fort was garrisoned by both black and white troops. It was said that Forrest, upon accepting the surrender, took the white troops prisoner but refused to honor the same conditions for the black troops. On his orders those troops were either shot or driven back into the fort to be burned alive as Forrest had the fort set ablaze. For the remainder of the summer Forrest skirmished with Union forces but was never defeated. As late as August he raided Memphis, Tennessee, fighting through the defenses, capturing the headquarters and destroying supplies. He then withdrew in good order, defying a large Union contingent.

At the beginning of May 1864 Sherman moved from Chattanooga into Georgia along the rail lines toward Ringgold. The Union army was soon brought up at the 1400 foot cliffs just outside Dalton. In the mountains of north Georgia Confederate troops held a ridge known as Buzzard's Roost and successfully blocked the Union advance. Sherman, believing that the Army of Tennessee was still nothing more than a ragged force whose fighting ability and morale were grossly deficient, threw Thomas' Army of the Cumberland against the Confederates. The Union attack was swiftly repelled.

General Joseph Eggleston Johnston, CSA, (1820–91) became commander of the Army of Tennessee and the defender of Atlanta.

Sherman later referred to the incident as a 'terrible door of death' which he had sent Thomas' forces to knock down but which had opened to swallow the lives of his troops. It was obvious that Sherman's impatience had caused him to sacrifice men unnecessarily. He decided to send McPherson's army south and outflank the Confederate position via the Snake Creek Gap. As Union forces reached the Gap more than 4000 Confederate reinforcements arrived to engage McPherson's troops in a running skirmish. McPherson, thinking that he had encountered the entire Confederate army, disengaged and sent word to Sherman that he needed immediate reinforcements. He dug in to await the arrival of the remainder of the Union army.

On 13 and 14 May Sherman shifted his army to the Gap and attacked the strengthened Confederate position commanded by Lieutenant General Polk. All through the night 'Fightin' Joe' Hooker, commander of the XX Corps of Thomas' army, launched a succession of attacks against the unyielding Confederate defenses. By morning Hooker was personally leading his troops, but they continued to waver as the number of losses increased. However, Hooker relentlessly continued the assaults and slowly the Confederate flank was turned, giving a small advantage to the Union forces.

With his troops wearying and having no

General Sherman outside Atlanta. The photograph was taken by Mathew Brady on 19 July 1864.

desire to endanger his army Johnston pulled back to Cashville where he once again positioned his men in a well-laid ambush. The element of surprise was accidentally lost by Lieutenant General John B Hood's impetuosity and with the attempted ambush thwarted the Confederates removed to the next defensible position in the Allatoona Range.

Sherman had gained a new respect for his opponent and believed that it would not be advantageous to strike immediately against the elevated Confederate position. Once again he sent a force to outflank the Confederates. On the second occasion, however, Johnston was one step ahead of Sherman, having sent Hood's Corps to the area around New Hope Church to block any flanking attempt.

On 25 May Hooker's XX Corps once more attacked the entrenched Confederates. In a battle dubbed 'Hell Hole' Union soldiers threw themselves against the Confederate position, sustaining enormous casualties. By the end of the day Hooker had initiated three separate charges and had gained nothing but heavy losses to his corps. So intense was the fighting that both Sherman and Johnston shifted their primary points of attack and defense to that area.

On 28 May Union forces once again took the offensive against the Confederates, but still no advantage was gained. By dusk they were subjected to a Confederate counterattack which was so intense that it drove the Union troops back with such fury that Union wounded had to be left behind to be captured on the

field. It had become obvious to Sherman that it was futile to pursue the fighting in that area and he withdrew his army toward the rail lines which he had originally followed into Georgia. In turn Johnston relinquished his position at Allatoona and fell back to the Kennesaw Mountains.

In mid-June General Polk was killed at Pine Mountain, a great loss to the Confederacy. At the same time rain became Sherman's enemy as it turned the Georgia clay into mud impeding the mobility of the Union army.

On 27 June Sherman, who had become impatient with the weather and the delays, decided to strike out against Johnston. The sun had dried the area sufficiently enough to give an attack a reasonable chance of success. At the chosen point of attack Sherman had assembled a grand battery of 140 cannon which laid a bombardment against the Confederate position for more than an hour. In two massive divisional columns General Thomas ordered his troops to advance against the Confederate center defenses while McPherson's army was to attack on the left. Thomas' troops were so closely ordered that the Confederate soldiers had only to aim in the general direction of the advance to hit a target. Some later accounts claimed that each Confederate soldier killed or wounded 80 Union troops.

Thomas' advance was broken but McPherson's attack on the left succeeded in attaining the Confederate position only to be thrown back by a determined counterattack. On the right Sherman attempted to deceive Johnston by feinting an attack with Schofield's Army of the Ohio. Although that attack was designed merely to draw Johnson's forces away from the authentic attack by Thomas and McPherson, Schofield's troops were able to outflank and capture a section of the Confederate line. Rather than risk the possibility of being cut off, Johnston pulled his forces back during the night to fortify positions at Smyrna on the Chattahoochee River. In spite of the fact that Johnston had his back to the river, Sherman realized that it was the strongest Confederate defensive position yet and without a doubt could totally absorb and destroy his entire army if he pursued the offensive.

Thus far Johnston's strategy of bleeding Sherman was working to perfection. Sherman, upon arriving at the new fortified position, decided that he had to find another tactic. Sherman left a force to hold Johnston at his position and swung northeast to Roswell, upstream of the Confederates. Fording the river at that point he outflanked Johnston and forced him to fall back to Atlanta.

Upon Johnston's withdrawal to Atlanta, politics once more entered onto the battlefield. Although Johnston had rebuilt the army and caused Sherman great losses at minimum cost to the Confederate force, Davis did not consider the

The Shenandoah Campaign in September 1864 was an attempt to destroy the last source of food for the South.

campaign satisfactory and called for Johnston's replacement. He accused Johnston of being a 'faint-hearted defeatist' unable to halt the Union advance. 'Before Atlanta could be lost by such an individual,' Davis and his military advisor Braxton Bragg, intended to assure that the army received a more aggressive commander. Although Davis secretly wished to make Bragg the army's commander once again, he knew that such a decision would result in chaos. His authority and the war effort would certainly be jeopardized by such a blatantly political move.

Instead Davis gave Bragg the authority to choose a new commander. His choice was Lieutenant General John Bell Hood. Hood had constantly argued with Johnston over strategy but it was clearly evident to Hood that Johnston possessed command qualities which made him invaluable to the army. Johnston had also become extremely popular with the troops, known as a commander who would not lightly throw their lives away as had so many previous commanders. Nevertheless Johnston was relieved of command

After two weeks of bombardment, Atlanta had not surrendered. Sherman decided to raise the siege and move his army to attack from the south.

Sherman's advance toward Atlanta was temporarily halted at Kennesaw Mountain, where the Army of Tennessee was firmly entrenched.

on 17 July 1864. Johnston found the situation so painfully intolerable that he left the state of Georgia.

Within several days of Hood's appointment Sherman too heard the news that his adversary Johnston was no longer in command. Sherman was elated. Johnston's dismissal was the realization of his fondest hopes. Sherman knew Hood's reputation as a 'scrapper' and would only have to bide his time. Soon, if Hood's past record held true, the Confederate army would be foolishly thrown against Sherman's superior forces on the open battlefield. Sherman considered Hood to be a gambler, willing to stake all yet unable to bluff.

Sherman also knew that Hood's temperament would, sooner or later, outweigh his better judgment. Perhaps of equal importance was Hood's physical condition. Even those on Hood's own staff considered the effects of the strain of command too great for an individual who had lost his left arm at Gettysburg and his right leg at Chickamauga. Hood also suffered, as did all the army, from excessive strain and poor diet. However Bragg and Davis wanted a 'scrapper' who would take the fight to the enemy and win a glorious victory, rather than a stable individual such as Johnston who knew the true capabilities of an army and could devise an overall strategy which might achieve ultimate victory.

The Confederate force had moved to the defense of Atlanta. With foresight the city had been heavily fortified by Colonel L P Grant, chief engineering officer of the Department of Georgia. Sherman's chief engineer, Captain O M Poe, viewed the fortification from a distance and reported that the defenses rivaled those at Vicksburg. He expressed the opinion that it would be suicidal to attack such fortifications. Sherman agreed and decided that it would be better to lay siege to the city and starve the Confederates into submission.

To accomplish this he ordered the armies of McPherson and Schofield east to Decatur to destroy the rail links to the city and to cut off the supplies and reinforcements from that direction. The Army of the Cumberland under Thomas crossed Peachtree Creek and established themselves along the perimeter of Atlanta. Although the tactic was sound, a large gap developed between Thomas's forces and those of the other generals. However, after the failure of the Confederate attack several days earlier, Sherman did not believe that the Confederates would dare come forward. Also, under the misconception during the earliest maneuvers that Johnston was still in command, Sherman did not see any true offensive threat.

Sherman underrated his rival. Although Johnston was no longer in command he had formulated a plan designed to exploit any gap or opportunity presented. Hood, recognizing the sound qualities of that plan, intended to follow it through.

On 20 July Hood sent his troops forward in an attempt to divide Sherman's forces, cutting them off from their lines of supply. In that manner he hoped to make the Union objective unattainable as they were in the heart of enemy territory. In spite of the fact that the plan was well conceived by Johnston, its timing was deplorable and in several uncoordinated attacks the Confederate troops were repulsed with heavy losses. Though surprised, Sherman and his staff were somewhat relieved as the engagement certainly meant that the loss of Confederate troops would force Hood to stay within the fortifications. Sherman could mount his siege in earnest.

However, Hood's tendency to gamble surfaced and on the night of 21 July he sent Lieutenant General William Hardee on a wide sweep around the left and rear of the Union army. Hood felt that if Hardee could strike the flank, as simultaneously a frontal assault took place against McPherson's forces, the Union lines could be shattered.

At noon on 22 July Hood launched his attack with Hardee hitting the flank of McPherson's army. At that time McPherson was having lunch with Sherman discussing whether or not Hood was considering the evacuation of the city. The attack interrupted that discussion and McPherson rode directly to the battle area to evaluate the situation. McPherson, who was a young impetuous officer of great fighting spirit, well liked by Sherman, became overly involved during the early moments of the engagement and accidentally rode through his own lines into the Confederate attack. He was quickly and easily shot down.

Confusion reigned in the Union lines but once again the Confederate command failed properly to coordinate and Hardee's flank attack had spent itself before the frontal attack was launched. Had those two attacks indeed been carried out simultaneously there is little doubt that the Confederates would have won the day. As it was, the attacks were staggered and without coordination and Union forces were able to move. After deflecting Hardee's attack they were able to rush forward and repulse the frontal attack by Major General B F Cheatham's division.

By nightfall more than 8000 men, Union and Confederate, lay dead and Hood had gained nothing. For Sherman the loss of less than 4000 troops could in no way compensate for the loss of McPherson. His death made Sherman even more determined to defeat his enemy.

On the outskirts of Atlanta, Sherman placed Major General Oliver Otis Howard in charge of McPherson's army. Hooker resigned in protest, feeling that he and not Howard should have been given the honor. Sherman later said that Hooker's presence was 'not much missed.'

For five days Union forces attempted to tighten their stranglehold around Atlanta, moving constantly to their right. On 28 July Hood attempted to halt that movement with an attack but it was easily repulsed and the Confederate forces sustained a large number of casualties. It became apparent to both generals that neither army was going to gain a quick victory and both sides settled in for a prolonged siege.

Sherman still believed that the key to the siege lay in the eventual outflanking and surrounding of his enemy. However, in early August, as rapidly as Sherman extended to his right, Hood would extend immediately to his own left. Sherman decided that the time had come to begin a bombardment.

On 9 August Sherman gave the order to destroy Atlanta with artillery fire. The first casualty was said to have been a small girl and her dog who disappeared when a round exploded on the street corner where she was standing. As the day wore on the indiscriminate fire took its toll in the city. In consideration for the inhabitants, the Mayor, James M Calhoun, and General Hood sent a message to Sherman calling for an end to such a 'barbaric act against the civilian population of Atlanta.' Sherman refused to halt the barrage saying that it was his duty to destroy the will of his enemy, whether civilian or soldier, to carry on the hostilities. That attitude so shocked the Confederate officers and inflamed the citizens that instead of breaking the city's will Sherman forged a more determined resistance.

After several days of artillery barrages by both Union and Confederate batteries Hood decided to send his cavalry, led by Major General Joseph Wheeler, around Sherman's forces to harass his supply and communication lines, hoping that the diversion would stop the awesome bombardment. Although Wheeler caused a great deal of havoc in Sherman's supply lines he was unable to relieve the situation in Atlanta.

Sherman was furious that the bombardment of the city had not brought immediate results and embarked on a new plan of attack. He decided to move the entire army, except for Slocum's XX Corps, around to the less well-fortified south-side of the city. He felt he could launch an attack from there which would take the city and cut off the few lines of supply still open to Hood.

On 26 August Atlanta awoke to silence No shells fell on the city from the bombardment which had become routine to the inhabitants. After waiting in expectation for the barrage which never came, Hood sent out pickets to discover exactly what Sherman might be planning. As the pickets pushed forward they came upon deserted Union trenches and assumed that Sherman had lifted the siege and returned north. For the next four days while Sherman maneuvered the Confederate soldiers

*Left:* Major General Philip Henry Sheridan, USA, (1831–88) was given command of the Army of the Shenandoah with the order to make the valley 'a barren waste.'
*Above:* Beginning the destruction that would run 'from Atlanta to the Sea,' Sherman's men pull apart the railyard in the center of the city.

and civilians celebrated what they thought was the end of the battle. Had Hood not sent Wheeler's cavalry to harass Sherman's supply lines their intelligence would surely have proved that Sherman was merely reorganizing the battle lines.

On the morning of 30 August Hood came to the grim realization that Sherman had surrounded the city. He ordered Hardee's corps to attack immediately. Although Hardee's forces, which still numbered some 24,000, fought bravely, they were no match for the numerically superior Union forces. By the night of 31 August Hardee's corps had dwindled to a mere 5000 and Hood had no choice but to evacuate the city.

On 1 September Hood ordered Hardee to hold Atlanta at all cost while he evacuated what remained of his army. For the entire day Sherman tried desperately to defeat the rear guard of the Confederate army but Hardee's 5000 survivors managed to foil him at every turn. As night approached it became obvious

The Army of Tennessee led the Union army commanded by Major General Thomas back through the south to a confrontation at Nashville.

that Hood had escaped and Hardee and his men broke off the engagement and began a trek which would bring them back to Hood in three days.

With the Confederate army gone, Mayor Calhoun rode out of Atlanta under a white flag on 2 September to surrender the city to Sherman. The Union army led by the Massachusetts Infantry marched into the city.

The capture of Atlanta silenced all opposition to Lincoln's reelection and his handling of the war. Although the Confederacy continued to fight with the desperation which made them a formidable opponent, Northerners believed that the war was almost over and that it was only a matter of time before Grant's strategy would triumph.

As Sherman held his position in Atlanta, opposition broke out again in the Shenandoah Valley. On 19 September Sheridan defeated Early's forces at Opequon Creek, 20 miles from Winchester. Three days later Sheridan again engaged the Confederates at Fisher's Hill, dislodging them from their position. By that time Sheridan had cleared most of the Valley of Confederate forces. He then turned his attention from the elimination of his enemy to the elimination of the main sources of food for Lee's army.

Sheridan felt that Early's force was not reckless enough to engage a Union force twice its size and chose to ignore the Confederate commander. Though Early had suffered setbacks in the Valley he believed that his forces were still capable and on 19 October he caught Sheridan's forces completely by surprise at Cedar Creek. That surprise attack almost succeeded in destroying the Union army, sending it in full retreat from the battlefield. Early halted his attack to allow his half-starved troops to forage for food before pursuing his enemy. That decision was fatal for it allowed Sheridan who had just arrived and had not been present during the initial attack the necessary time to reorganize his troops. Their confidence restored under Sheridan's personal command, the Union army counterattacked and destroyed Early's force, ending the fighting in the Shenandoah Valley.

In Georgia Hood's army, after leaving Atlanta, was still on the move. By October Hood had recaptured Allatoona and Dalton but when threatened by Union troops he retreated once more to Alabama. Sherman himself was faced with a perplexing problem. His supply lines were over 400 miles long and it was obvious that Hood's intentions were to sever the Union supply lines so that the army would be forced to relinquish Atlanta and withdraw along their previous line of advance. Since the surrender of Atlanta, Sherman had followed Hood's army, but it was impossible to hold Atlanta and chase Hood.

By November Sherman had made his decision. He ordered Thomas' Army of the Tennessee, to pursue Hood, and detached two extra corps to support Thomas. Sherman and the remainder of his army would march to the Atlantic. Sherman had set himself a deadline with the statement that he would be in Savannah by Christmas and he was determined to fulfill that promise. It was necessary to begin his new campaign as soon as possible. He decided to sever his normal supply lines and live off the land as he marched. Sherman was aware that he could not leave Atlanta intact, giving Hood the opportunity to march back in and reclaim the city. To prevent that possibility he destroyed the few standing factories and set the city on fire.

On 15 November Sherman took 60,000 men and began his now infamous 'March to the Sea,' cutting a path 60 miles wide across the heart of Georgia. Sherman's march burned its way across the state, destroying everything in its path. His destruction horrified the Southern populace and a strong outcry was heard from the Southern newspapers. On 21 December 1864 Sherman entered Savannah victorious, declaring the city's capture to be a Christmas present to the Union and President Lincoln.

As Sherman marched the Southern people and the Confederate government begged Hood to engage the Union army and stop the rape of Georgia. However, Hood remained convinced that a campaign against Tennessee with Nashville as its ultimate objective would force Sherman to abandon his goal and turn around to counter the Confederate threat. With approximately 40,000 men in the Confederate Army of Tennessee Hood began an offensive in the hope of drawing Sherman from his destructive course. Major General John Schofield was ordered to stall Hood's forces until General Thomas' army could reinforce Nashville. Hood had placed himself in an excellent position to cut off a Union retreat and by the time Schofield reached Spring Hill, Tennessee, about 25 miles south the Confederate army was by far the closer to Nashville.

In spite of his advantages, Hood lost control of his army which bivouacked indiscriminately that night at Spring Hill. That chaotic condition allowed Schofields troops to slip past the Confederate outposts and pickets and entrench themselves in the safety of Franklin. On the following morning, 30 November Hood realized his grievous mistake. He had lost the best opportunity to capture Nashville as well as the opportunity to destroy the Union force while it was on the move. Enraged Hood blamed everyone, especially Lieutenant General Benjamin Cheatham, for the mismanagement of the operation. His anger did not stop with just his subordinate officers and it soon became known throughout the ranks that the blunder was not Hood's but the entire army's.

In that frame of mind Hood and his army

pursued their enemy to Franklin to dislodge the Union forces from their position. Although Hood's army was numerically superior to Schofield's the Union troops were in a strong defensive position. As months of earlier campaigning had shown, dislodging an entrenched enemy was not only costly in lives but was only successful when strategy, tactics, and a degree of luck were on the side of the attacker. This was not the case at Franklin. Hood threw his army against the lines as they arrived on the battlefield. Confederate troops fought with a fury seldom seen and had almost succeeded in dislodging the Union defenders when the arrival of a Union reserve brigade plugged the gap at the last moment.

Throughout the day and well into the night 13 separate Confederate attacks were launched by Hood in attempts to secure the breastworks. In effect the Battle of Franklin was Hood's way of

A popular engraving depicting various aspects of Sherman's March to the Sea.

relieving the frustration he had felt since he had fallen for Sherman's ruse at Atlanta. Hood's bitterness cost over 6000 Confederate lives including five generals, with seven more captured and wounded. Among the dead was Major General Patrick Cleburne, whose division had been the backbone of the Army of Tennessee since Chickamauga.

Hood pushed on toward Nashville. Thomas had entered the city and carefully prepared for battle. However Hood's drive had been slowed and at best he could only send Forrest's cavalry to conduct raiding operations in the area. Finally Hood decided that he would besiege Nashville in spite of the fact that he lacked the forces necessary to accomplish a viable siege. Over the following two weeks both armies did little but entrench along lines south and east of Nashville waiting for an improvement in the weather.

Thomas was willing to wait Hood out as each day it became more and more apparent that Hood was in no position to dislodge the Union army from the city. However pressure was applied by General Grant in the form of orders to Thomas to take the initiative and destroy Hood's army. Thomas had no choice but to obey and on 15 December 1864 he attacked Hood's Army of Tennessee. Thomas' attack was not only perfectly executed but his numerical superiority gave the Confederates no chance whatsoever. Hood's losses at Franklin, in men and officers, took their toll and although his army fought bravely their fate was sealed.

By nightfall Hood's army had been dislodged from their positions and were delivered a second blow. Hood should have resigned himself at that moment to the fact that the battle was over. Instead of retreating he fell back to new lines to continue the fight. On the second day, 16 December, the Union victory was even more decisive than on the first. The Confederate troops had nothing more to give and the battle became a retreat to the Tennessee River with the Confederates hotly pursued every step of the way.

With that defeat the war in the West was ended. Hood requested that he be relieved of command. What remained of the Army of Tennessee was sent to the Carolinas. Although a minor campaign would be launched in 1865 in the Carolinas, Hood's disastrous campaign was the last serious threat. On all major fronts the New Year heralded bleak prospects and dark inevitabilities for the South. The war was essentially lost and it was only a matter of time before the gunfire ceased.

The capture of Fort Fisher, North Carolina, gave the Union a base for reinforcements below Richmond.

# THE FINAL DAYS

By January 1865 there was little doubt who the victors of the Civil War would be. The previous year the Union armies, under the command of Grant ably assisted by General Sherman, had conducted an awesome campaign which ripped through the heart of the South. The Confederate ability to fight had been damaged but even more important was the erosion of the South's will to fight. From Sherman's campaign to Atlanta and the Union army's ravishment of Georgia on its way to Savannah to Grant's war of attrition in the East, the new strategy of total war cost the South dearly in both lives and property. Each day that prolonged the war meant further hardship.

The events of 1864 meant an end to any hopes that the South may have cherished of English or French intervention on behalf of the Confederacy. Many of the once proud Confederate armies had been reduced to little more than armed rabble while others simply ceased to exist. By February 1865 both the Confederate Congress and Jefferson Davis had come to the grim realization that their interference in military appointments, strategy and objectives had cost them dearly. Although the end was near they passed legislation which called for a General in Chief to be appointed with complete and absolute power over the mechanics of the war effort. That legislation was passed in the dim hope for a miracle. Regardless who they appointed it would take no less than a miracle to turn around the events of the past months.

Only one man was seriously considered for the position and on 6 February 1865 Jefferson Davis appointed General Robert E Lee General in Chief. Lee realized that the legislation and appointment were nothing but the game of politics played by men who did not want to have the blame cast upon themselves when the inevitable conclusion was finally reached. Yet to some degree it was a victory for Lee. He knew that it was only a matter of months before the armies of the South would be

*Below:* Despite a route through the difficult coastal swamps, Sherman's army managed to march over 10 miles a day and reach Columbia by 17 February. *Right:* Grant's veterans waiting for another attack on the Confederate trenches at Petersburg.

incapable of offering any resistance whatsoever, but he could at last set upon a course of action which could possibly forestall the inevitable long enough to allow for some effort to be made to bring about an honorable peace.

Lee also could appoint competent commanders who could be trusted to implement plans without sacrificing soldiers' lives. With politics no longer playing a role in the command structure Lee felt certain that it was possible to stop the Union advance. Troops could be brought to bear on crucial fronts rather than being strewn across the country at the whim of the government. Realistically Lee knew that the centralized military command had come three years too late. He would strive to do his duty for his country as he always had done but the war was essentially over.

By February the final campaign lines were beginning to form. Sherman's army moved north from Savannah while another large Union force was being formed at Fort Fisher, North Carolina. Sherman's plan was to march through South Carolina and capture its capital, Columbia. He felt that Columbia was an essential target as the city had suffered little from the effects of the war thus far. Charleston, the more prominent military objective, had been subjected to constant bombardment, leaving it not much more than the skeleton of a city and a fortified mass of rubble. It was also evident that any Confederate troops left in Charleston would be immediately outflanked once Columbia fell and would have no alternative but to withdraw from the city or surrender.

On his march to Columbia Sherman's troops accomplished one of the greatest military feats of the war. It was decided that the army would take the most direct route to its objective. That route took it through swamps which were considered impassable, yet Sherman's army managed to cover 10 miles per day. On 17 February they entered Columbia. The Confederate militia there was taken by surprise but succeeded in evacuating before any engagement took place. During their retreat Confederate troops set fire to warehouses and storage areas which held materials which could possibly have been used by the Union army, particularly stores of cotton. In the confusion of a departing army and an enemy advance the fire burned out of control. Before it could be extinguished half of the city had burned to the ground.

By the end of February Sherman's army had marched to within a few miles of the border of North Carolina, on a course toward Fayetteville. At the same time troops from Fort Fisher had occupied Wilmington, North Carolina and prepared to move on toward Goldsboro, North Carolina where they were to rendezvous with Sherman. With Georgia and South Carolina under Union control and North Carolina facing the same fate,

Lee asked his friend General Joseph E Johnston to come out of retirement and take on the unenviable task of defending North Carolina while Lee tried desperately to stall Grant's forces at Richmond and Petersburg.

Johnston could not refuse. He took command of what remained of Hood's Army of Tennessee, which had been reinforced by militia and other Carolina troops. Along with the threat of Sherman and the army at Fort Fisher a third Union force was moving inland from the coast. Johnston knew that if all three could unite his troops would be overwhelmed. Considering the troops marching inland as the immediate threat, Johnston engaged and defeated them at the Battle of Kinston on 8 and 9 March. The Union force withdrew along its previous avenue of advance.

On 11 March Sherman marched into Fayetteville and Johnston knew that if his army could gain a victory against Sherman, or even a stalemate, it would buy Lee the time for which he had asked. On 19 March Johnston attacked part of Sherman's army at Bentonville. The initial stages of the battle favored the Confederate army, but the attack soon lost impetus as more and more Union troops were brought on to the battlefield. By late afternoon Johnston was no longer attacking but had been forced onto the defensive. Two days later he was forced to retreat from the battlefield, allowing Sherman to march into Goldsboro and rendezvous with the troops from Fort Fisher.

With that retreat and Sherman's advance it was evident that the war was in its final stages. There was however one last great battle yet to be fought. That confrontation had extended from June 1864 through the events which took place in the spring of 1865. This was the Battle for Richmond and Petersburg.

Grant had begun this campaign in the East with the strategy that a war of attrition and dogged fighting would bring the Army of Northern Virginia to a point where its total collapse would be imminent. However Lee had managed to maintain his army's cohesiveness and to wound Grant's forces at every engagement. The Wilderness, Spotsylvania and Cold Harbor failed to give Grant the decisive edge which he had sought and in many ways those bloody engagements served to erode not only the Union army's strength but its self-confidence. Lee had succeeded in positioning himself to protect the Confederate capital. Grant realized that an extended siege of the city was not possible as long as the city could be resupplied with food and troops through its smaller sister city, Petersburg. Essentially the supply base and railhead for the whole tidewater area, Petersburg was the key to Grant's offensive. By capturing Petersburg the Army of Northern Virginia, would be isolated in Richmond and Lee would, Grant thought, have only two alternatives. He could surrender, an option

which Grant considered highly improbable, or he could leave the protection of his defenses and engage Grant's superior forces in the open.

The defense of Petersburg had been assigned to General P G T Beauregard. There he commanded a small garrison of a single Confederate brigade, comprising soldiers who were either too young or too old to fight with Lee's army or who were invalids whose wounds had rendered them no longer fit for service in the field army. Petersburg was ringed with 10 miles of trenches, with 55 redoubts and fortifications known as the Dimmock Line. Although on the Southern military maps those lines of fortification seemed strong, commanders in the field knew that there were several places where men on horseback could conceivably ride through unnoticed until they had reached the inner defenses. That flaw was due to the hills and valleys through which the defenses were interwoven.

Beauregard had another problem. Not only was his force composed of men whose abilities were questionable but their numbers were inadequate for the protection of the area he had to defend. When his brigade was stationed on the defense works there was a gap of four or five feet between each soldier. For an era when the massing of fire power was becoming more and more crucial, it was evident that any major Union assault launched against Beauregard's forces would easily push them aside.

By 9 June 1864 Grant had sent Major General Benjamin Butler and his Army of the James plus a division of cavalry to attempt to capture Petersburg. In a battle that has been called 'The Battle of Patients and Penitents' Beauregard and his army of militia and invalids managed to bluff Butler into believing that the hills which lay before him were far better defended than they actually were. The only redeeming factor of the initial confrontation for the Union was that Butler's cavalry managed to reveal several weaknesses in the defenses. When those were reported to Grant he was convinced that he had found Lee's Achilles' heel.

On 12 June Grant decided to move his army from Cold Harbor, where it was securely entrenched, and march 50 miles to Petersburg. The orders for that maneuver came as a surprise to the troops of the Union army but more importantly, Lee was baffled and could not accept the reports that Grant was on the move. Lee considered it another trick or trap and refused to believe his reports until the location of Grant and his staff was positively confirmed.

Grant's plan was simple. Major General William F Smith's XVIII Corps was to position itself in front of the entrenchments at Petersburg. They would then attack, driving Beauregard's forces out of their trenches and capturing the city before Lee could react and send major reinforcements. On 15 June the XVIII Corps arrived at the point where it was to assemble for the attack.

Smith apparently decided that it was in his best interest to conduct his own reconnaissance of the battlefield and enemy trenches before launching the attack. He justified that belief with the fact that his entire corps had not yet arrived. By the time they formed he would have conducted his reconnaissance and be prepared to make a clear evaluation of the conditions. Beauregard on the other hand became aware of the nature of the situation immediately and sent an urgent request to Lee for reinforcements.

By late afternoon Smith and his corps were ready to attack. Smith gave orders for a bombardment of the Confederate defenses and for the troops to launch their attack with the sound of the artillery. For several minutes everyone waited tensely along the Union lines for those first shots to ring out. The rounds never came. In utter disbelief Smith and his staff came to the grim realization that no artillery had been brought forward to begin the attack. When the artillery units were finally located and the chief artillery officer confronted with the situation his only reply was that he had not been told that the attack was so imminent and had released all the horses for watering after the long march.

It took three hours for the corps' artillery to assemble. Once in position the bombardment began with artillerymen firing a steady stream of rounds at the Confederate position to cover the advance of the corps. Almost immediately Beauregard's forces began to crumble. A Union division of black troops participating in the attack themselves captured five fortifications, 12 cannon, and more than 100 prisoners in the initial stages of the battle. Beauregard hastily reassembled his troops one mile behind the original lines to form a viable defense.

In keeping with recent errors, Smith halted his attack rather than continue against the nearly routed Confederate soldiers. The battle had gone too quickly and too simply. The legend of the fighting ability of the Confederate troops led Smith to believe that Beauregard's apparent weakness was not weakness at all, but a feint to draw the XVIII Corps into a trap. Although a 5000-man division was funneled into Petersburg from Richmond later that night, Beauregard had no reinforcements at the time and Petersburg was virtually free for the taking.

As Smith's corps was digging in, Major General Winfreld Scott Hancock's corps arrived on the scene. Hancock's troops were considered the Union elite. They had participated in all the major battles of the Army of the Potomac. If Union field com-

Lee was appointed General in Chief of the Confederate army in February 1865 which freed him from the political wranglings in Richmond.

Petersburg, Virginia, was a railhead and the supply base for the Army of Northern Virginia.

manders could chose who would reinforce them in a battle the unanimous choice would be Hancock and his II Corps. However, by the time Hancock reached the battlefield his corps had marched and counter-marched for the entire day, unable to find the reference points illustrated on their maps. The corps had once halted for five hours waiting for food and supplies which never arrived. Finally, it was evening on 15 June before a messenger from Smith's Headquarters found Hancock and gave him proper directions to the battlefield.

By the time they reached Petersburg Hancock was furious. He was tired and in pain from the wound he had received at Gettysburg which refused to heal; and his professional pride had been so seriously injured that he sent a message to Smith refusing to enter the battle at night on terrain with which he was unfamiliar. The order went out to his troops to bivouac. As they arrived the men of Hancock's corps received word from Smith's troops about how easily the fighting had gone. The black soldiers had managed to capture more than any other unit in the initial assault and had claimed 'bragging rights' which further goaded the men of Hancock's corps. They were used to that honor for themselves.

Hancock's men gathered and pleaded

with the general to let them go into the battle. Although they were tired they were sure that they could easily take their objectives and demanded to be allowed to fight. Their pleas fell on deaf ears. In his present state Hancock put his pride before his better judgement and once again ordered the corps to bivouac. His soldiers were incredulous at his attitude and the incident came close to destroying the morale of the II Corps.

By the morning of 16 June 1864 Burnside's IX Corps and Warren's V Corps had

also reached the battle area. In the early morning Hancock's corps, supported by the troops of Burnside's corps, attacked Beauregard's reinforced and entrenched forces. The results of Smith's misjudgment of the situation, the delay of the Union forces and Hancock's injured pride were soon felt. As the Union troops had feared the Confederate forces had re-

The army travelled with its own sutlers, farriers and blacksmiths.

covered and the attackers were repulsed in complete disarray.

Grant arrived at Petersburg on 16 June and Lee was notified. Aware of his previous error, Lee sent his army as soon as possible to Beauregard's aid. There remained a large gap between the two Confederate forces. Butler's army again entered the battle in an attempt to isolate Beauregard from Lee. Butler's forces were turned back by Major General Richard Anderson's Division, which had just arrived and was making a great effort to stabilize the situation. The following morning Pickett's Division attacked Butler's forces crushing any hope Butler may have had of regaining the lost initiative.

On 17 June the Confederate force totalled more than 14,000 and was opposed by a Union force of approximately 80,000. Major General George Meade had also arrived. After studying the location he decided that the key to the Confederate defense lay on two hills which guarded the main road to Petersburg. If those two positions could be captured the Confederate defense would crumble and the city would easily be taken. Burnside's and Hancock's corps were again called

The black troops in the Federal army were renowned for their bravery, which was proved again and again at Petersburg.

upon to initiate the attack. The plan was to take the hills in a swift, silent attack which Meade hoped would catch his enemy off guard and result in few Union casualties.

The surprise attacks worked perfectly and the two hills fell almost immediately. However the offensive halted with the capture of the hills. Burnside's support, in the form of Brigadier General James Ledlie's troops, did not advance. Quickly Burnside sent a staff officer to discover what the delay was. Ledlie was found, still asleep, and when asked why he had not advanced he replied that he had not been given any specific orders.

Burnside reacted by sending another division in Ledlie's place but the element of surprise was gone and the Confederate forces were able to turn the attack and repulse it. Hancock's wound was by then painfully inflamed and had become seriously infected. No longer capable, he relinquished his command to General David Birney. Birney knew little of Hancock's objectives and much less what the attack was intended to accomplish, but he was the only available officer for the command. Confused and without orders Birney made no further advance beyond the hill and halted to consolidate his forces at their position.

The Union attack was chaotic, but it managed to scatter Beauregard's troops,

Grant arrived at Petersburg in June 1864. The Union attacks failed and Grant settled down to siege and trench warfare.

forcing the Confederate commander to pull his men back to just outside the city in one last desperate effort to hold until Lee arrived. As he maneuvered Beauregard sent another urgent message to Lee pleading for the general to come to the aid of Petersburg. Beauregard considered the last hour of the Confederacy would be at hand if Lee failed to reinforce him in time and the city fell to the Union army.

As Beauregard was contemplating his ability to hold on, Meade was in a blind rage which he directed at his corps commanders. They appeared to be incapable of taking the initiative necessary to capture the city and destroy the Confederate forces. Meade chastised all of them for halting to consolidate as if at any moment a Confederate army of unbelievable magnitude would charge out of the defenses against them. Meade knew that the enemy was in his grasp yet each delay by Union troops gave Lee time to assemble his army and cross the gap from Richmond to Petersburg.

Meade issued his final orders. The army would not only attack in its entirety, but all commanders were free to exploit on their own initiative any opportunity which was presented to capture Petersburg. On the morning of 18 June, 1864 the Army of the Potomac charged out *en masse* to attack the Confederate position. Within minutes the attack was in utter chaos. The Union troops, reaching the Confederate lines, found the positions deserted. Not only were the troops and regimental officers confused but Meade too was caught completely off guard.

It was several hours before a new plan of attack was developed and it was not until noon that the Union army again began to advance. It was by then too late for a swift and easy victory. Lee's veteran units had reinforced Beauregard's position just outside the city and before noon Lee himself had taken command of the front.

As the battle was renewed it became

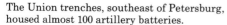
The Union trenches, southeast of Petersburg, housed almost 100 artillery batteries.

evident to the average Union soldier that the advantage and impetus was lost. They spent the remainder of the day throwing themselves against the Confederate positions but those positions would not yield and the only result was a growing number of Union casualties. As evening approached the Union command conceded that the day was lost and Grant ordered a halt to further attacks before the casualty rate went any higher.

The army paused to recover and two days later Grant attempted a flanking maneuver to sever the Jerusalem Plank Road. It was decisively repulsed, by General A P Hill's III Corps. Grant was well aware that the initiative he had possessed two weeks earlier had slipped away. Casualties had reached an alarming proportion. In four days not less than 12,000 men had been killed and the Eastern Campaign had to date cost some 70,000 killed, wounded, or taken prisoner. With Lincoln facing the elections and with a loud public outcry over the casualty count, Grant decided that siege was the only way that Richmond and Petersburg would be taken.

The Union forces entrenched in lines parallel to those of the Confederates holding Petersburg. Both armies resigned themselves to a siege rather than the constant mounting of attacks. Both the Union and Confederate pickets declared their usual truce by refraining from shooting at each other while on guard duty. If the situation should make it necessary for shots to be exchanged, neither side would shoot to kill but merely to force the other back. Incidents along the lines of new recruits shooting at opposing pickets and wounding them met with harsh reprisals from their fellow soldiers for disrupting and threatening the undeclared truce. The 'truce' at Petersburg was carried to

such an extent that when a Union officer, using binoculars to inspect the Confederate lines, was spotted by Confederate pickets, they threw a note wrapped around a rock to one of the opposing Union pickets. That note politely asked the Union pickets to inform the officer that he must either leave the area or make himself less conspicuous, otherwise the Confederate pickets would be forced to open fire on him.

Throughout the remainder of June and most of July 1864 the deadlock continued. Whenever an attack was mounted it seemed that the Union soldiers accomplished nothing more than running toward then away from the Confederate trenches. At the end of July the 48th Pennsylvania Veteran Volunteers Regiment, comprised mainly of coal miners from that state, took part in a skirmish against the Confederate fortifications. One commanding officer overheard a soldier of his regiment proclaim the idiocy of attacking above ground. He claimed that if they would give him half a chance and a pick and shovel he would personally dig a mine shaft beneath the fortification and 'blow it sky high.' As absurd as the

The mine shaft was packed with explosive in an attempt to breach the Rebel lines. It created a huge crater when it finally exploded.

idea might have sounded to anyone else, it was not absurd to the regiment's officer who was a mining engineer.

The idea was put before General Burnside for his approval and later before General Grant. The army engineering corps scoffed at the plan and refused to have any part in it, but Grant's approval was secured and the 48th Regiment went to work digging the shaft.

By 30 July 1864 a 500-foot tunnel had been dug and a magazine of powder had been placed under one of the Confederate fortifications. To capitalize on the destruction of the stronghold when the charge exploded, an assault on the Confederate line at that position was planned. Initially two brigades of black troops, positioned directly behind Burnside's front lines, were to lead the assault. The black troops, proud of their earlier exploits, were exuberant at the opportunity of playing such an important role in the impending battle. Although the plan was well conceived, politics soon destroyed it. Grant was reminded by his staff that such an attack by the black troops would be viewed in many circles as a reckless use of those troops. Grant might well find himself accused of sending them to slaughter because they were black and not as precious as his white troops.

Although the troops themselves begged Grant not to change his mind, they were relegated to the reserve. Ledlie's division was given the task by Burnside of replacing them. It was a poor choice as Ledlie's forces were considered some of the worst in Burnside's corps and Ledlie himself was often found at the rear drunk.

The attack was to be launched at half past three on the morning of 30 July. With the explosion Union troops were to rush forward and take the area. They were then to move out from that central point and exploit the attack as far as possible with the ultimate objective of routing the Confederates. At the appointed hour everyone

A Pennsylvanian regiment of coal miners suggested digging a mine shaft beneath the Confederate trenches.

stood ready for the explosion. After a substantial wait two men bravely crawled into the shaft to discover the fuse had gone out. It was eventually relit and the mine was detonated at four forty-five. An enormous crater, by which the battle became known, was blown in the Confederate lines obliterating the fortifications and troops within.

As the initial assault of the Union troops began the Confederate army around the blast site was in complete confusion. A Union victory seemed only a few hundred yards away but on reaching the crater Union troops advanced no further. They halted to huddle in its protective cover. As more lines advanced the available space in the crater became smaller and smaller but no one seemed willing to move forward, in spite of the fact that the Confederates were incapable of responding to the attack. Soon the crater, which had earlier been a hellish scene for the defenders, became a hell-hole for the Union troops crowded within it.

At seven o'clock in the morning Burnside finally committed the reserves. Ledlie's mismanaged offensive had resulted in chaos. The black troops charged forward across the front and through the mass of milling troops in the Crater. They reformed on the opposite side and launched themselves against the recovering Confederate troops. The fighting became furious, perhaps because the Confederates were confronted by the black troops who attacked them so successfully in the earlier days of the battle for Petersburg. Although the black soldiers carried their initial assault with great success the Union troops still cowering in the crater would not come to their aid and the advance was soon halted.

Grant ordered Meade and in turn Burnside to withdraw their troops. The Battle of the Crater was viewed by all as a monumental fiasco. The black soldiers who fought so bravely suffered the greatest number of casualties and an outcry from citizens and politicians was raised, reviling Grant for allowing those troops to bear the brunt of the attack. Grant would later say that the Battle of the Crater was the saddest affair he witnessed during the entire war. Burnside, through his indecisiveness and his assignment of Ledlie to the lead position, bore the blame for the failure of the Union assault.

From the time of the Battle of the Crater until the end of the year Grant resorted to probing attacks and maneuvers which he hoped would force Lee out of his position. The result was the loss of more lives and greater frustration. Even more embarrassing for the Union command, Early's Corps moved back into the Shenandoah Valley and Grant was forced to dispatch

A romantic view of the Battle of the Crater, which shows that black troops were in the forefront of the assault.

The Union cavalry, led by General Sheridan, attacked the Confederate line.

troops under General Sheridan to deal with the problem. General Wade Hampton, who had taken command of the Confederate cavalry after Stuart's death, attacked a supply depot on 16 September, capturing not only 300 Union soldiers but also several thousand head of cattle. Hampton's troopers then drove the cattle into the city of Richmond to help feed the undernourished army and the civilian population.

That incident, referred to as the 'Beefsteak Raid' infuriated Grant so much that he ordered Meade to initiate offenses at either end of the Confederate line in the hope of recovering some of the lost self-respect of the Army of the Potomac. Meade's attacks met with small success, and Lee was able to maintain and safeguard his lines of communication with the South and Richmond, leaving Grant once more empty handed. In spite of the difficulties he was experiencing Grant's received a letter from President Lincoln commending him for his stubbornness and telling him to continue his efforts to wear down his opponent and to 'hold on with a bulldog's grip.'

From September 1864 until March of 1865 the battle for Petersburg became one of trench warfare. Neither army gained any substantial advantage, taking losses which only Grant's Army of the Potomac could afford. By February 1865 it was evident to the Confederate government that not only was the war nearly lost but that if there were any hope of forestalling defeat it could only come with appointing a single General in Chief to direct the military operations. That fact is significant to the Petersburg Campaign because Lee could finally follow through with a strategy which he felt necessary. The salvation of the Confederacy, not merely Richmond, was in the balance. Lee's

strategy was to launch an attack which would throw Grant and his army off-balance and enable Lee to execute a withdrawal of the main body of the army to rendezvous with Johnston's forces in the south.

Early on the morning of 25 March 1865 a group of Confederate engineers passed themselves off as deserters to the Union pickets outside Fort Stedman. When they were certain that they had been accepted by the Union troops the Confederate soldiers overpowered their captors and captured the Union fortifications before an alarm could be given. Confederate troops under Major General John B Gordon then attacked all along the front, hitting Fort Haskell, Fort McGilvery and several Union battery positions. Gordon's force numbered nearly one-third of Lee's total army and although it appeared that the assault would succeed as planned, Gordon was soon confronted by stiff resistance. As the battle raged the Confederate assault began to collapse. Grant was able to readjust his army and repulse the successive Confederate advances.

When the battle finally ended 10 percent of Lee's army had been lost while the Union losses were less than one percent. Grant knew that Lee had launched his last possible offense and that the gamble had failed. After stabilizing the front Grant sent Sheridan's Cavalry Corps, supported by infantry, to cut off any possible Confederate path of retreat from the Petersburg–Richmond area.

Weather became a serious factor. It rained constantly, flooding the rivers and washing out most of the roads in the area. However these impediments to Union mobility were not enough to save Lee. On 1 April Sheridan attacked the Confederate forces in an effort to rendezvous along the White Oak Road in the Battle of Five Forks. By the end of the day the Confederates had been outflanked, out-gunned, and were finally on the brink of com-

plete collapse. Pickett's Division, which had assumed most of the fighting on the Confederate side, had simply ceased to exist.

On 2 April Grant ordered the Army of the Potomac to capture the Petersburg trenches. Small pockets of Confederate soldiers tried to stall the Union advance but it was only a matter of hours before the Army of the Potomac finally captured its long-sought objective. On the same day General A P Hill, commanding a sector of Confederate resistance, was killed in action while trying to rally his men for another assault.

On 3 April black troops from the Army of the James marched through Richmond

in triumph. Lee tried valiantly to complete his rendezvous with Johnston's army but without success. Union troops were everywhere and no matter which way Lee turned Sheridan's cavalry was ready and waiting to cut him off. Lee had one last chance. If his troops could reach the railhead at Appomattox Station there was a chance the army might escape. However Grant was well aware of that possibility and had sent two corps to sever that last

*Below:* On 2 April, after a final assault, Petersburg fell. On the evening of 2 April Richmond was also evacuated.
*Right:* The Confederate forces set fire to the factories and military stores before evacuating Richmond.

approach. With less than 13,000 troops
and 60 cannon Lee brought his army to a
halt at Appomattox Courthouse where
Sheridan and two infantry corps had once
again blocked his way.

On 9 April Palm Sunday 1865, Lee accepted the inevitable and conceded to
Grant's terms for surrender. The Army of
Northern Virginia had fought long and
hard and had distinguished itself as a
brave and determined fighting force.
Grant was generous in his terms, as he
had been at Vicksburg, making the surrender easier for Lee and his generals to
bear.

Several weeks later, on 26 April in
Greensboro, North Carolina, General
Joseph E Johnston surrendered his army
to General Sherman. With Lee defeated
there had been no hope for further success
and Johnston, too, bowed to the inevitable.
Although the two largest Confederate
armies had officially surrendered, other
regions of the South continued to fight
until 26 May when General Kirby Smith
made the final surrender of Confederate
forces west of the Mississippi River.

After four long years the American Civil
War was over. Although the shooting had
stopped, in many men's minds the war
would never end. The memory would continue to burn in their hearts until, like
many of their relatives and friends, they
too were laid to rest.

*Above:* Lieutenant General Ambrose Powell Hill,
CSA, (1825–65) was killed by a Union skirmisher
after the fall of Petersburg.
*Below:* Grant and his staff saluted Lee as he rode
away from the McLean House after the surrender.
*Right:* The Court House at Appomattox (Virginia)
where the Army of Northern Virginia was trapped
by Sheridan's forces. Only his soldiers confidence
in him got Lee this far.
*Below right:* The ruins of Richmond at the end of
the war. It would be years before the city would
return to its prewar prosperity.

Confederate and British-owned privateers attacked Federal shipping.

# THE NAVAL PICTURE

The naval aspects of the Civil War are often overlooked because most of the best-documented events took place on land. The navies' role was somewhat limited in scope and purpose.

On 19 April 1861, only a few days after the surrender of Fort Sumter, Lincoln ordered the United States Navy to blockade the Southern ports and coastline. The early blockade has often been referred to as the 'paper blockade' as the United States Navy did not have the power to enforce it. Prior to the outbreak of hostilities the then Secretary of War, John B Floyd, dispersed the vast majority of the American fleet on ficticious missions and displays of strength to the various corners of the world. Floyd, a Confederate sympathizer who later accepted a position as a brigadier general in the Confederate army, sent five ships to the East Indies, seven to the African coast, seven more to the Pacific, three on patrol in the Mediter-

ranean and another three to Brazil. Their orders were to take up positions in those regions to protect vital American interests. Only two ships of any consequence, the 25-gun *Brooklyn* and the two-gun *Relief* were in condition for deployment in February 1861 with the *Relief* under orders to carry supplies to the African Squadron. It was little wonder that the blockade was derided as an absurd Union fantasy.

The United States Navy had a reserve of 28 ships, in various states of repair, stationed at ports along the coast. Congress had consistently failed to allocate funds to update those vessels and make them seaworthy. It was true that Congress had appropriated such funds but arrangement for the actual repairs had not been made. At the out-set of war, the United States Navy had a total of 90 ships of various sizes and types. Twenty-five of its first-line vessels had already been sent abroad. The remainder were those in for

repairs or in such poor condition that there was no possibility of their being able to patrol the 3500 miles of coastline as the President commanded.

In manpower the navy rivaled the sad condition of the army, having only 9000 officers and men. Although highly professional, they were too few to tackle the task they had been given.

In addition to the blockade, the navy was ordered to move troops and supplies for strikes against Confederate fortifications and ports. The opening engagement against Fort Sumter proved how difficult that would be as the *Brooklyn* found it impossible to enter Charleston Harbor to support the garrison.

Later in the war, the navy would also supply gunboats to support troops along the rivers and open those waterways to the United States forces.

To cope with the urgent need for naval vessels, the United States government bought or chartered any available, serviceable vessel and placed orders for eight new ships and 23 gunboats. The newly appointed Secretary of the Navy, Gideon Welles, embarked on an aggressive program which would bring the Union fleet to more than 500 fighting ships. The typical ship considered for renovation as a fighting vessel was the wooden steam sloop. These were armed with 22 nine-inch cannon, 11 to each side and two 30-pound rifled cannon, one on the forecastle and the other on the poop deck. Such ships

*Right:* USS *Brooklyn* was one of the few ships in service in home waters when war was declared. *Below:* Three of the gunboats of the Mississippi River Fleet had superstructures adapted from the Confederate ironclad *Virginia*.

were the standard American vessels on which the duty of blockade enforcement would fall.

At the same time, almost any ship which could navigate the rivers was considered as either a design for or conversion to a river gunboat. Different in style from the deepwater ships, the ironclad gunboats were steam-driven paddle wheelers with a shallow draft suitable for navigation on the treacherous river tributaries. Protection varied from full armor plate to none at all. Gunboats were heavily armed, used as support for army operations and against enemy fortifications. There was no actual standardization of the arma-

ment on those vessels, however, a typical vessel carried eight to 12 cannon ranging in size from 100 pounders and nine-inch smooth bore to 12-pound Napoleons and 24-pound howitzers.

By contrast, the Confederate navy at the beginning of hostilities was non-existent, and the South lacked the facilities for the construction of even the most simple vessels. It became evident that if the South were to possess a naval force which could challenge the Union she would have to seek foreign aid. Both England and France had an interest in the war because of economic ties with the cotton-rich Southern states and were,

therefore, the obvious countries to approach. Such ships as the CSS *Alabama* and the CSS *Florida* were built in England and had long careers as commerce raiders. The Confederacy also employed privateers to run the blockade and to bring much needed manufactured items and weapons from Europe.

There was an additional difficulty to the establishment of a Southern navy. When war was declared, the Confederacy benefited from the cream of the United States officer corps resigning their commissions to rally to their native Southern states. Officers such as Robert E Lee gave the Confederacy an enormous advantage on land. Although one of every six men in the United States Navy returned to the South, among them the Commandant of the Washington Naval Yard, Franklin Buchanan, it was not enough. The people of the South were not seafarers, having always relied on the New Englanders or foreign ships to transport their goods. As a result they had to solve the additional problem of manning their ships by using highly-paid volunteer British crews.

In spite of the difficulties, the Confederacy established a naval strategy. They were fully aware that their lifeline to Europe had to be maintained. They must also harass the commerce and trade of Northern ships. Yet another consideration was the maintenance of control and integrity on the major rivers. The protection of the inland waterways required the building of Southern ironclads and gunboats.

In the naval aspects of the war, the Confederacy realized that it must be on the defensive. Considerations for the defense of major ports and coastal cities were of high priority. To defend their harbors against invasion or bombardment, the South employed both ironclads and side-wheel gunboats. In total the South produced 37 armor hulled vessels to add to their numerous commerce raiders and blockade runners, but the Confederate fleet would never be more than 20 percent the size of the Union Navy.

The early days of the Union 'paper blockade' were a farce. As the Union navy grew in strength, the blockade became a reality. Blockade runners became an important factor in the economy of the South. They made short trips, primarily to the Bahamas and other Caribbean ports where England and other European countries had shipped the South's much needed supplies in exchange for cotton and other raw materials.

The ships used for blockade running were small, chosen for their low silhouettes which made them more difficult to see, particularly at night. They were also chosen for their capacity to carry a maximum load at a maximum speed and were much swifter than the Union warships which chased them. This capacity for speed was their major protection.

It has been estimated that more than 90

*Below left:* In the early years of the war, fortunes were made running the blockade in fast steamships such as the *A D Vance*.
*Left:* Nassau and Bermuda were two of the main transshipment points for the blockade runners.
*Above:* Captain Raphael Semmes, CSN, (1809–77) commanded Confederate commerce raiders.

percent of the blockade runners were British-built. Many were also owned and commanded by officers of the Royal Navy who had been granted leave status for an indefinite period by the English government. England was the first of the European nations to realize the immense profits that might be made through such activities. In the early days, blockade runners carried the luxury items which had become rare owing to the exigencies of war. Later the South would regret its indulgences as war materials grew scarce. In any event, the more hard-pressed the South became, the more profiteering flourished. There were claims that the captains of blockade runners made more than $5000 on shipments which in times of peace might have brought less than $200. It was little wonder that officers of a foreign country chose to take the risks that blockade running presented.

In addition to the blockade runners, the South hired privateers to harass and disrupt Union merchant vessels. A few were American-built, but, for the most part, the privateer was approached because of his ability to contract armed vessels from the European powers. They were extremely successful in their ventures. A neutral commission set up after the war in Geneva, Switzerland, awarded the United States Government more than $15,500,000 for damages caused by privateer vessels which had sailed from British ports.

The best known privateers, the CSS *Sumter* and the CSS *Alabama*, were both commanded by Captain Raphael Semmes. The *Sumter* was a 500-ton vessel armed with an 8-inch swivel gun and four 24-pound cannon. She began her voyages on 29 June 1861 after running the gauntlet past the USS *Brooklyn* which had been stationed at the mouth of the Mississippi River to deter the departure of Confederate ships. After only six and a half months of cruising the Atlantic the *Sumter* had destroyed 17 United States merchant ships. However the voyage and engagements had taken their toll and in a state of considerable disrepair she put into Gibralter. Rather than wait for the *Sumter* to be refitted, Semmes sold the vessel to a prominent British shipowner for use as a blockade runner.

Successful though she was, the *Sumter*'s career was not nearly as glorious or romantic as Semmes' second vessel the *Alabama*. That vessel was one of three built in 1862 by the British government for specific use as a privateer. The ship was sent to Egypt for final outfitting since to have fitted out the ship in England would have violated neutrality and drawn England actively into the war. Captain

Semmes took command of the vessel and enlisted a crew primarily from the British Isles. That crew, who Semmes described as '110 of the most reckless boozers from Liverpool pubs,' was extremely difficult to manage. The problems stemmed mainly from the liquor which had been smuggled on board and in more than one incident, Semmes was forced to use leg irons and confinement to discourage the excesses of his men.

Initially known as *Ship No 290*, the ship was a three-masted vessel with an auxiliary engine which could attain a speed of 13.5 knots without armament which was an extraordinary speed for that time. After playing out a charade to confuse Union spies, Semmes took her to the Azores. There, the Portugese government turned a blind eye as a British ship rendezvoused to transfer coal, arms and ammunition to Semmes' vessel.

On 24 August 1862, conversion into an armed raider had been completed and the ship sailed. Captain Semmes read the letter from President Jefferson Davis of the Confederate States of America formally commissioning the vessel as the armed steam-sloop CSS *Alabama*.

The *Alabama* successfully cruised the North and South Atlantic as well as the Indian Ocean and the China Sea. By 1864 Semmes had captured or sunk a total of 71 ships, causing so much damage that Union merchants had begun to sail their ships under foreign flags.

In June 1864, after her seventy-first victory, the *Alabama* entered Cherbourg, France for an overhaul and refit. Union representatives in Europe lodged strong protests with the French government for allowing a known privateer access to French harbors. Union representatives were well aware that the sympathies of many European countries, though not openly expressed, lay with the Confederacy. They realized that if there were to be an end to the *Alabama*'s raiding, a Union warship would have to be brought on station at the harbor. Messages were sent, and within three days of the *Alabama*'s docking, the USS *Kearsarge*, commanded by Captain John Ancrum Winslow, a friend of Semmes before the war, stood off Cherbourg Harbor.

Semmes was faced with the decision of either spending the remainder of the war interned by the French government, as they could no longer protect the *Alabama* without jeopardizing their own neutrality, or engaging Winslow, who defiantly sailed his ship just beyond the harbor as if baiting his old friend to fight. Of the two vessels, the *Kearsarge* had the larger crew and one more cannon. Altogether, the ships were fairly evenly matched. However the *Alabama* had not been able to complete its refitting.

The possibility of a major naval confrontation in the English Channel was greeted as a momentous event which brought spectators out in small boats and yachts. On the morning of 19 June 1864 the two vessels met three miles offshore. For over an hour, the ships circled one another maneuvering for well-placed exchanges of fire. Finally, the *Alabama* received a hit which destroyed her engine and the ship began to sink. Semmes struck the colors and hoisted the white flag.

Shortly after noon the *Alabama* disappeared beneath the Channel waters.

Among the *Alabama*'s victims was the fast mail steamer *Ariel*, captured off Cuba in December 1862.

Semmes and 40 of his crew were rescued by an English yacht which returned them to the French shore. The remainder of the crew, except for 12 members killed in the action, were taken prisoner aboard the *Kearsarge*. Union losses were one killed and two wounded.

The romanticized legend of the *Alabama* was increased with her sinking. The ship's doctor, David Herbert Llewellyn, a Welshman who had signed on to the privateer, refused to abandon ship with wounded on board and went down with the ship. Although the *Alabama* was by no means the last of the Confederate privateers, she had been the most productive. Her destruction caused a great sigh of relief from northern merchantmen.

As privateers conducted economic war on the high seas, a new type of warship revolutionizing naval warfare was being born. Those vessels were commonly known as ironclads.

*Above:* Semmes and part of his crew were rescued by the English yacht *Deerhound,* one of the fleet of spectators off Cherbourg.
*Right:* The Confederate commerce raider *Alabama* captured or sank over 70 Federal merchantmen during her career.
*Below right:* Captain John Winslow and his officers photographed aboard USS *Kearsarge* after sinking the *Alabama*.

The idea of a ship protected by armor plate was not an entirely new concept. Three warships had appeared during the Crimean War which attempted to utilize iron armor. The ironclads of the Civil War were a new generation, a vessel which was designed to withstand the fire power of the more powerful cannon and have the ability for a maximum fire capacity itself.

Despite the humorous outlook of certain European papers, the ironclad was fast accepted as the warship of the future.

The Confederate concept of the iron-clad was a vessel which would be impervious to Union gunfire yet capable of breaking the blockade around the major ports and river waterways. The Confederacy had opted for a defensive naval strategy and the ironclads would be employed in a basically defensive role. Unlike its northern counterpart, the Confederate ironclad was designed to be augmented by the fortification cannon of the city ports it protected, not by other naval vessels. The lack of proficiency in naval areas within the Confederacy made that type of strategy an intelligent choice. It was clearly impossible to attempt to meet the Union navy on an equal footing. It was better to employ that which was available to the best advantage.

The South's first true ironclad was the CSS *Virginia*. Its hull was that of a Federal ship, the USS *Merrimac*, which had been refitting when war broke out and was unable to put out to sea. To avoid having the vessel fall into the hands of the Confederacy, she was scuttled by her crew.

In July of 1861 Stephen R Mallory, former United States Secretary of the Navy and then Confederate Secretary of the Navy, ordered the *Merrimac* refloated to serve in the construction of the new ironclad. Once recovered, it was obvious that the ship with its 23 foot draft would be

*USS Cumberland was the first ship sunk in action by the ironclad Virginia.*

unable to move at more than five knots once armor, armament and redesign were applied. The vessel, christened the CSS *Virginia* not only had the thickest armor of any ship to date but carried three 8-inch cannon, two 6-inch cannon, two 7-inch swivel guns and a steel lance for use as a ram at its bow. The design emphasized fire-power and protection rather than speed.

The *Virginia*'s crew was composed of 350 men, 80 of whom had seaman's experience. Her commander was Captain Franklin Buchanan who had been the First Superintendant of the Naval Academy of Annapolis and Commander of the Washington Naval Yard.

The ship's primary objective was to break the Union blockade of the Chesapeake Bay and the river approaches to Norfolk, Virginia. On 8 March 1862 Captain Buchanan took his ship out of Norfolk under tow down the Elizabeth River. The *Virginia* sat low in the water and under its own power proved to be an unwieldy vessel, taking from 20 to 30 minutes to complete fundamental maneuvers. In spite of that Buchanan was confident that his ship would ravage the Union fleet although his crew had yet to fire even one of the ship's cannon.

Opposing the *Virginia* on her maiden voyage were five Union screw-driven frigates, three of which were of the same class as the *Merrimac*. Those three were the *Minnesota*, the *Congress* and the *Roanoke* carrying 50 cannons each. The remaining

two vessels were the 52-gun *Saint Lawrence* and the 24-gun *Cumberland*. All five were anchored under the protection of the Union batteries at Newport News.

The Union fleet was completely unprepared. One ship's captain was ashore and several of the vessels displayed the crew's laundry hanging from the rigging. For the most part all the ship's crews were on stand-down status, going about their daily non-combatant duties.

When the *Virginia* was within 1500 yards of the *Congress* her crew opened fire. The distance allowed the crew of the *Congress* time to rally and react with a broadside volley from its 25-pound cannons. To the sailors amazement, the shots ricocheted harmlessly off the *Virginia* while the oak hull of the *Congress* had been severely damaged. The *Virginia* then turned on the *Cumberland* firing and then ramming the ship, killing crew members and causing the ship to begin sinking. Witnesses to the attack on the *Cumberland* stated that the hole the *Virginia* ripped in her side was large enough to drive a carriage through. The crew of the *Cumberland*, however continued to man their guns while making desperate attempts to keep the ship afloat. The *Virginia* pulled away to avoid being dragged under by the sinking *Cumberland* while raking the decks with shot and killing many of the gun crews. The situation was hopeless and the *Cumberland* settled to the bottom of the bay.

Buchanan then turned his attention once again to the *Congress* whose crew had beached her before she could sink. From a distance of 150 yards, shell after shell from the *Virginia*'s cannon tore at the immobilised vessel. Finally, after all the *Congress*' guns were silenced and her captain dead, the senior ranking officer decided there was no option open to him but to surrender.

Buchanan paused to send a boarding party to the *Congress* to claim his prize. As the boarding crews approached the vessel, Union troops arrived on the shore and, supported by shore batteries, brought heavy fire to bear on the Confederate sailors. Buchanan hastily recalled his men and in a defiant gesture fired red-hot shot into the *Congress* setting her afire. During that exchange, Buchanan was severely wounded and surrendered his command to a Lieutenant Jones.

The remaining three Union vessels had run aground in the shallow waters in their efforts to aid the *Congress* and the *Cumberland*. Darkness was approaching and Lieutenant Jones broke off the engagement to withdraw across the bay to the protection of the Confederate batteries at Sewell Point.

As the *Virginia* sailed away, she left destruction in her wake. She had completely destroyed two vessels and caused damage to a third, killing more than 200 Union sailors and naval officers. Damage to herself was limited to that sustained by her bow in the ramming of the *Cumberland*. The most encouraging note for the *Virginia*'s crew was the fact that at no point had her hull been penetrated by the Union cannon fire. The *Virginia* was in excellent shape to return on the following day and complete her task.

News of the 8 March victory spread rapidly throughout both the North and the South. In the South the news was met with great celebration. Optimistically,

*These diagrams are accurately drawn to scale.—In Fig. 2 the exterior solid line represents the entire surface of the deck, including armor-shelf and overhang at bow and stern. The exterior dotted line represents the top of the proper hull; the interior line shows the dimensions of the flat bottom.—Fig. 1 is a profile of the vessel; the portion visible when the vessel is afloat is shown by the place of the water-line.—Fig. 3 is a vertical section of the turret.—The reference letters are the same throughout: A, Revolving Turret.—B, B, Smoke-pipe.—C, Pilot-house.—D, Anchor-well.—E, Rudder.—F, Propeller.—G, Iron Armor.—H, Braces for Deck Beams.—K, K, Water-line.—L, Gun.—M, Gun-carriage.*

many believed that it would only be a matter of time before the Union blockade threat was laid to rest by the challenge of vessels like the *Virginia*. In the North, the news was greeted with both despair and anxious anticipation.

On the same day as the Battle of Hampton Roads, a Union ironclad approached Chesapeake Bay. Its crew must surely have felt some anxiety as they surveyed a harbor lit by the flames of the still burning *Congress*. The newly-arrived ship, upon which so much faith had been placed, was none other than the *Monitor*.

The *Monitor* was designed by a Swedish engineer, John Ericsson, known primarily for his work in steam-driven ships. Ericsson's vessel was the first ever designed as an ironclad. Until that time ironclads

USS *Monitor*, the first American vessel designed as an ironclad, revealed a much lower profile than the adapted *Virginia*.

were merely adaptations of wooden ships.

Construction had begun on Ericsson's *Monitor* nearly two months after work on the *Virginia* was underway. Ericsson's idea was simple. He had designed a ship which was both small and maneuverable with a low superstructure which gave the enemy the minimum area upon which to concentrate its guns. The result was that the *Monitor* resembled a flat barge, pointed at bow and stern, with a large metal cheese-box in the center. The ship had a draft of only 12 feet which meant she could navigate in the shallows of bays and rivers.

The *Monitor* carried only two cannon, though they were the largest of that period, being Dahlgren 11-inch cannon. They were mounted in the nine-foot high by 20-foot diameter revolving deck turret. The turret itself was protected by one-inch iron plate and had an independent auxiliary steam engine to turn it, thus drawing no power from the ship's main propulsion engines.

The *Monitor* left New York City on 6 March 1862 and almost sank on the following day. Although Ericsson had designed a revolutionary vessel for warfare, it was not seaworthy in open water. Her captain, Lieutenant Commander John L Worden, almost ordered her abandoned twice during the voyage but the crew managed to keep the vessel afloat, arriving safely at Chesapeake Bay on the night of 8 March 1862.

On the morning of 9 March 1862 the crew

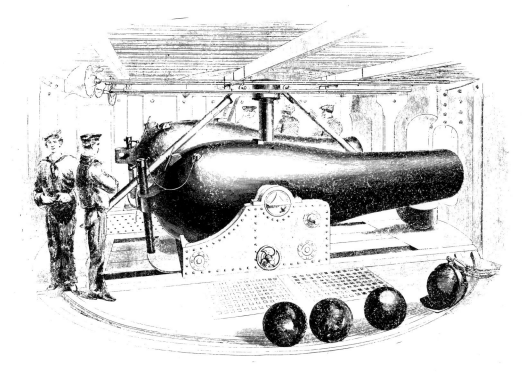

The *Monitor* was armed with two 11-inch Dahlgren smoothbore guns in a single revolving turret.

of the *Monitor* received their first view of the Confederate vessel that had caused the destruction which greeted them in the bay. The *Virginia* was steaming across the bay on a course to engage the *Minnesota* which remained stranded in shallow water. Worden had guessed that the *Minnesota* would be the most likely target for the renewed attack and positioned his vessel to protect that ship. As the *Virginia* closed on the *Minnesota*, Jones mistook the *Monitor* for one of the many buoys floating in the harbor and ignored it. He had been warned that a Union ironclad was in the area but was expecting a vessel that looked much like his own. His mistake was soon made obvious as the *Monitor* opened fire.

In the shallow water, Jones was quick to realize that the *Monitor* was by far the superior vessel in both speed and maneuverability. The crew of the *Virginia* found it difficult to lay effective fire against the smaller more-responsive vessel. However, as the ships exchanged shots it became evident that neither could inflict serious damage on the other. Much frustrated, Jones decided to take the offensive by ramming his opponent. The result was a glancing blow damaging the bow of the *Virginia* but the *Monitor* was unscarred.

With that failure, Jones decided to turn away from the *Monitor* and resume his attack against the *Minnesota*. After several broadside volleys, the *Minnesota* began to burn as the *Monitor*'s crew tried desperately to come between the other two vessels. As the *Virginia* maneuvered for a final assault on the frigate, the *Monitor* cut across her bow forcing Jones to swing his vessel to avoid further damage to the bow. In the course of this action, the *Virginia* went aground in the shallows.

The Confederate ironclad was now at the mercy of its opponent. As the *Monitor* closed in, the *Virginia*'s gunners fired a lucky shot which struck the *Monitor*'s armored control cabin, temporarily blinding her captain. Without orders to the contrary, the helmsman maintained his course, carrying the *Monitor* away from the helpless *Virginia*. This lapse gave the Confederate crew time to free their ship and they promptly withdrew across the bay.

Although the battle of Hampton Roads was actually over, the captain of the *Minnesota*, having seen the *Monitor* steam away before the *Virginia* had been freed, thought the Confederate ironclad was the victor and blew up his ship so it would not be captured by the Confederates.

The battle of the ironclads ended in a stalemate. Both ships, though they had received numerous hits, suffered little damage beyond the fracturing of a few armor plates. The *Virginia* had suffered slightly more damage by ramming the *Cumberland* and the attempted ramming of the *Monitor*.

After a momentous beginning, neither ship would meet with a glorious finish to its days as a fighting vessel. The *Virginia* was scuttled by her crew in May of 1863 when it was feared she would be captured in port by advancing Union troops. The *Monitor* sank in a gale at sea several months after the demise of the *Virginia*.

The Battle of Hampton Roads was the first true battle of the ironclads but by no means the last. Ironclads became the vessels upon which both the North and South based their fortunes. Southern ironclads continued to resemble the *Virginia* with the purpose of defending the Confederate ports. The Northern ironclads remained consistant with the original *Monitor* though improvements made them more seaworthy and an extra turret was added to increase the firing capabilities. The North envisioned their ironclads as little iron fortresses which could bring their fire power to bear against

*Above:* The more maneuverable *Monitor* was able to drive the *Virginia* aground in shallow water, but inflicted little damage.
*Right:* The crew of the *Monitor* photographed while cooking on deck in July 1862.

coastal fortifications and batteries. This aspect of their use came under much criticism as the war progressed. The limited capabilities of the ironclads when focussed against land fortifications created a great deal of controversy.

It was eventually discovered that the most profitable use of Union ironclads was in conjunction with standard naval vessels such as the frigate. The cooperation proved that the two classes of vessels complemented one another and the Southern threat was swiftly neutralized as more ports were captured by the Union naval operations.

By 1864 Admiral David Glasgow Farragut, Commander of the Western Gulf Blockading Squadron, had succeeded in capturing New Orleans, Galveston, Corpus Christi, Port Hudson and other strategic coastal cities and garrisons of the Mississippi River and Gulf of Mexico. For some time Farragut had advocated a naval assault against Mobile to close that important Confederate port.

Farragut's squadron consisted primarily of wooden ships. He realized that his operation would not be approved unless he had ironclads to support his efforts. He also had some difficulty in finding troops for a complementary land assault against the garrisons of Fort Morgan and Fort Gaines which protected Mobile Bay.

Compounding Farragut's frustration, the Union government approached the entire situation with indifference. Mobile's defenses had been strengthened as the war progressed. They included a small naval squadron, the pride of which was the *Tennessee* a ram built in Selma, Ala-

bama and reputed to be the most powerful, heavily armed Confederate ironclad.

Farragut was not willing to adopt the same pessimistic attitude. Mobile and its defenses had put little strain on the Western Gulf Squadron but Farragut decided that the time had come to eliminate the major Confederate port still open on the Gulf Coast.

Mobile had constructed a formidable defense since Admiral Buchanan had taken command of the port. Buchanan's experiences with ironclads was well matched by the skills of Brigadier General Gabriel J Rains, an inventive mine expert. Buchanan strengthened the fortifications

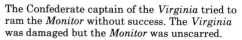

The Confederate captain of the *Virginia* tried to ram the *Monitor* without success. The *Virginia* was damaged but the *Monitor* was unscarred.

which guarded the harbor and increased their fire power by adding cannon and rifled weapons whenever and wherever he could find them. However, Buchanan was not satisfied to trust his fortunes to those garrisons and also reduced the main channel to 500 yards of open water through the use of pilings and torpedo mines. Rains oversaw the laying of those channel defenses. Buchanan was confident that any Union attempt to enter the harbor would result either in its being engaged by the full force of the garrisons or destroyed by the minefields while attempting to navigate a clear passage through the bay.

Buchanan's most important ship was the CSS *Tennessee*, which was the same class as the *Virginia*. Her superstructure was armored by three layers of 2-inch iron plate. The layered effect convinced Buchanan that the *Tennessee* could withstand any assault, including fire taken at point-blank range.

The *Tennessee* carried six heavy cannon four 6.4-inch Brooke rifled cannon for broadside attack and two 7-inch Brooke rifled pieces on pivot mounts at bow and stern. The pivot mountings allowed those cannon to be used in broadside assaults as well as to the front and rear, permitting her crew to employ two-thirds of its total fire capabilities to either port or star-

CSS *Tennessee* was forced to capitulate when the constant firing shot away her steering chains and destroyed her smokestack.

The Confederates increased the defenses of Mobile by laying a minefield in the deep-water channel to Mobile Bay.

board. In addition, she possessed a forward ramming device.

The *Tennessee* was impeded by the same faults as her predecessor, the *Virginia* with regard to maneuverability and a maximum speed of only six knots. Although Buchanan viewed the *Tennessee* as a monster which would devour her enemies, the vessel had several flaws. Her engines had been cannibalized from an old river boat and were driven by a series of wooden gears which diminished the horsepower rating. Her gun portals were protected by a crude, make-shift shutter system which could be easily damaged or jammed if hit by the shell of an enemy cannon. Yet those were not considered her worst features. The vessel's steering chain was exposed across her rear deck, a design flaw which had been temporarily corrected by bolting a one-inch iron plate over the chain. That attempted protection was insufficient, revealing a point vulnerable to enemy fire. A direct hit on the chain could disable the vessel.

Buchanan reconciled the maneuverability problems by intending to employ the three lightly armed gunboats, the *Morgan*, the *Selma*, and the *Gaines* as support for the cumbersome ironclad. That strategy was equally flawed as the gunboats would be forced to avoid close

Captain David Glasgow Farragut, USN, (1801–70) commanded the Western Gulf Blockading Squadron.

Gunboats and paddle steamers were used to move troops along the Mississippi.

contact with enemy vessels which might expose them to raking. The cannons and crews located on the decks of the gunboats would fare badly in such close quarter exposure. Buchanan appeared to project his initial experience with the *Virginia* to the current situation and remained confident in his defenses, his vessels and his strategy in spite of the problems presented.

In July of 1864 Admiral Farragut received three *Monitor*-class ironclads to aid his impending attack on Mobile. Of those three vessels the *Manhattan* was a single turret design. The accompanying *Chickasaw* and *Winnebago* were twin turret, river-class designs. A fourth single turret vessel, the *Tecumseh*, was to join Farragut's squadron sometime in early August.

The problem of additional ground troops was resolved as the commander of the Military Division of West Mississippi detached some 5000 men under the command of Major General Gordon Granger to Mobile. By early August Farragut was prepared to institute his intended attack on Mobile.

Before Farragut undertook his attack, he gathered all available information about the bay and its defenses. Small blocks of wood were fashioned to resemble ships by the flagship carpenter and Farragut began to explore the best means and methods for the attack. With his aide, Lieutenant Commander J C Watson, Farragut experimented in miniature wargames attempting to insure that the best possible strategy and tactics were implemented, leaving nothing to chance. Watson stated that it was far better to make

mistakes with miniature wooden replicas than with the lives of men in combat and without a doubt Farragut agreed.

A strategy was finally fixed. Farragut's fleet was divided into two columns. The first, closest to the fortifications, would consist of the ironclads and would proceed in single file. The second column would include all of the 14 wooden ships, lashed together in pairs; one large frigate coupled with a smaller class gunboat. The pairing of the vessels was intended to protect the smaller vessels as they ran the gauntlet of the Confederate fortifications. Once within the bay the vessels would cast off their cables and the lighter gunboats would engage those enemy vessels which were not ironclad. The *Tennessee* was to be the focus of attention for the four monitors and the seven larger Union ships.

On the foggy morning of 5 August 1864 the Union fleet with the *Brooklyn* leading the column of wooden ships and the *Tecumseh* leading the ironclads formed for battle and awaited the dawn. At five-thirty in the morning Admiral Farragut finished his morning tea and gave orders for the attack to commence. Approximately one hour later the *Tecumseh* was the first vessel to fire a shot. The flotilla approached Fort Morgan, maintaining a steady barrage of fire. Shortly after seven o'clock the remainder of the fleet arrived to add the weight of their cannon. By that time Fort Morgan's guncrews had recovered and reorganized enough to return fire. A half hour later the wooden ships began their cannon assault on the fortress, delivering full broadside strikes in a concerted effort to destroy it. For a full 30 minutes the exchange between the ships and the fortress continued. During this bombardment the *Tennessee* moved

out past Mobile Point and the fortification at the head of a small gunboat contingent.

The Union fleet found itself in a precarious position. The *Tennessee* had blocked the narrow passage between the port and the minefields and the Union vessels were caught in a crossfire. Farragut, in his flagship the *Hartford*, signaled ahead for the *Brooklyn* to proceed on her predetermined course. The *Brooklyn* began to falter and turned back into the column of wooden ships. As the *Brooklyn* swung around, she placed the *Hartford* and the rest of the column on a direct course with the minefields.

In the confusion, the *Tecumseh* broke formation and steamed directly toward the *Tennessee* which had positioned itself on the opposite side of the minefield. The *Tecumseh* drew to within 200 yards of its enemy before striking a torpedo and plunging bow first into the depths of the bay. So quickly did the *Tecumseh* sink that she took her captain and 90 members of her crew to the bottom. It was reported that in the course of abandoning the ship the pilot and the captain met at the foot of the ladder which led to the turret and safety. There they paused to argue over who should ascend first, each insisting that it was the other's perogative. Their delay raises the question of whether more lives than the 22 who were saved could have been spared.

All seemed lost for the Union. Both the *Brooklyn* and the *Hartford* were receiving a devastating barrage from the fortress guns and the decks of both ships were slick with the blood of their crews. Farragut appeared to have lost control as all signals to and from the leading vessels were misunderstood or not acted upon. He decided to push on with the attack rather than allow the fortress batteries

*Right:* Farragut ordered the wooden ships of his fleet to be lashed together to pass the Confederate defenses into Mobile Bay.
*Below right:* Farragut's flagship USS *Hartford* fired numerous broadsides at the ponderous but invulnerable *Tennessee.*

to destroy his fleet in the passage. He signaled to the ships of his flotilla that he intended to take the lead in the renewed assault. Farragut's only route around the disabled *Brooklyn* was through the mine-field. The *Brooklyn* frantically signaled to Farragut that he was rapidly approaching the mined area, to which Farragut made his famous reply, 'Damn the torpedos, full steam ahead.'

There were many in those fateful moments who believed that Farragut's frustration would ultimately bring destruction to the fleet, but all the ships followed their Admiral's flagship into the mined waters. Lieutenant Commander Watson later recorded that the crew expected to be 'blown all over the bay' as they listened to the sound of primers being set off against the hull of their ships. Miraculously, not one of the torpedo mines detonated and the fleet passed through the field without incident. For the moment, the flotilla was saved as the ships left the minefield and entered the inner bay.

No longer at the mercy of the fortress batteries, the fleet was nevertheless disadvantaged by the confining channel. The *Tennessee*: responded by attacking the Union vessels as they attempted to maneuver in the restrictive waters. Buchanan recognized Farragut's flagship and steamed forward with the intention of ramming it. As he made that attempt the *Hartford* managed to turn aside and fired a full broadside into the Confederate ironclad. Union sailors looked on in amazement as the barrage which would have laid open a wooden vessel, glanced harmlessly off the plated hull of the *Tennessee*. Although the *Hartford*'s volley failed to damage the ironclad, it succeeded in frightening off the Confederate gunboats *Gaines* and *Morgan*. They retreated to the safety of cover fire provided by the port batteries.

The *Selma* on the other hand, managed to maneuver directly in front of the *Hartford*, there delivering round after round into the bow of the Union vessel. Unable to withstand or allow the continued damage being wrought on his vessel, Farragut cast off the *Metacomet* to actively engage the *Selma*.

Although she had missed her mark, the *Tennessee* was more than willing to attempt another ram against one of the smaller gunboats. For a second time, the slow, cumbersome movements of the ironclad prevented it from achieving a hit. In frustration, Buchanan turned away and set course for the protection of Fort Morgan.

The engagement appeared to be over and the Union fleet paused to tend its wounded. Farragut plotted a new tactic. He was convinced that the only way he could destroy the *Tennessee* was by using his three remaining ironclads against her, under cover of darkness, to avoid a confrontation with the batteries of Fort Morgan. Farragut was certain that Buchanan was considering a similar night attack. If Buchanan could destroy several of the larger Union ships, he would have the advantage and Farragut would be forced to withdraw.

The Union crews removed their dead and wounded, scrubbed the decks and were preparing breakfast when a sudden cry went up throughout the fleet. The *Tennessee*, still some four miles away, had turned around and was launching another attack. The reappearance of the ironclad caused a great deal of confusion within the Union fleet. Not a confusion bred of panic but one of ships jockeying for position, contending with one another for the glory of the kill.

As the *Tennessee* drew near, the wooden Union ships made desperate attempts to ram the ironclad. The *Monongahela* and the *Lackawanna* were the first to make contact with the ironclad, doing little damage to the *Tennessee* but much to their own hulls. Farragut then maneuvered the *Hartford* for a ramming attempt, but the angle of the *Hartford*'s approach caused her to glance off the ironclad. Both the *Hartford* and the *Tennessee* fired broadsides into one another. The ironclad suffered no damage, but the *Hartford* was badly mauled and eight of her crew were killed.

Success in the battle was dependent on the destruction of the *Tennessee*. To that end Farragut brought the *Hartford* about for another pass on the ironclad. In the process of that maneuver, the *Hartford*

and the *Lackawanna* collided, causing added damage to the flagship and placing the vessel in a critical state. The *Lackawanna* proceeded on her second attempt to ram the *Tennessee*.

Farragut had become irritated and frustrated by the course of events. He ordered his signal officers to flash a message to all ships, particularly the *Lackawanna*, to get out of the way and allow the monitors to enter the fray. As that message was sent, the *Lackawanna* again barely missed a collision with the *Hartford*. The ramming attempt on the *Tennessee* failed and the *Lackawanna* drew off, obeying Farragut's orders.

The Union *Chickasaw* approached to within 50 yards of the *Tennessee* and commenced fire on the Confederate ironclad. So rapid and devastating was the *Chickasaw*'s fire that she soon had the armor plates of the *Tennessee* ripping away from the main structure. The other Union vessels joined the assault and it was not long before the *Tennessee* had lost her steering chain and smokestack and all of her gunports were jammed.

The situation within the *Tennessee* was grim. Buchanan knew that unless he was able to repair the gunports and fire his cannon his vessel was doomed. Buchanan, one of the ship's engineers and members of the crew struggled desperately to open the ports. Bombardment from the Union vessels increased and in a rapid succession of volleys, one projectile crashed through the *Tennessee*'s hull and landed near the engineer who disappeared in the explosion which followed. In the same explosion Buchanan was seriously injured when his legs were crushed by part of a casemate which had been jarred loose by the explosion. It was obvious to all on board that their ship, unable to maneuver or return fire, would soon be destroyed. The ironclad lay dead in the water when the union monitor *Manhattan* raked the vessel and sealed the fate of the *Tennessee*.

At 10 o'clock in the morning less than five hours after the battle began, the *Tennessee* surrendered. With the elimination of the *Tennessee*, Farragut knew that the battle was won.

The two forts at the mouth of the bay fell after a brief engagement but the city of Mobile held out until the end of the war. Although Mobile was not captured, Farragut had achieved a victory by eliminating it as an effective port. The Confederacy had only one major open port, Wilmington, North Carolina.

Union casualties in the Battle of Mobile Bay were 319 with 145 killed. The loss of the *Tecumseh* and her crew was singled out as the worst American naval disaster in combat and would remain so until World War II. Confederate losses were 12 killed, 20 wounded, 280 captured, compounded by the destruction of the *Tennessee*.

As the war progressed, the significant role that the rivers played in the war

effort became increasingly more evident. For both the Union and Confederacy the rivers were essential to the movement of troops and supplies. The opening of the Mississippi was of high priority to the Union government as its closure threatened the commerce and stability of the western states.

To conduct the campaigns on the inland waterways, river gunboats were developed. For the most part, they were nothing more than paddlewheelers, some armored, others not, which could be used to transport troops and supplies or as floating batteries to engage troops and fortifications along the rivers. In February of 1862, five armored gunboats were employed to carry Grant's troops along the Tennessee River for the attack on Fort Henry. Those gunboats aided Grant immensely in silencing the fortification's batteries and forcing its surrender. That same flotilla, shortly after the fall of Fort Henry, destroyed bridges and rail links along the river, harassing and disrupting the Confederate Army in that area. Later, those vessels helped Grant in the destruction of Fort Donelson on the Cumberland River and similar vessels were employed against Vicksburg and on other military expeditions which used the rivers as their main avenues of approach.

The ironclads and gunboats of the river war developed some of the basic doctrines for naval support of land troops and were a welcomed ally to the soldiers fighting on the fields of battle. At the Battle of Shiloh, three Union gunboats helped to repulse the Confederate attack at one of the most crucial moments of the battle, laying down support fire on the night of 6 April 1862. However, gunboats also had their limitations. On many tributaries they were at the mercy of land troops who could easily block or bottle up the vessels. That tactic was used on various occasions by Confederate forces and the Union flotilla commanders quickly learned their lessons and were careful to observe the limitations of their vessels.

Although river gunboats never received the glory which was attached to other aspects of naval warfare, their contributions to the war effort could not be denied. One final aspect of naval warfare of both interest and insight to the future was the 'submersible torpedo boat,' the submarine. The idea of a submersible vessel was not a new concept, but attempts were being made to perfect the vessels and several designs were built. The vast majority of submersibles appeared to have been more dangerous to their own crews than to their enemies. The only weapon of the combat submersible was a spar torpedo, placed at the end of a pole and mounted on the bow of the vessel. The submersible attacked by ramming that spar torpedo into the hull of an enemy ship, resulting in an explosion which could be equally devastating to both vessels. The most successful of the

*Left:* Many riverboats were converted to gunboats by the addition of armor and armament.
*Above:* Gunboats frequently supplied support fire in land engagements.

Confederate submersibles was the CSS *H L Hunley* which on 17 February 1864, sank the USS *Housatonic*. Unfortunately, the *H L Hunley* accompanied the *Housatonic* to the bottom of Charleston harbor.

The Union also experimented with the idea of submersibles. It produced one vessel, the *Intelligent Whale* but the war ended before she was brought into service.

The naval war, although important in its own right, was merely a sideshow in comparison with the land campaigns which almost exclusively occupied the main efforts of both the Union and the Confederacy. Placed in a proper perspective, it was obvious that the Union could not have enjoyed the successes of 1863 and 1864 nor its ultimate victory in 1865 had it not been for the naval blockade which isolated the South from its industrial suppliers in Europe. In a war of attrition, the Confederacy, for all its bravery on land and sea, lacked the means to fight on indefinitely. The days of wooden ships and sail were drawing to a close and the future belonged to engine driven vessels of iron and steel. The naval powers of Europe would soon follow the trends set by the American States.

The first recruits to the Union army had to be taught everything, including learning their right from their left.

# SOLDIERS, ARMS
# AND ARMIES

core of veteran troops around which to build its army.

On 15 April 1861 Lincoln called up 75,000 militiamen for active service, only to discover that the militia system had deteriorated over the years. It was evident the militia system was totally inadequate for the number of troops needed to carry out the wishes of the President and his military staff. Compounding that problem, available militiamen would need almost their entire three months duty period to become sufficiently trained for combat.

In frustration, Lincoln implemented the same system applied by Confederate leaders for raising troops. A call was made

The outbreak of the Civil War clearly revealed the deterioration in the United States' military services. The regular army was small, consisting of an established force of fewer than 13,000 officers and men. In the years prior to the war, Congress had regulated the permissible size of the army. By law it could consist of no more than 10 regiments of infantry, four regiments of artillery and five regiments of combined regular cavalry, dragoons and mounted riflemen. Not only was the army small in numbers but its concentrated size had been decreased even further by the dispersal of units for duty along America's borders and frontiers and in the manning of coastal fortification. Fort Sumter was a vivid illustration that such garrisons were wretchedly undermanned.

The principal reason for the restrictions placed on the military services was the fact that the United States considered a large standing army a threat to the nation's independence. In the place of such a standing army, it had been decided that the military forces would be composed of individual citizens. The expansion policy of the United States was one which was basically limited to its own natural boundaries. An isolationist policy had been adopted toward the rest of the world.

It seemed unnecessary and unwise to promote a large regular army simply for defense, thereby paying to maintain a force that could feasibly be directed against its own government.

The citizen army, the militia, seemed an appropriate compromise. By decree such militiamen could only be called for active general service for three months in one calendar year; 90 days of either consecutive or non-consecutive periods of service. If any acts of war extended beyond that three-month period, a volunteer system or a policy for conscription would be implemented.

In the days following the secession of the Southern states, both the Union and the Confederacy discovered that their ability to act and react was curtailed by the necessity to raise and train troops. Strangely enough, although the officer corps was torn apart by the resignation of its members to support the Confederate cause, the vast majority of enlisted regular soldiers remained loyal to the army and the Union. While the Confederacy was blessed with able officers, the Union retained a strong

*Calling the militia for active service was the usual way of enlarging the small regular army, but the efficiency of these citizen soldiers could not match that of regular troops.*

for 100,000 volunteers for one year of active service. Commissioned regular army officers would be used to command such troops whenever possible. As the war progressed, requests for additional volunteers for longer periods eventually up to three years were made.

The armies of the Union and the Confederacy began on relatively equal terms with volunteers and militiamen forming the main bodies of troops. The balance would, in the long run, favor the North with its higher population. The Confederacy, however, had an advantage as the cream of the United States Army officer corps were primarily of Southern

background. The majority of those officers rallied to the call of their home states, as Robert E Lee did. General Winfield Scott, Union Chief of Staff, compared the loss of Lee's services and expertise to the Union with the loss of '50,000 veteran troops to a campaign.' Although it was not acknowledged at the beginning of the war, the experienced Southern officers would make a great difference in the first two years of the Civil War.

Little information has been preserved describing in detail the criteria used by the Confederacy in raising its volunteer army. Extensive material exists on the requirements set for the Northern male

population which was called into service. There were subtle differences but it could be rightly assumed that the requirements were relatively the same.

Entrance into the service was initiated by a medical examination of all prospective recruits. In fact, examining physicians did little more than give a descrip-

The artillery batteries, like the rest of the Confederate army had the advantage of a higher percentage of regular army officers. A large part of the prewar regular officer corps was composed of southerners and most of these men sided with the Confederacy. However most regular enlisted men remained loyal to the Union.

Many immigrants were recruited for the Union army straight off the boat, so acute was their need for manpower.

tion of the recruit's height, complexion, visible physical condition and a reference to previous occupation. The primary objective of medical examinations was intended to screen recruits for diseases or ailments which would make them unfit for military service. By the end of the first year of the war, it was apparent that a more thorough method of examination was needed as chronic ailments resulted in the discharge of many recruits. The Medical Director of the Army of the Potomac reported that a large number of those men had been forced into enlisting. The burden of their care was put on the army, relieving their families or communities of that responsibility.

Another problem was the discovery that the ranks of the army held many young boys between the ages of 14 and 18 and men of 60 years or older. The adolescents lacked the maturity and physical development necessary to enable them to withstand the rigors of war. At the opposite end of the spectrum, old men were equally unsuited to the hardships of battles and campaigns. The enlistment of those age groups during 1861 and 1862 resulted in the ultimate discharge of more than 200,000 troops.

By 1863 the North had adopted a much more stringent enlistment code. Minimum and maximum age limits were set at 18 and 45 respectively. There was also a minimum height requirement, set at five feet three inches. Although no maximum height was stipulated, it was standard practice for examining physicians to dismiss a man who was more than six feet three inches tall. Physicians were required to make more thorough examinations of potential enlistees. Men who showed signs of imperfect development, particularly in the chest and legs, were rejected. Men who suffered from varicose veins or hernias were also turned away. Weight limitations were set as guidelines for the examiners with a minimum of not less than 110 pounds and a maximum of not more than 220 pounds. The latter was often overlooked if it reflected the well-developed stature of the man rather than a case of obvious obesity.

Another criterion resulted from the experiences of the first year's fighting. Musket cartridges were made of paper and had to be torn open with the teeth. Recruits had to have a sufficient number of healthy teeth to perform that basic function adequately. Although men with false teeth were admitted into the service, they first had to prove that their dentures fitted properly and could be used as effectively as real teeth.

Further requirements were laid down in 1863 which would appear to be basic common sense but which it was deemed necessary to include. A man would be disqualified if insane or mentally retarded. He had to have full function of all limbs and a sufficient number of fingers on both hands to load and fire a musket and to grasp tools and other implements used by a soldier to perform his duties or defend himself. A man could not be blind in either eye and he had to have good hearing in at least one ear.

Finally, by regulation, three conditions were set forth which warranted disqualification. A man could not be a convicted felon. He could not be a known drunkard, though that regulation could not have been strictly adhered to as drunkeness was a major problem for both armies. Lastly, he could not exhibit signs of venereal disease.

If an individual could fulfill the stated requirements, he would be considered eligible for induction into the army. Within six days of his enlistment, the soldier took an oath of allegiance given by a civil magistrate or regular army officer. He was then mustered into a unit for six weeks of training.

For the Confederacy, the majority of volunteers were from a cross-section of all walks of life within the predominantly agricultural Southern communities. The officer ranks attracted those of the gentry and professional classes. Many of those officers received their commissions because they either raised their own units or had political influence with state officials.

In the North the officer rank was recruited in the same way. However more than 20 percent of the volunteers who served in the Union Army were of foreign birth. Immigrants enlisted, but not necessarily for the sake of patriotism. They joined for the bounty that was paid for fighting in the army during the early days of the war. However, the immigrant frequently had another reason for volunteering. The American Emmigration Company brought both skilled and unskilled laborers from Europe. Along with a small passage fee, the company established a contract between the immigrant and an employer in the United States. That contract stipulated that the immigrant had to repay the company the expenses incurred for his passage. The immigrants soon learned that if they enlisted in the army the government would then be responsible for their debt. This was made into a business arrangement and the Union government was forced to issue a resolution making it illegal to enlist immigrants abroad. Only after arriving in the United States were immigrants permitted to enlist, of their own free will.

Many foreign soldiers fought with as much bravery and distinction as native-born troops, but they were often denied acceptance in the ranks. Commanders referred to them as 'worthless foreigners' and the Irish particularly were the butt of jokes. In spite of the difficulties some 500,000 immigrants, mainly from Germany, England and Ireland fought and died for the Union.

The American Indians and blacks were also allowed to enlist. Together, the Union and Confederacy enlisted 3500 American Indians, more than 1000 of whom lost their lives. 186,000 blacks served in both armies and more than 2500 were killed in action. Blacks were originally detailed to perform menial tasks as they were not believed to possess sufficient intelligence to react well in battle. Such prejudice was completely without foundation, as black units which did see combat fought with much courage and valor. Both the Union and Confederacy attempted to recruit Mexicans to fill in their ranks but their efforts were unsuccessful.

Based on the statistics of the Union army, the average enlisted soldier was white, native-born, approximately 25 years old, five feet nine inches tall and weighed 145 pounds. Although the average age of Confederate soldiers decreased as the war continued, the basic statistics were the same.

After enlistment, the transformation of citizens to soldiers began. Initially, the Union and Confederacy relied on the superficial drill of the militia system to set

the foundation of training. Instruction was given by veterans of the Mexican War but consisted of little more than teaching a recruit his left foot from his right and how to march in a relatively straight line. Neither the North nor the South considered it necessary to employ professional instructors to train their troops.

One exception was General Thomas J Jackson, previously an instructor at the Virginia Military Institute who invested a great deal of time and effort into the training of his units at Harper's Ferry. However, the effects of inadequate training became obvious. Young officers could not control the troops, identify the enemy and maintain a substantial degree of controlled fire. There was a marked inability to move troops from one area to another without scattering them over the surrounding countryside.

Training camps were established but were conducted in more a civilian than military manner. In the initial days of recruitment, the soldiers had no uniforms and more often than not, no weapons. Until a regiment was actually formed or they were sent to a staging area, most men lived in the nearby towns or were billeted in government barracks. Drill, when it was accomplished, often lasted for as long as eight hours a day. Even then, it was usually a chaotic mass of individual units acting independently.

Blacks enlisted in the Union army and fought bravely at a number of battles, including Petersburg.

Regard for personal hygiene was also lacking and the performance of the troops was affected by epidemics of communicable diseases which swept many of the camps. As time went on, those troops who survived apparently became immune to disease.

Perhaps the most important training was in the use of the musket. Weapons were generally the last of the essential supplies to appear at the camps and when finally procured, they were often found to be antiquated and of inferior quality. Until the actual weapons arrived, recruits drilled with wooden muskets or broom handles. Repetitions of the loading sequence were fundamental, as many of the recruits had never handled a musket before.

Once the loading procedure was sufficiently understood and practiced, the actual firing technique could be taught. It was not an easy task. The inferior quality of the weapons was obvious not only in their inaccuracy but also their unpredictable nature. Frequent accidents and a lack of familiarity with weapons caused a great many troops to flinch with every shot they fired. In general, they would aim their muskets in the direction indi-

Punishment drill in the Union army varied with the severity of the offense committed.

cated, close their eyes, turn their heads and fire on command. Their accuracy with the musket was consequently poor and as ammunition supplies were precious, the average recruit was only permitted to fire 10 rounds per week.

While the ability of the average infantryman improved with experience, it was demonstrated that as late as Gettysburg insufficient training was not unusual. The 24,000 muskets which littered the battlefield were randomly examined. Less than 25 percent had been properly

Sports such as 'foot-ball' were encouraged especially when the army was in winter quarters.

loaded. More than 50 percent contained double charges and another 25 percent had been loaded from three to 10 times without ever being fired. One particular example of the effects of confusion and inadequate training was a musket which had 22 balls, 62 buckshot and a proportionate quantity of powder rammed into its barrel.

If individual training was inadequate, so too was instruction of drill and maneuver at the company and regimental levels. A complete absence of realism prevailed as there was little training in the combined efforts of the infantry, cavalry and artillery. The application of cooperation between the three branches was left to the battlefield. The prevailing consensus appeared to be that experience would be gained through battle for those fortunate enough to survive.

Attempts were made to instill discipline in the new recruits. It was generally believed that poor discipline stemmed from poor leadership. Even the most highly motivated regiment could be ruined in a short time by an ineffective commander. Discipline and a sense of purpose were essential to the development of trained soldiers. Such discipline had to go beyond the rules and regulations of military service. It was the central core which gave the soldier the confidence with which to perform his duties and follow the orders given him. An excellent example of training discipline was to be found in the troops commanded by 'Stonewall' Jackson in their performance at the First Battle of Manassas. Jackson's brigade had no more courage or experience than any other brigade at that time. Their primary asset was a confidence in themselves and their commander, a confidence born of the training they had received and the discipline it had instilled. In that sense, a good commander consistently made the difference in the outcome of any given battle.

Army regulations were also of importance to the maintainence of discipline. Punishment was relatively straightforward, but commanders were recommended to make punishment reflect the crime committed. Drunkenness, gambling and absence without leave generally resulted in extra duties or confinement. Blacklists of persistant offenders were often kept and their names were likely to appear on duty rosters for the purpose of digging latrines, burying dead animals or other disagreeable tasks.

Court-martial was another alternative. One board sentenced a soldier who had been absent without leave for five days to no less than three years hard labor at a fortification with the loss of all pay except for those allowances to cover his laundry expenses.

The most drastic of the lesser punishments was torture, used in the hope of making an example of the offending soldier. The rack was the most widely used implement for such punishment, varying from a simple wooden frame to the use of a spare wagon wheel for that purpose.

The most serious crime, in both armies, was desertion. In his final days as commander of the Army of Northern Virginia, Lee complained bitterly about desertion calling it his greatest enemy. In the North commanders adopted a policy of executing a few men guilty of desertion as an example. In the Army of the Potomac, it was believed that the executions of 'bad' soldiers in 1862 actually improved discipline and saved the lives of many 'good' soldiers in the future.

One such execution was described in the diary of a young soldier in 1863. Three men were to be shot for desertion and the entire corps was assembled to witness the event. After waiting for over an hour a wagon appeared bearing three coffins which were placed next to the graves

Gambling and cardplaying were tolerated, but soldiers would frequently throw cards, 'devil's pastboards,' away before going into battle.

which had been dug by the deserters themselves. A second heavily guarded wagon arrived carrying the condemned who were then seated upon the coffins, tied and blindfolded. After a short prayer, they were shot by a firing squad which had been drawn from men of different units in the corps. Men who were themselves under disciplinary action were sent forward to put the bodies into the coffins, seal the lids and fill the graves. Little attention was given to whether or not the men were actually dead. No soldiers were excused from participating in or witnessing the executions and the harsh price for breaking regulations was not soon nor easily forgotten.

Major and minor crimes such as thievery were punishable by being 'drummed' out of the corps as fife and drums played the 'Rogue's March,' branding and even mutilation. The rigors of war were harsh indeed, and the need for stern discipline in preparation for what lay ahead was recognized and enforced.

However the soldier's life was not completely grim. When not on duty or in drill practice, sports were encouraged and regiments formed teams to participate. Such regimental competition was not always restricted to sports. In one incident,

several regiments engaged in a snowball fight which mushroomed into a brawl during which the entire camp was wrecked, eyes were blacked, teeth knocked out and bones broken. The damages were done 'all in fun' and served to relieve a great deal of tension within and between the regiments.

Boxing, chess and a form of football were popular and among Southern troops,

horseracing was a much indulged sport. Another game, developed by General Abner Doubleday in 1839, was baseball. Though still in its infancy, it was nevertheless a widely-played, popular form of diversion. Some armies even had their

Dancing, especially jig contests, was a popular entertainment.

and available in large quantities. However, the many styles and colors of uniforms in the early days proved a problem to commanders and troops alike on the battlefields, making it difficult to distinguish friend from foe in the heat of an engagement. It was obvious that a standard had to be set. In the North, it was decided that a dark blue tunic jacket with trousers of various shades of blue would comprise the basic uniform. In the South, a gray tunic jacket with light blue or gray trousers was adopted for the simple reason that the material was easily accessible.

Not only were the early uniforms indistinguishable, they were also elaborate, impractical and cumbersome. One popular style was the French uniform known as the 'Zouave.' It consisted of baggy trousers, a vestlike tunic and an exotic turban, all elaborately embellished with gaudy embroidery. Soldiers of both armies adopted it and it was one of the styles which created difficulty of distinction on the battlefield. In any given regiment, the uniforms varied from company to company,

*Above:* Amateur minstrel shows and theatricals were performed in the camps of both armies.
*Right:* With the development of photography, it was possible to send a portrait back home. They were especially treasured if the soldier was killed, as in the case of this Louisiana private who fell at Gettysburg.

own periodicals, formed clubs and had travelling theatrical companies for the entertainment of the troops.

Commissaries were established where soldiers could purchase soap, tobacco and even whiskey as well as other items which could supply some of the meaner comforts of home life. Furloughs and visitor privileges were also permitted. One recent invention, the camera, fascinated soldiers of both armies and men would stand in line for hours to have their pictures taken.

The soldiers' lot was not, nor ever will be an easy one, but these diversions helped to offset the rigors of drill and discipline.

In the transformation of civilian to soldier, nothing was more obvious than the issue of that soldier's uniform. It set him apart and reflected his position as a member of the military. When war began and men flocked to the service of both armies, young volunteers paraded proudly in the uniform of their companies or regiments. Unlike the European armies, most Union and Confederate army uniforms were not standardized. Militia and volunteers wore whatever uniform fitted their particular taste. Although the United States Army had a regulation uniform the influx of new troops created a demand which could not be met. It was impossible to insist on regulation dress for the vast majority of troops. The newly formed Confederate Army faced the dilemma of both adopting and providing a regulation uniform. Soldiers of both armies were generally dressed in 'cadet gray' as that particular cloth was popular with the men

being blue, gray, dark green or of the Zouave style. With the passage of time, the uniforms were eventually, of necessity, standardized, creating a more unified appearance and a more effective distinction between the opposing armies.

Aside from their uniforms and military paraphernalia, troops were permitted to retain necessary personal items. Although they disappeared during the course of the war, knapsacks were originally used to carry personal belongings. However the knapsack was found to be cumbersome and not always in sufficient supply. Following the southern custom, the use of the 'blanket roll' became more usual. The average soldier carried a jacket, shirt, pair of trousers, pair of shoes and socks and a change of underdrawers plus personal items and mementos. These would be rolled inside a rubber blanket if one were available, then in a woollen blanket. The roll was then tied off at several points to hold the contents in place, then tied to form a loop which was slung over the left shoulder and across the body.

The haversack was another basic item which came into use as the war progressed. It seldom carried clothing and was used to transport food, coffee and the equipment and utensils for the soldier's meals. Each soldier carried a canteen which was attached to a strap and slung across his body with his blanket roll. Made of wood and later of metal, canteens were often marked with regimental numbers, state's name or another individualized pattern

traced on them by their owners. As a supply of water was not a major concern to the majority of troops, the canteen was often discarded for a strong tin cup. In the latter part of the war, the discovery of a discarded metal canteen of a Union soldier by a Confederate troop was considered quite a prize as they could be cut to serve as a cooking pan.

Other articles included a belt upon which a cartridge case and often a knife were hung. Civilian footwear was worn or boots were provided. As the war progressed, footwear for the Confederate troops ranged from hide to rags and those fortunate enough to possess a pair of shoes, even those whose soles were worn through, treasured them and would replace the soles with wood or even horseshoes.

The period of uniformity in military dress was shortlived, particularly in the South. The longer the war continued, the less available replacement uniforms became. Army supplies were supplemented with articles which the troops could scavenge from the battlefield. It was not unheard of for Confederate troops to be shot as spies when captured in Union dress salvaged after a battle. Civilian clothing augmented the scarce uniforms to the extent that Confederate troops looked completely civilian. In some cases they were only distinguishable as soldiers by the weapons they carried and their response to orders from their officers.

In the officer corps, the emblems of rank were another source of confusion. For

*Above:* Typical of the exotic and impractical uniforms of Zouave regiments in both armies are those of Ellsworth's Chicago Cadets which had bright red trousers.
*Below:* Civil War campaign medal issued to the veterans of the Union army.

*Above:* Sutlers attached to the Union army sold canned goods and occasionally liquor at high prices, in addition to standard rations.
*Left, right and below:* Posed photographs lend a romantic air to soldiers whose actual life, despite pets and corn liquor, was quite harsh.

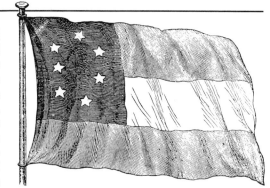

The first Confederate flag, which was confused with the 'Stars and Stripes' of the period.

the enlisted men, the markings of rank were firmly established in both armies, represented by the number of stripes on the sleeves of their uniforms. The Union army retained the use of bars, oak leaves, eagles, and stars to classify its officers. Those items were cast in silver or gold which also had a recognized significance. Shoulder boards were worn with backing colors indicative of the particular branch of service; yellow for the cavalry, light blue for the infantry and red for the artillery.

In the Confederate army, rank was denoted in a multitude of ways, the lacing on the sleeves and cap and the gold badge of rank on the collar. The number of bars and stars on the collar and the braiding on the sleeves also gave indication of the officer's rank. The higher the rank the more gaudy the uniform. Not all officers rigidly abided by that system. The rank of general in the Confederate army was to be denoted by three gold stars and a laurel wreath on the collar and four gold braids intricately looped up the sleeve, ending midway up the bicep. However, the highest ranking Confederate general Robert E Lee, wore only the three stars and three braids of the full colonel.

One aid to distinguishing opposing armies on the battlefield was the development of battle flags. The 'Confederate Jack' with a field of blue in the upper left hand corner, studded with seven stars and three horizontal stripes of red, white, red, bore a great resemblance to the Union 'Stars and Stripes' at a distance. During the most crucial moment of the First Battle of Manassas, when Early's brigade arrived on the battlefield, neither army could distinguish whose reserves were approaching because of the similarity of flags and uniforms. The new nation of

The Federal flag still carried stars for the states which had seceded.

the Confederate States of America decided to adopt a original design, the 'Stars and Bars,' a red field, blue diagonal bars bordered in white with 13 white stars spaced upon the blue. Although there were actually only 11 Confederate states, the designers of the flag and the sentiments of the people influenced the decision to include the sympathetic states of Kentucky and Missouri so that the flag would contain the same number of stars as the original flag of the American Colonies. It was hoped that fate would prove as favorable to the Confederate's fight for independence as it had to the original colonies. Although state flags continued to be flown proudly in battle, the 'Stars and Stripes' and the 'Stars and Bars' represented the distinct separation of the Union and the Confederacy.

Although the military paraphernalia of the individual soldier was important to his effectiveness as a fighting man, nothing equalled the importance of his weapons. At the start of the war, several models of rifle-musket and standard musket were used by both armies.

For the Union, two rifle-musket types were the basic infantry weapon. The United States Rifle Musket, 1855 replaced earlier percussion weapons used by the American military. It was considered accurate up to 500 yards when fired in a volley from an entire line of soldiers. Individually, the weapon was virtually useless beyond a range of 150 yards. More than 47,000 were produced between the years of 1857 and 1861, making it one of the original weapons issued in the early years of the war. Several different versions of the United States Rifle Musket, 1855 were produced. The most popular and widely used of the modifications was the Harper's Ferry Rifle, a shorter version of the '1855.'

The other basic Union weapon was the United States Rifle Musket, 1861 which

had a few principal modifications. This weapon, produced at the Springfield Armory in Massachusetts, was consequently nicknamed the 'Springfield Musket.' It is estimated that some 900,000 were produced before 1863. The '1861' was essentially the '1855' rifle-musket except that the '1861' used a normal percussion cap for its primer system which made the weapon more reliable in inclement weather. The Maynar Tape Primer System of the '1855' was notoriously prone to misfire. The accuracy of the Springfield Musket was effective to a range of 300 yards for individual targets. When fired in mass volleys up to regimental strength, it was known to inflict casualties to a distance of up to 1000 yards. Its rate of fire was almost twice that of other rifle muskets produced to date and an experienced soldier could fire six rounds per minute. Even the rawest recruit, with the most minimal training, could fire three rounds per minute. That factor placed them at an effectiveness equal to veteran troops who carried older styles of rifle muskets. The Springfield Musket was a favorite prize of Confederate troops who were said to have used more than 150,000 of them, most of which were captured in battle.

In the Confederacy, the standard weapon used until after the Battle of Gettysburg was the United States Percussion Musket Model 1842. Because the South had few factories manufacturing firearms, the Confederate soldier relied on weapons which had been seized from the militia's arsenals. The old-fashioned smooth-bore muskets were typical of the armaments stored in those arsenals. They had an effective range of only 100 yards and a rate of fire which permitted two or three shots per minute. For all its faults, the one redeeming factor of the musket was an extremely low tendency for misfire, set at only one out of every 160 shots. Nevertheless, its limited range put the Confederate soldier at a distinct disadvantage as 100 yards placed Confederate troops within easy distance of the enemy forces.

To counter the obvious deficiencies of the '1842,' the Confederacy bought weapons from European nations and attempted to produce its own copies of United States rifles and muskets. One such effort was the 'Richmond Sharps Rifle,' and while several

other models were also attempted, their workmanship and performance was far inferior to the originals and the European weapons.

Several other rifles and carbines were used, but most in small quantities. However, the 'Enfield,' a British made weapon purchased and used by both the North and the South was considered superior even to the 'Springfield.' The accuracy of the 'Enfield' was described as being superior to all other rifles of the time. Some accounts claimed that it could consistently hit an individual target at a range of 500 yards. That was an extremely long range for a weapon of that period and a more accurate account would probably place its range just slightly longer than the 'Springfield.' With respect to volley fire *en masse*, the 'Enfield' was known to be effective to the distance of 1100 yards. The primary draw-back of the 'Enfield' was its rate of fire which stood at two or three rounds per minute. It had been intended that the 'Enfield' would represent the standard weapon for the Confederacy but owing to the effects of the blockade and the shifting fortunes of war, the number of weapons actually delivered was far less than the demands of the Confederate Army. Some discrepancy exists over the exact number of British 'Enfield' rifles actually shipped to both the Union and the Confederacy. Estimates range from 200,000 to 800,000.

While the rifle musket was the infantryman's favored weapon, the cavalryman's requirements were best met by the carbine. The carbine was small enough and simple enough to be carried and reloaded on horseback. The most widely used cavalry weapon was the 'Sharps' single shot, breech-loading, lever-operated carbine which could fire up to ten rounds per minute. It was highly immune to malfunction as each round was an individual cartridge. More than 100,000 'Sharps' carbines were used. The accuracy of the 'Sharps' was listed at 400 yards. If the cavalry troopers were dismounted and in a position to fire on advancing troops, as did Buford's Cavalry at Gettysburg, the troopers proved that they were worth two to three times their actual numbers.

Two other carbine type weapons gained great favor with the cavalry. One, the 'Spencer Carbine' was a repeater rifle whose magazine held eight rounds. Properly employed, the 'Spencer' could deliver up to 21 rounds per minute. Approxi-

mately 200,000 of that particular carbine were used during the war.

The other carbine, the predecessor of the 'Winchester' lever action rifle which gained great fame in the West after the war, was the 'Henry,' a .44 caliber rifle. It had a magazine which could deliver 15 rounds in as little as 11 seconds. In a five-minute period of load and fire its user could direct more than 120 rounds against his target. Such a rapid fire rate contributed to the fact that the weapon had a tendency to jam. That tendency was overlooked by those who desired the qualities it possessed but no more than 10,000 'Henry' rifles were used during the war.

The basic weapon for both officers and

*Top:* At the outbreak of the war, both armies were primarily armed with the US Rifle Muskets of 1855, firing Minié balls.

cavalry, several models and copies of revolver were used during the war. The two most extensively used pistol revolvers were the 'Colt' and the 'Remington.' Imported models from England and France were also popular.

The 'Colt' was available in three basic designs; the 'Dragoon' which weighed an unbelievable four pounds, and the 'Army' and the 'Navy' which were the preferred models. Approximately 150,000 'Colt' revolvers were recorded as purchased during the war but it was more likely that some 500,000 were actually used. The

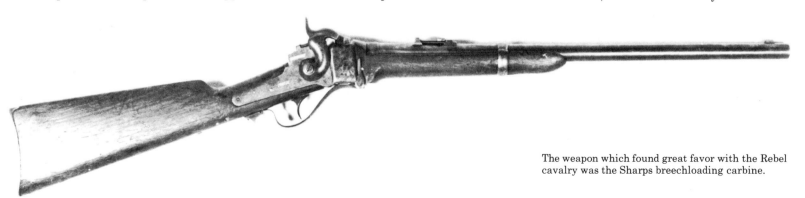

The weapon which found great favor with the Rebel cavalry was the Sharps breechloading carbine.

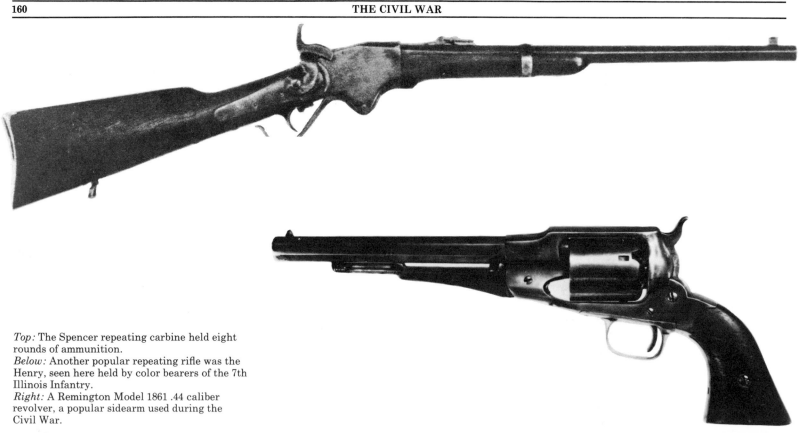

*Top:* The Spencer repeating carbine held eight rounds of ammunition.
*Below:* Another popular repeating rifle was the Henry, seen here held by color bearers of the 7th Illinois Infantry.
*Right:* A Remington Model 1861 .44 caliber revolver, a popular sidearm used during the Civil War.

effectiveness of the 'Colt' was best suited to a range of 20 to 50 yards. All 'Colt' revolvers were single action which required the hammer to be cocked before each firing.

The 'Remington', which was not quite as popular as the 'Colt,' was also a six shot, single action revolver. It was available in .44 and .35 caliber. The .35 caliber was most widely used by naval personnel and more than 120,000 'Remingtons' found their way into service during the course of the war.

A third revolver type was the 'Starr.' Only some 40,000 such pistols were ever produced, the most popular being the 'Starr' army .44 which was a six shot, double action model which fired a self-consuming cartridge or could also be hand loaded with loose powder and ball. Although the 'Starr' was never very popular with the troops, its self-cocking mechanism was incorporated in the future designs.

Other weapons used by the soldiers, both Union and Confederate included the sword, the sabre, the bayonet, which was primarily a socket type, and, of course, the knife. The cavalry lance, popular in Europe, met with minimal success.

Most edged weapons were little more than morale boosters and remnants of a previous era, particularly the bayonet. Few soldiers in either army were actually killed or wounded in an action where bayonets were involved. Of the 250,000

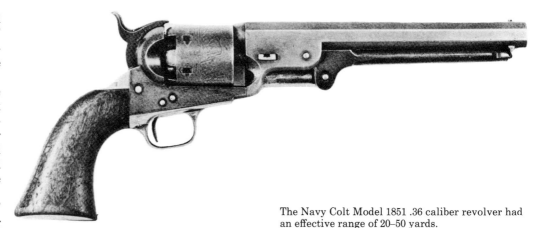

The Navy Colt Model 1851 .36 caliber revolver had an effective range of 20–50 yards.

men treated in Union hospitals, less than 1000 had wounds inflicted by sword or bayonet. In fact, the majority of wounds from those sources were accidentally self-inflicted.

One of the most unusual weapons considered for use during the Civil War was the pike. Owing to the scarcity of arms for the Confederacy, at the beginning of the war, an effort was made to reintroduce the pike as an infantry weapon. As late as 1862, plans were underway for 20 pike regiments and further consideration was being given to the incredible idea that two companies of every regiment should be issued with pikes. Even Lee, during his service as special adviser to Jefferson Davis, lent his support to the proposal. After much time and material were wasted the idea was shelved without one pike

actually being issued. That was indeed fortunate for the infantry soldiers who would have been called upon to participate in the scheme. They would surely have been slaughtered in their efforts to use pikes on a battlefield dominated by gunpowder.

The most generally destructive of the weapons on land and at sea were the artillery. On the battlefield, artillery performed two basic functions. In an offensive role, it was employed to disperse or destroy enemy artillery and as support to disorder and inflict casualties on units which were scheduled to be attacked. In defense, artillery, with the use of

The Parrott Rifle, easily identified by the wrought-iron jacket reinforcing the breech, was one of the first rifled field guns used by the US army.

cannister and shell, was directed against oncoming enemy forces in an effort to weaken or break an advance. Artillery was also employed against fortifications but such heavy cannon were not easily transported with the moving armies and usually were kept as special units of the artillery reserve.

The primary artillery piece for both the Union and the Confederacy was the 12-pound Napoleonic Gun-Howitzer. Considered the work-horse of the artillery, they were used extensively throughout the Civil War. The '12-pound Napoleon' was a smooth bore cannon which could fire two aimed shots or four cannister rounds per minute. It had a maximum range of 2000 yards which made it extremely effective in either offense or defense. There was also a six-pound version of the Napoleonic Gun-Howitzer. Its range was 1500 yards and that decrease was coupled with a

The army commissariat was responsible for feeding the troops, issuing a certain number of loaves of bread and a certain weight of meat to each company.

marked decrease in fire strength. Although the 'six-pound Napoleon' was used by the South primarily as a lighter horse-artillery piece, its obvious flaws made Lee replace it whenever possible and to melt down older cannon to cast 12-pounders.

Another popular artillery piece was the 'three-inch Rodman,' also known as the three-inch Ordnance Rifle or Gun. It was a rifled, 3.00 caliber weapon, developed by the United States Ordnance Department in 1863. As a rifled piece, it could achieve a higher degree of accuracy than the conventional smooth-bore cannon. It was also small and lightweight enough to be easily transported or moved in position. As rifled cannon became larger, heavier and more unwieldy, the 'Rodman' filled a definite need. It could fire all the standard ammunition of rifled cannon and was exceedingly effective as a close range, anti-personnel weapon. Used extensively by horse artillery batteries, it was put to use in all batteries whenever possible. Primarily a Union weapon, the 'three-inch Rodman' was considered quite a prize by Confederate artillerymen when captured.

The effective range was equal to the maximum range of the '12-pound Napoleon' and when manned by an experienced artillery crew, was known to hit a target as far away as 4000 yards.

The design of the 'Rodman' followed that of the rifled 'Parrott.' The 'Parrott' was available in 10- and 20-pound models. It had been developed for accuracy and had a range which was equal to that of the 'Rodman' and was used by both the Union and Confederacy artillery batteries.

The only other artillery pieces of any consequence were the breech loading models, most of which had been imported from England. Those used were the 12-pound 'Whitworth,' the 12-pound 'Blakely' and the 12-pound 'Armstrong.' All were rifled and could fire a round to a distance of six miles. Unfortunately they were prone to premature explosions while the shell was still in the breech. Such explosions destroyed the weapon and mutilated the unfortunate crew. Although initially favored by the Confederacy, they soon fell into disuse, occasionally aiding other cannon to fix a point for bombardment.

Both the 'Blakely' and the 'Armstrong' used several types of shells, but all were small and accommodated a limited degree of explosive power. Another innovation was applied to heavy siege artillery pieces during the Civil War. Not known for ease in maneuverability, such cannon were mounted on railway cars which could be stationed near strategic points.

In the same general catagory with artillery, another form surfaced during the Civil War – the rocket. The Confederacy used the British 'Congreve' which had changed little since the British Army employed it at Leipzig and Waterloo. For a time, a rocket unit was attached to Jeb Stuart's cavalry but they saw limited action. The Union put two types of rockets into service, six-pound and 16-pound models developed by William Hale. More accurate than their British counterpart, their maximum range exceeded 2000 yards and carried either an explosive or incendiary device. However sophisticated, rocket design was far from perfect. Troops distrusted rockets as they possessed a marked tendency to explode on the ground or fly off in a direction other than that in which they were aimed. One artillery officer recorded that the rockets of his day were as dangerous to the army using them as to the army at which they were directed. It became a standard jest that the safest place on the battlefield to be during a rocket barrage was in the ranks of the intended target.

Explosive hand grenades were another weapon of pre-Napoleonic origin to reach the Civil War battlefields. Nearly 100,000 were purchased by the Union government for use primarily in siege operations. However, most remained untouched in arsenal storage depots as troops quickly realized that frequently they exploded before they could be thrown.

In spite of the armament developments in the Union and the Confederacy, it was the individual soldier which truly made the difference on the battlefield.

As previously stated, the infantry ranks of both the Union and Confederate armies were mainly filled by volunteers rising to the call of their individual states. Once massed, the volunteers became companies which in turn formed regiments, the basis of the Civil War armies. Regimental organization varied. The United States Regular Army regiments, of which there were few, consisted of between two and four battalions per regiment. Each battalion was composed of eight companies of approximately 100 men each.

The Union decided that new volunteer infantry regiments would have ten companies each, eliminating the battalion classification. Each company would have approximately 100 men, though in actual battlefield conditions their strength usually ranged from 60 to 80 men. The companies were to have three officers and 97 enlistees divided into 13 non-commissioned officers, two drummers, one wagoneer and 81 privates. The regiments were to have an attached staff section which would consist of a colonel, commander of the regiment and his aides; a lieutenant colonel, a major, an adjutant and a quartermaster. In turn, those officers would be

The more familiar Confederate flag or 'Stars and Bars' flying over Fort Sumter.

*Above:* Major General Wade Hampton (1818–1902) raised an independent Confederate legion which fought with Longstreet's Corps.
*Below:* Federal artillery going into action on the south bank of the Rappahannock River on 4 June 1863.

assisted by a sergeant major, a quartermaster sergeant and a commissary sergeant. In the early days, each regiment was also equipped with a 24-man band but they were soon replaced by only two musicians, usually drummers. Another important addition to the regiment was a surgeon with his accompanying assistant and a hospital steward.

Generally the regimental strengths of the Union and Confederacy varied from 800 to 1000 men, depending on the recruitment capabilities which prevailed.

In combat, the regiments of both armies were employed in relatively the same manner. It was in the area of handling their losses where they showed a marked variation. Once a Confederate regiment was formed, new recruits were added to fill the ranks and maintain regimental strength status. The Union command believed that men fought best in the company of men from the same general area. They felt that a man was less likely to show cowardice or desert when he was surrounded by neighbors and friends. Such pressure on the individual instilled discipline and confidence in all members of the company and consequently, in the regiment. When a regiment was reduced to 25 percent of its original strength, it would be transformed into a company which would then join with others to form new regiments. However the Confederate view was equally logical as their method of replacement put new recruits with veteran soldiers where they could more quickly learn the methods of fighting and staying alive on the battlefield. In either case, the availability of manpower played a crucial role. The North had a larger male population on which to draw, while the South had to make the most of every available man.

Organization of the cavalry branch differed between the North and the South. A Union cavalry regiment consisted of four to six squadrons. Each squadron had two or three companies of 100 men each. Ideally that meant that a Union cavalry

regiment would be at least 800 men in strength. In actuality their strength was usually between 250 and 350 men. That discrepancy between the intent and the fact was due more to the lack of good horses than a lack of volunteers.

Southern cavalry regiments, many of which were individually formed and financed, had no strict organizational standard. However, it was generally accepted that each regiment would consist of ten companies of 100 men each. The average regimental strength was intended to be at least 500 men, but as the war went on, the Confederate cavalry suffered as much as the Union through an inadequate supply of horses. By the end of the war, it was not uncommon for a Confederate cavalry regiment to be able to muster only 100 mounted troopers at one time.

The Union Army supplied its troopers with horses, whereas the Confederate cavalryman owned his horse or string of horses. That meant that the Confederate

trooper was mounted on an animal he knew, trusted and loved. His care and treatment of his horse had a much greater priority than his Union counterpart. The Confederate cavalryman in the opening days of the war was a much more efficient horseman as well.

The composition of the cavalry regiments was very similar to the infantry with reference to command and support personnel except that more assistance was provided to aid the troopers in the care of their animals and equipment.

The Confederacy also used a mixture of infantry, cavalry and artillery in reviving an old European-style organization, the Legion. It was a combination of the three branches in a fighting force of regimental size. Such organizations were usually privately recruited, armed, outfitted and commanded by influential men of the individual states. One of the most famous Confederate legions was created and commanded by a rich planter from South Carolina, Wade Hampton. Hampton's

Legion had six infantry companies, four cavalry companies and six 'Blakely' 12-pound field pieces. They were involved in First Battle of Manassas and distinguished themselves with honor and bravery while serving with Longstreet's Corps and during the Peninsular Campaign. However, like most legions, the monies supplied by their commanders began to disappear, making it difficult to maintain the organization of the units.

Eventually, the legions were forced to disband, usually to be absorbed into the regular army. The commander and creator of Hampton's Legion rose to the rank of Major General during the war and went on to become Governor and later Senator of South Carolina.

The artillery, referred to as the 'queen of battle,' was attached to large units and even formed its own divisions as reserve support for the army during battle. Artillery was subdivided into light and heavy classes. The light ones were intended to be field pieces used in direct support on the

battlefield. The heavy, larger caliber pieces were destined for use during sieges, against fortifications and in static defense.

Each Union battery was composed of four to six guns of the same type. Each cannon had a crew of six or seven men, a limber drawn by six horses and a caisson for ammunition drawn by a similar team. Artillery batteries also boasted a travelling forge, extra caissons, baggage wagons, spare limbers and horses and whatever else was necessary to maintain the cannon and men in action. Each battery was expected to have the capacity to reforge or rebuild a damaged gun.

Union horse artillery batteries travelled with the cavalry. They consisted of six to eight guns, six or seven mounted crew members per gun and at least two extra horses.

The basic distribution of the Union artillery was two to five batteries per battalion and two to four battalions per brigade. It was standard practice for each Union corps to have an artillery brigade attached to it.

Confederate artillery was employed and maintained in the same manner except that a battery could consist of between two and eight guns, four being the norm. An important difference, which caused no small degree of complication for the Confederates was the use of different type and caliber cannon in the same battery. The mixing of weapons was a result of necessity, not intended design. In the early days of the war it was difficult for the Confederates to field well-formed batteries and in the latter days, Confederate pieces which had been lost or destroyed were usually replaced by Union ones which had been captured on the battlefield. Complications arose in keeping an adequate supply of the various types of ammunition required by the different guns within the batteries.

The basic arms and subdivisions of the army were gathered into higher grouping orders and commands which were basically the same for both the Union and Confederate armies. Brigades usually consisted of an average of four or five regiments. On average, three brigades equalled a division in the Union army, making a division approximately 6000 men. Confederate divisions were much larger, usually having four to six brigades totalling 9000 men. That Confederate numerical superiority per division was a bonus in that more troops under a single command could be brought to bear on a given point. It often eliminated the necessity to coordinate assaults with other units which frequently caused difficulties on the battlefields.

The corps was the backbone of both the Union and Confederate armies, averaging four divisions per corps in both instances. This meant that a Confederate corps was larger than its Union counterpart, 50 percent larger in fact.

Infantry tactics during the Civil War were similar to the tactics of the Napoleonic Wars and European methods which had been applied since that time. However, after the first major engagements and such disasters as the Battle of Fredericksburg, where large dense columns were pushed forward to be slaughtered by rifle and artillery fire, those tactics were abandoned. It was evident that the increased range, power and accuracy of both rifles and artillery could inflict devastating losses before the advancing enemy infantry was able to reach its objective.

Several new tactics were formulated. First was the movement of troops in open order. Assaults of that type resulted in a decrease in the effectiveness of both artillery and rifle fire. Second, rather than plod forward *en masse*, troops attacked in rapid bursts or rushes toward the enemy. By rushing a position, the advancing infantry were subjected to the least amount of time exposed to enemy fire. Reserves were kept which could quickly be moved forward to capitalize on the initial assaults. Commanders soon discovered that those tactics reduced their losses and increased their ratio of successes.

In defense, infantrymen were drawn up in shallow lines, rarely more than two ranks deep, which allowed the maximum number of rifles to be brought to bear. Contrary to the traditional tendency to form lines in open terrain, Civil War commanders quickly learned that the best results were achieved when some form of natural protection was employed in a defensive position. When no natural protection was available, the tactics began to include digging trenches. Entrenched troops could often hold off an enemy two or three times their own size, as was seen at Vicksburg, Petersburg and Atlanta.

By the end of the war, infantry tactics had evolved into massive flowing formations of skirmish order troops attempting to bring more fire power to bear on the enemy that the enemy could bring against them. It was becoming obvious that firepower would decide battles. The changes in both offense and defense were indicative of the trend to the modern tactics

which were emerging and are only today being altered once again.

Cavalry tactics were also changing. Although some commanders continued to believe in the glory of the charge, very few such charges actually occurred. The terrain over which most battles were fought lent itself to the grand charge. However, the increase in the rates of fire was a deterrant, as more rounds could be directed at the approaching cavalry. Artillery, firing at charging cavalry at a distance of 1000 yards could direct 11 solid or shrapnel shots and five cannister rounds before that cavalry could reach the gun emplacements. Supporting infantry could add up to six rounds of rifle fire during the last 500 yards of such a charge. Death and destruction were the only rewards for such futile attempts.

The deployment of the cavalry underwent a revision. It became a rapidly moving force whose primary functions were to conduct raids, create diversions and gather information, as well as harass and destroy enemy lines of supply and communication. No longer the shock troops of the battlefield, cavalrymen discovered that in battle their most effective role was to move forward quickly, dismount and apply the firepower of their 'Sharps,' 'Spencer,' or 'Henry' carbines.

Once again, the groundwork was being laid for twentieth century warfare as new objectives and methods of deployment with increased mobility and firepower laid the foundation for the principles of mechanized warfare.

Artillery tactics changed very little. It was the advances in technology which allowed artillery to reap a larger harvest of lives on the battlefield which marked the most noticeable difference. Massing the improved weapons in 'grand batteries' often determined the outcome of a battle before the infantry even made contact. Artillery advancement was a key factor in forcing the infantrymen into trenches and behind fortifications. Increased ranges allowed imaginative minds to project a future where guns could be brought to bear against troops who had never been seen and who might be miles away.

The Civil War made evident that the face of warfare was indeed changing. Long-standing traditions were being broken. Large numbers of men and armies were being deployed over extended, independent areas, each with different objectives and priorities. Advances in technology resulted in an ability to kill more and more troops and expanded the restricted size of the battlefield. Napoleon had said that a good general must develop a new, innovative method of waging war every 10 years if he were to keep ahead of his peers. The innovations which were developed and to some degree perfected during the Civil War, marked a new era in the art of war which the rest of the world could not afford to ignore. The developments in warfare which first emerged in this conflict were to reach a bloody culmination on the Western Front in World War I. Trench warfare and strategies based on attrition were pointers to the future.

Advances in artillery technology forced the infantry into trenches or behind fortifications to escape the devastating effects of artillery pieces massed into 'grand batteries.'

A contemporary engraving of a Federal mortar
battery in action.

# THE CHANGING FACE

The American Civil War was an important stage in the evolution of the art of war. Its scope and effects separated warfare from the last great revolutionary era, that of the Napoleonic Wars, and the birth of modern warfare. The impact of certain technological advancements caused other aspects, such as the change in tactics and a broadening concern for the scope of strategic objectives, to be transformed. The basis of war can be reduced to one very brutal fact: the ability of one army to eliminate the soldiers of another. That can be done in many ways, but the more effective the better. Reflecting that fundamental characteristic of war, much attention was directed at the most basic weapon of the infantryman, the musket.

The musket, which was the principal weapon of the infantryman since the 1700s, carried over onto the battlefields of the Civil War. It had an extremely limited range and was known for its inaccuracy. The United States Precision Musket, Model 1842, had an effective range of less than 100 yards. In the hands of a trained soldier it had a low rate of fire of only two or three rounds per minute. Those characteristics meant that for maximum effect the musket had to be fired in volleys, that is, troops grouped together in large formations so that a maximum number of rounds could be fired at the advancing enemy.

Hitting a target at a full 100 yards with a musket was usually the result of luck rather than any skill on the part of the soldier. Consequently tactics had remained simple with massive numbers of troops facing each other and exchanging volleys. When one side or the other displayed a weakness as a result of the fire, a thrust would be made to overpower the enemy at that point.

Napoleon expanded that practice by forming dispersed open order troops called skirmishers. Skirmish order troops were harder to hit but they drew fire away from the columns they moved before. Skirmishers in turn produced effective offensive fire as they were aiming at close order troops. Once within charge range the skirmishers would move aside and the columns would attack. As a result, on the battlefields of the Napoleonic Wars the skirmishers did the bulk of firing while the columns applied their weight of numbers to the melee.

As time went on other advances were made in infantry weapons and the rifled musket was introduced. Before its application to military use, prototypes of the rifle musket existed, primarily as individual hunting weapons. Any rifle formations were not standardized since each man might own a rifle of a different caliber and range.

The British army had been the first to experience the devastating potential of frontiersmen armed with rifles during the American Revolutionary War. As a result the British began to lead the field in the production and utilization of rifled weapons, most notably the Baker Rifle. By the 1840s a great deal of effort was being focussed on the development of rifle muskets. In the following decade it became the principal infantry weapon, replacing smoothbore muskets of most European armies. Again the British took the lead by employing rifle musket formations in the Crimea. By the time of the American Civil War the use and value of the rifle had been firmly established.

Ammunition for the new rifle pieces standardized in 1847. Claude Minié, a French captain, developed a projectile which was an elongated ball, rounded at one end with a flat hollow base. When fired it expanded to fit the rifling of the barrel. Its inventor's name became synonymous with that new projectile which was dubbed the 'Minié ball.'

It became obvious that two important elements had to be incorporated into the rifle musket: Range with accuracy and a more rapid fire capability. By increasing long range accuracy infantrymen could engage targets at greater distances with better results. Consequently fewer troops could be employed to achieve the same effect. Similarly, making the weapon easier to load would mean an increase in the rate of firing, making a single infantryman worth two or three of his musket carrying counterparts. A modern company of 100 men armed with such a rifle would have a fire effectiveness equivalent to three companies of the previous era.

At the start of the Civil War both the Union and Confederacy realized the value of the rifle musket to their troops. The North was able to produce a large quantity of arms, but in the South industrialization had remained underdeveloped. Representatives of both governments were sent to buy weapons overseas, primarily in England, to compensate for the deficiencies which existed. The most popular foreign rifle was the British 'Enfield' which had a range of 1000 yards with assured accuracy up to 500 yards. More than 800,000 'Enfields' were recorded as purchased by American buyers. Although the 'Enfield' was considered a superior weapon of its time, it had a low fire rate.

In the North a new rifle musket, 'Model 1861' was in production. Known as the 'Springfield Musket' some 900,000 were manufactured during the Civil War. The weapon employed a percussion cap firing mechanism which simplified its reloading procedure and increased its rate of fire to six rounds per minute. That rate was twice that of the 'Enfield' but its longest range was slightly less with an effectiveness at about 300 yards. Incorporating both essential factors the 'Springfield Musket' became extremely popular with the troops and was recovered from the battlefields by Confederate soldiers whenever possible.

The development of the rifle musket was far from complete. The idea of a muzzle-loading weapon was a more accepted, concept, although it required several steps or operations to reload, making six

The weapons and behavior of the colonial frontiersmen in the American Revolutionary War were responsible for changes in traditional infantry tactics.

Both armies used sharpshooters armed with high-powered rifles, which were fitted with specially developed sights.

rounds per minute the maximum rate which could be achieved. The evolution had two steps: breech loading and the use of an ammunition magazine cartridge. Such a reloading system required the development of a round which was a self-contained unit of powder, shot and primer device. The cartridge would undoubtedly be made of metal, allowing for easy removal of the spent round and rapid insertion of a new one. A breech loading weapon had basically the same requirement, but the main difficulty was the creation of an air-tight seal at the breech once the round was loaded. The breech-loading weapon also required a movement in removing the spent round and loading a new one with every shot fired. However, that technique would prove vastly more efficient than muzzle loading weapons as each cartridge would be self-contained.

The most widely used of the breech loading rifles was the 'Sharps Rifle', more than 100,000 of which were manufactured during the Civil War. The 'Sharps' fired approximately 10 rounds per minute with an accurate range to 600 yards. It was three times faster than the muzzle loading weapons to operate and had twice the effective range.

With the first metal cartridges being put to use during the Civil War the concept of designing a magazined rifle was within reach and the magazine fed or 'repeater' rifle made its debut. Two such weapons gained fame during the Civil War. One, the 'Spencer Rifle' had a magazine which held eight rounds and could fire up to 21 rounds per minute. That more than doubled the rate of the breech loader and was seven times the rate of a muzzle loading weapon.

The other, which caught the imagination of those interested in the field of infantry weapons and was the predecessor of the Winchester Rifle, appeared late in the war. The 'Henry Rifle' had a magazine which could hold 15 rounds, all of which could be fired in approximately 11 seconds. The 'Henry' applied a rearming system in which a lever was pushed forward then returned to its original position. That simple motion ejected the spent round, cocked the weapon, and fed a new round into the chamber. In a five-minute time period, a soldier could fire more than 120 rounds, using less than one minute of that time for the reloading procedures.

The military beauty of the 'Henry's' reload system lay in the fact that inexperienced troops were not required to learn complex loading sequences, which they had a tendency to forget in the heat of battle. Blunders such as loading the

powder and ball out of sequence, multiple loadings, or simply firing the ramrod away were common with muzzle-loading weapons. The 'Henry Rifle' averted those blunders and in the hands of even the greenest troops produced devastating effects on the enemy. Cavalrymen also reaped the benefits of the 'Henry Rifle' in a combined capacity for rapid movement and increased fire strength. The tactical value of speed in maneuverability and fire power would not be so startling again until the development of tank and blitzkrieg warfare.

Not only did the metal, self-contained cartridges permit the development of breech loading and magazine fed rifles, but they also paved the way for those who saw the possibility of a rapid fire weapon capable of holding more rounds than any rifle. The concept gave rise to the weapon known as the machine gun.

In July 1856 United States Patent Number 15315 was awarded to C E Barnes for his crank operated machine cannon. That weapon was far ahead of its time and met with little acceptance. Although there were many other attempts at creating a suitable machine gun, little progress was made until 1861. That year saw the development of the Union Repeating Gun, often referred to as the 'Ager Gun' or the 'Coffee Mill' since it resembled the kitchen coffee grinders of that era. The weapon was

operated by turning a crank on its top, which in turn operated a hopper feed mechanism for the presentation of the rounds. While it could fire 120 rounds per minute to a range of more than 1000 yards, the Union Repeating Gun had several glaring faults. It had a tendency to overheat rapidly and rounds often became jammed in the hopper mechanism. Not of least importance it simply was not popular with the troops or general staff. It was only at Lincoln's personal insistence that the weapon ever saw combat. Although in one instance it virtually destroyed two squadrons of Confederate cavalry at a distance of more than 800 yards, the 'Repeating Gun' continued to be labelled unreliable, potentially dangerous to operate, and extremely wasteful of ammunition.

In 1862 two new weapons came to the forefront. The first, the 'Williams Gun' was dubbed the 'Confederate secret weapon.' It was a small, single-barrelled, breech-loaded weapon which fired paper cartridges and could only sustain 18 to 20 rounds per minute. More than seven batteries of that gun were formed. The weapon was prone to overheating and jamming with extensive use, but with a

range of 2000 yards it made quite an impression.

The most famous of all machine gun class weapons was the 'Gatling Gun' designed by Richard Jordan Gatling. That weapon had an unusual firing mechanism. Six barrels rotated before a loading mechanism and when turned by a crank fired one round from each barrel in rapid succession. The 'Model 1862 Gatling Gun' could fire 250 rounds per minute at an effective target range of 1000 yards. Because of that weapon Gatling was given the distinction of being the 'father of the modern machine gun'. He presented his weapon to General J W Ripley, Chief of Ordnance for the Union army, but Ripley refused to have anything to do with it. Not until General Butler personally ordered 12 of the weapons for use at the siege of Petersburg, was any interest shown in Gatling's invention. One of Gatling's difficulties did not concern his invention but lay in the fact that he was born in the South and lived there until 1844. Many believed that Gatling was actually a Confederate sympathizer who was trying to cause the Union to spend time and money on a worthless weapon.

Although Gatling improved his design in 1865, it was not until 1866 that the United States Army officially adopted the weapon. If it had not been for the prejudices shown to Gatling, two of the machine guns could have been attached to each regiment. The devastating fire which could have been brought against enemy troops would have been so great that such a weapon would have dominated the battlefields. Machine guns did exactly that during World War I.

One area where little in the way of technological advancement was made was artillery. For the most part it remained the same as it had been during the Napoleonic era. However, one truly influential advance was made in the design of gun carriages during the Civil War. Designs were developed to compensate for the larger caliber, heavier field pieces, but an overall conversion was made which was more compact and often lighter than previous carriages. The cannon and mortar pieces themselves continued to be forged in bronze or iron.

Artillery pieces, like muskets, were divided into two types: those which had smoothbore barrels and those with rifled

barrels. The standard smoothbore piece throughout the Civil War was the 12-pound 'Napoleon' which had a fire rate of either four cannister or two aimed shots per minute. Five basic classifications of ammunition could be used in such smoothbore pieces. For long ranges of 750 to 2000 yards they could fire solid shot, spherical case, or explosive shell rounds. Solid shot was generally preferred by gunners as both spherical case and explosive shell rounds had a tendency to detonate while still in flight or just after leaving the barrel. Many anxious moments were spent dealing with those types of ammunition, and on the battlefield it was usually left to the howitzers and mortars to fire spherical case and explosive shell.

For shorter ranges of less than 750 yards grapeshot was preferred. The round consisted of three layers of lead balls separated by iron rings with an iron plate on the top and bottom holding it all together. Grapeshot rounds were, in effect, a replica of an extremely large shotgun shell and were quite devastating against targets in the 300 to 750 yards range. Once the enemy moved to within 300 yards the artillerymen automatically switched to cannister

rounds, which were nothing more than large metal containers filled with lead balls. Quite often other metal objects were placed in the barrel with the cannister to add to its destructive effectiveness. The results achieved by cannister fire at short ranges were awesome and the 12-pound 'Napoleon' had no equal when it came to firing that particular type of round.

The largest of the smoothbore artillery pieces were the 32-pound howitzers, though the 24-pound cannon was usually the heaviest employed by battlefield artillery brigades.

In 1860 the United States Army intended to convert most of its artillery to rifled barrel models. Although the maximum range of rifled pieces was slightly more than 1000 yards greater than the 'Napoleons,' accuracy was vastly improved. The two best known and most widely used were the 'Parrott,' available in ten or 20 pound classifications, and the Three-inch Rodman Ordnance Gun. The 'Rodman' could consistently, with precision, hit a target at a range of 1800 yards and had a maximum range of 4000 yards. It fired basically the same classifications

The most obvious change in naval warfare was the introduction of the ironclad. Although such warships had already been developed in Europe, the Civil War saw the first test of ironclads in battle.

of ammunition used by the smoothbore cannon but was disadvantaged by an inability to fire an effective cannister round at close range.

Although the precision of rifled cannon was being improved, those weapons had one unusual drawback. The increased power behind the rounds launched from a rifled barrel often buried explosive rounds into the earth when they reached their targets. The ensuing explosion was therefore muffled and its destructive potential diminished.

Some cannon, such as the Confederate 'Wentworth,' could only fire a solid shot or 'bolt' as it was often called. Although it was destructive when employed against fortifications or 'hard' targets, it was not explosive and was virtually useless on the battlefield against enemy troops.

As the war progressed smoothbore and rifled artillery were assigned to particular roles. Smoothbore weapons were used

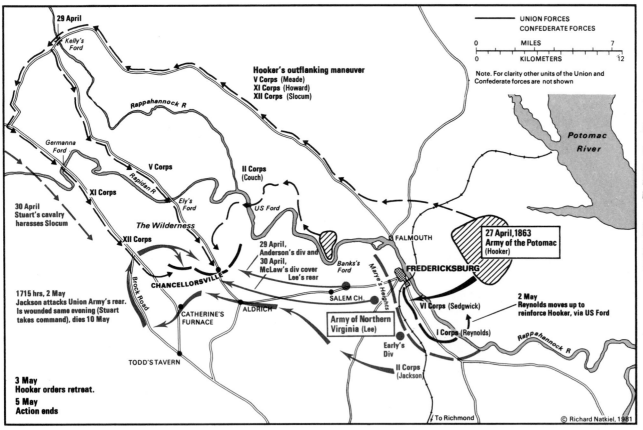

primarily in defense, for which they were best suited because of their close range potential. Rifled artillery was used primarily in offense as support by applying concentrated fire at longer ranges.

The principal alteration in naval artillery reflected the development of ironclad vessels. Of necessity naval cannons became more powerful in order to pierce the protective armor of the ironclads.

The only real experimentation with artillery during the war occurred in the South. Southern inventors and ordnance personnel attempted several innovative designs. One design incorporated a pair of revolving cannon, mounted on a single carriage. It was hoped that the revolving barrels would allow for a more rapid rate of fire. In its very first test one of the guns exploded, killing the crew. The experiment was abandoned.

Another novel idea was a cannon which used steam as a propellant instead of gun powder. A prototype for that weapon was captured by the Union in 1861 and although it sparked the interest of several inventors and political figures, its impracticality soon eliminated it from further consideration.

The Confederacy also experimented with several double-barrelled cannon designs. The most notable model consisted of two 6-pound guns, joined together and mounted on one carriage. Both barrels were intended simultaneously to fire a round shot connected between the barrels by a length of chain. The projectiles would act much like a giant 'bola' against advancing infantry. The major difficulty encountered was achieving a truly simultaneous fire. One barrel consistently fired before the other, sending the two rounds off to either the right or the left. With each attempt to master the technique for simultaneous fire the crew lived in fear of one of the barrels failing to discharge, which would inevitably wrap the ball and chain around the gun and kill or maim the crew. That possibility never actually occurred, but the testing proved that further development was not feasible. During its debut the weapon managed to cut down several small trees, destroy the chimney of a house adjacent to the test site, and kill a cow in a nearby pasture, none of which were particularly glorious recommendations.

One of these cannon still exists and stands in the town square of Athens, Georgia. In fact, almost every style or model of cannon used during the Civil War can be found scattered throughout the countryside or standing as monuments in the eastern United States, just as rifle muskets still hang as heirlooms in many American houses.

With the development and advances made in the basic weapons of war, alterations in the tactics which were employed naturally followed. As previously stated, most of the early Civil War tactics reflected the same line and column formations as the Napoleonic wars. Military theory had its foundations set in the European tactics and few generals applied themselves to the consideration of new methods. The concepts of volley lines and massive columns continued to be the accepted norm. One of the most notorious examples of the employment of the outmoded Napoleonic tactics was displayed in Burnside's attack on Fredericksburg against entrenched Confederate troops on the heights above the city. The devastat-

ing slaughter of the Union troops was in direct contrast to the minimal losses suffered by the Confederates.

The average soldier not only had increased range but a far greater rate of firing and accuracy. A change in tactics had to be devised or mass carnage would ensue. The Confederates were the first to realize that troops defending an established position, or entrenched, compensated for any lack of numbers. As time went on both armies realized that some type of entrenchment or advantage in the lie of the land would have to be utilized to protect the troops from the increased destructive potential of their enemy.

Innovations in tactics were actually quite simple and straightforward. Success on the battlefield became dependant on a maneuver which would put the odds in favor of the attacker. Generally that meant some sort of flank attack or sectioning-off of the enemy so that a large number of troops could be brought to bear against a lesser number. A primary example of that tactic was Jackson's flank maneuver at Chancellorsville. Lee was to hold the attention and the mass of Union troops concentrated against himself while Jackson, taking the majority of the army, would march his troops to a point from which they could strike against an important flank. The intention was to gain an advantage which would dislodge Hooker's army. The North was less apt to take advantage of entrenching its troops in the early days of the war, thus making such a Confederate maneuver plausible.

It was soon obvious that soldiers moving from one point to another had to assume fortified positions once they reached their destinations. By 1864 Lee's army had be-

Increased fire potential led to the development of sophisticated systems of trenches, presaging those of World War I.

come quite proficient at entrenching. Union observers wrote that the Confederate army on its first day at a new position would entrench itself into strong rifle defenses. By the second day such rifle pits would be joined together by trenches or parapets and artillery positions that afforded the crews and guns a degree of protection would appear. By the third day the Confederate field works would consist of entrenched artillery positions, generally of a size which could hold a full battery, and extensive trench and parapet works arranged in a wedge-shaped formation. From such a position Confederate soldiers could hold off three or four times their own strength. At Spotsylvania in 1864 Confederate troops took Grant totally by surprise when within one day they had managed to dig themselves into positions which were normally not seen until the third or fourth day of action.

The development of sophisticated entrenching systems was the forerunner of what would be seen fifty years later during World War I. Obviously the increased fire potential no longer permitted masses of troops with glistening bayonets marching forward in great columns against standing lines of enemy soldiers. Warfare had been transformed. Soldiers were burying themselves like moles and cutting their enemies down with solid walls of lead, fired from rifles which killed long before the enemy maneuvered within range of a charge.

That is not to say that the infantry attack was not employed, but the method of such attacks was changed. Attacks had to be properly coordinated so that large numbers of troops could surge quickly forward in unformed open order, presenting the smallest possible target for defending rifle fire. Only the most determined assault had any chance for success against entrenched troops.

Such determination and bravery were simply not enough. Until 1864, though new tactics were evolving, generals continued to entrust victory to valiant displays of raw courage rather than to their soldiers' abilities to take advantage of terrain or the enemy's miscalculations. Lee at Gettysburg, like Burnside at Fredericksburg, was an excellent example of commanders' reliance on the extraordinary fighting capabilities of a particular group of soldiers. Pickett's Charge proved that in light of the developed rifle potential and the increased cannon fire a reversion to the Napoleonic advance would result in wholesale slaughter. Why Lee, often acclaimed as a military genius, chose to allow such an assault remains a mystery. The bravery of the Union and Confederate troops in both cases was beyond reproach. The blame for failure must rest with the implementation of outmoded tactics.

By the middle of 1864 US Grant had introduced another new concept in the Civil War. It dealt not with a new weapon or battlefield tactics but the application of the strategic concept of attrition. Grant realized that one Union advantage lay in its greater resources of men and materials, and that both were becoming scarce in the Confederate states. Although Union losses in troops and supplies greatly outnumbered those of the Confederacy, they could be more readily replaced while Confederate deficiencies could not. Ultimately, an army is on the road to defeat when it realizes that it is impossible to match its enemy indefinitely.

Grant also brought forward another major strategy, that of 'total war.' Before Grant took command, there was little coordination between the Union campaigns on different fronts with regard to the total picture of achieving victory. The commands of both the Union and Confederacy concerned themselves with bat-

Many Civil War guns like this 30-pounder Parrott can be found throughout the United States, kept as memorials to the war dead.

The folly of ignoring the advances in battlefield tactics was made horribly obvious by the number of Confederate dead after Pickett's Charge.

tlefield engagements as the key to breaking the resistance of their enemy, and sought to destroy their opponent's operation in specific areas. They were also bound by the mystique of capturing the enemy's capital city.

Grant's concept of war was different. As he so positively demonstrated during the Vicksburg campaign, one must eliminate the enemy's capacity to wage war. In so doing, his willingness to conduct or continue the war is also destroyed. When Grant sent Sherman on his famous 'March to the Sea' he was ultimately annihilating the South's ability to wage war by destroying the areas of manufacturing and munitions supply and by inflicting the ravages of war on the heartland of the South. Grant firmly agreed with Sherman's much quoted phrase, 'War is Hell,' The essence of war is death and destruction, but a true commander wages total war, not for glory nor self-gratification, but to bring war to a swift end. Grant's philosophy may appear to be a contradiction in terms, but he proved that by waging war viciously and completely the sufferings of war would ultimately be

brought to a more rapid conclusion.

In the development of technology typical of the nineteenth century, other inventions were also finding their way to military application.

One such invention was the steam engine, whose value to the war effort became increasingly evident. Steam-powered ships opened an entirely new era for naval warfare. No longer were ships forced to rely on the providence of nature for their ability to move across the seas. As the size and capabilities of steam-driven engines grew larger ships increased in size, weight and speed. The greatest advantage was the capacity for a vessel to use armor plate to protect its superstructure without making it too slow or cumbersome.

Although the Civil War ironclads were not the first to employ the armor plating on a war vessel, they were the first to be used in combat against one another. Their abilities against wooden ships marked them as vastly superior vessels and heralded the end of an era.

The railroads played their own important role. Trains could be used not only to carry supplies but to transport troops and their equipment rapidly from one area to another. Since the 1830s, more than 30,000 miles of track had been built

in the eastern half of the United States connecting the major commercial cities of the country.

In the North, the railroads grew through the need of transportation between the major industrial areas. They were then expanded to link the agricultural regions of the midwest with the demanding markets of the eastern cities.

The South, on the other hand, used its rail lines primarily for the hauling of cotton, connecting railheads near the major plantations and the coastal city ports. Surprisingly, during the great expansion period, neither the North nor the South made any concerted effort to link together. In fact, northern railroads often deliberately isolated the South for economic and political reasons, which stemmed from the fact that the North looked to the West as an ally because of its dependency on the agriculture of the West to feed its growing population.

When war broke out, the North was in a much more advantageous position than the South. The Union had an abundance of links to the West and had standardized its rail gauges. Southern railroads were usually independently owned and operated and ran on three different gauges of track. That difference hampered rail operations for the Confederacy, requiring them

to load and unload troops and supplies at various stages along the route.

Another major difference was to be found in the condition of the tracks as the war began. As a result of the poor state of repair of Southern tracks, train speeds were limited to 20 miles per hour and, more often than not, to less than 15 miles per hour. By contrast, 25 to 30 miles per hour was the average in the North, though higher speeds were attainable.

In spite of the problems, the Confederacy was the first to demonstrate the possibilities offered by the use of railroads when they moved troops from the Shenandoah Valley to reinforce General Beauregard at the First Battle of Manassas. Railroads had been employed during the Crimean War, but the Civil War used the railroad on such a grand scale that its longterm strategic value was firmly established.

Due to their increased importance, the railroads and tracks became strategic objectives. Raiders of both armies destroyed and disrupted rail movement, causing delays and confusion during many campaigns with their 'hit and run' tactics.

One item did appear on the tracks which was considered the first of its kind. Railroad flat cars were adapted to transport

mobile guns and mortars which could be fired from their platforms at military objectives within range of the lines.

Another invention extensively used during the Civil War was the telegraph. Invented in 1844 by Samuel F B Morse, the telegraph allowed immediate communication between generals in the field and the government. Although the telegraph did not immediately replace the more conventional means of communication, the courier and dispatch rider, it was used early in the war to transmit information and orders to generals in distant field areas.

As the war continued, the manner in which the telegraph was used differed between the North and the South, although both sides determined that extensive use should be made of existing civilian telegraph facilities. In the North Lincoln's Secretary of War, Edwin Stanton, formerly an executive of the Atlantic and Ohio Telegraph Company, not only secured the rights for the Union government to use existing telegraph lines but brought the operation under the direct supervision of the Federal Government. Stanton was also responsible for creating a military telegraph system under the control of the Army Signal Corps which used both civilian and military operators.

Sherman's theories of 'total war' included destruction of the railroads to prevent their use by the enemy.

In the South the idea of cooperation between the Confederate Government and Southern telegraph companies never actually materialized. Jefferson Davis held the conviction that the government should not hamper civilian business with government regulations on private industry. The Southern telegraph system would continue as it always had, carrying government messages on the same basis and often with the same priority as civilian messages. Consequently, the efficiency of the Southern telegraph system was often less than might have been desired.

Both sides paid for their messages although Stanton got a reduced rate in the North. Southern military messages, regardless of how crucial they were, were charged at the same rate as civilian messages.

Grant used Stanton's system far more efficiently than anyone else. From 1864 until the end of the war, Grant had his own system of telegraph lines, linking his headquarters with Washington. That gave him the ability to remain with his forces while carrying on communications with those who dictated policy from the capital.

*Above:* The Confederate 'scorched earth' policy is well illustrated by this photograph of Manassas Junction in March 1862.
*Below:* Rails were made useless by heating the middle of the tracks over a fire. The weight of the cold ends would bend them.
*Right:* The military railroads were used for transporting troops and supplies.

The poor quality of track and rolling stock in the South frequently resulted in accidental derailments, adding this hazard to the dangers of sabotage to the railroad by enemy raiding parties.

For the first time, commanders in the field could be immediately apprised of a change in policy or have immediate approval or disapproval for any changes they wished to make in their operations.

Another invention which had little effect on the war effort but added much to the later understanding of events was photography. First used as a money making device by enterprising men taking photographs of the troops, the photograph took on a completely different aspect in the hands of Mathew Brady.

Brady travelled throughout the country during the war taking pictures of battles, soldiers, weapons and the dead to record them for posterity. Those photographs became invaluable to future historians but, more importantly, they sparked the idea that the camera might hold future possibilities for application as a military device. However the potential of photography as an essential intelligence gathering tool was unrealized.

The use of balloons as a means of observing enemy fortifications and troop movements resurfaced during the Civil War. The French were actually the first to experiment with balloons as a military device. Napoleon at one point considered an invasion of England by massing vast numbers of balloons to transport his army across the English Channel. Although that dream never materialized, balloons had appeared from time to time on the battlefields as a method of observation.

The Union army took the balloon very seriously and Professor Thaddeus Lowe was made commander of the Balloon Corps. Lowe's Corps reached a maximum strength of seven balloons and was used in the Seven Days Battle. Unexpectedly, his small air force was disbanded shortly after Chancellorsville. Its value appeared to stand on too limited a base to withstand the changing times and pessimistic views which were taken of the early flights.

During its brief existence, Lowe's corps pioneered an important military concept. Not only could the balloon be used for direct observation of troops and fortifications, but as an aid to the directing of artillery fire. In one instance Lowe experimented with placing a telegraph operator in an observation balloon for the purpose of calling the accuracy of artillery fire. The idea of 'forward observers' was not

*Above:* Railroad batteries were another
technological advance made during the American
Civil War.
*Right:* Dispatch riders were still used in the midst
of battle to transmit orders.
*Left:* An observer in a 'buzzard's roost' or signal
station would obtain information then relayed by
telegraph or dispatch rider.

taken seriously until World War I, but
Lowe's experiments proved that it did
have an important contribution to make.

Although the Union service was better
organized, the Confederacy also used balloons. However Southern balloonists did
not fully understand the service which
balloons could render, either. One Confederate balloon made out of silk strips
cut from dresses and undergarments do-
nated by the belles of the Confederacy,
was captured by Union forces early in the
war. Southerners viewed the capture as a
'dirty Yankee trick' since much sacrifice
and sentiment was invested in the balloon.

Balloons had little impact on the war as
both sides realized their potential and
countered them very efficiently. It was
obvious that an observer could make a
quick, accurate count of troops and assess
positions. General Beauregard, after view-
ing a Union balloonist observing a Confederate position, suggested that the

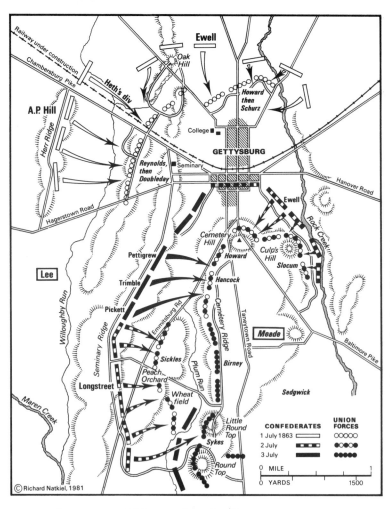

The hand grenade, though not a new invention, proved useful in protracted sieges such as Vicksburg and Petersburg. However they were prone to explode prematurely.

enemy observer could be used to the Confederate advantage by deceiving him in one of two ways. One idea called for the creation of false positions to give the impression that there was more strength and firepower than actually existed. 'Quaker Guns,' which were nothing more than the trunks of trees, shaped and blackened to resemble artillery pieces entrenched along fortified lines, were used. Balloon observers often mistook such guns for real artillery and consequently returned false intelligence reports.

Measures were also taken to camouflage positions in the hope that observers would be unable to distinguish hidden troops or cannon, drawing enemy forces into a false belief that there were fewer troops in an area than there actually were.

The South achieved one 'first' when a camouflaged artillery battery opened fire on approaching balloonists with explosive shell. Confederate troops claimed that a balloon was shot down but McClellan's files of 1862 recorded no such loss. However, a precedent of antiaircraft fire had been set as an excellent countermeasure to the aerial observer.

As the war evolved and static positions became the norm on the battlefield, with both armies developing trenching systems, another invention appeared which foretold gruesome consequences. Designed originally as an inexpensive fencing material, barbed wire was introduced onto the battlefield in May of 1864 at Drewry's Bluff. The wire was strung in front of Union positions and attacking Confederate soldiers became entangled in the wire and were slaughtered. After the battle, Confederate commanders described the use of barbed wire as 'a devilish device which could only have been thought of by Yankees.' The South saw no honor in using such a device against the infantry, but the idea would be developed in World War I.

Another weapon which became increasingly used as a result of sieges and trench warfare was the grenade. The grenade was not a new weapon but both the Union and the Confederacy immediately realized its applicability in stagnant siege situations. More than 100,000 grenades were purchased by the Union government and an unknown quantity were procured by the Confederacy.

The grenade had advanced little over the years and was still a small exploding shell which was detonated by either fuse or impact. Grenades saw extensive use by Grant's army at Vicksburg but were unpopular with the troops because of their tendency to explode before they could be thrown.

The South expanded on the grenade concept by taking six pound spherical case shells and rolling them down hills at charging troops. Such shells were detonated by fuse and if properly employed had the same effect as artillery support.

Grenades were taken one step further with the idea of gas grenades. Generally, they contained a substance which produced an obnoxious odor when exploded.

It was hoped that the stench would force entrenched troops to abandon their positions before they became helpless and violently ill. Dubbed 'stink bombs,' they were the forerunners of the deadly morbid gases used in World War I.

The rocket was also added to the military arsenal. The development of rockets had been ignored and they were basically the same weapon that appeared during the Napoleonic wars. Although the effects of the rocket were more psychological than destructive, its inaccuracy and unreliability eliminated it as a feasible weapon. If either government had given time or consideration to the development of the rocket, it might have been proven to be an inexpensive, effective weapon which could have raised the army's fire capability. The South, especially with its lack of industrialization and shortages of arms and ammunition, might have found the rocket to be an answer to some of their deficiencies.

The final innovative weapons brought forward during the Civil War were the torpedo mine and a device which had been experimented with during the Revolutionary War, the submarine.

The marine torpedo or river mine was a constant threat to the Union navy throughout the War. The Confederacy found mines to be an effective defense

*Above:* The CSS *C L Hunley,* the submersible which sank USS *Housatonic,* was trapped below the water by her adversary.
*Left:* Electricity for the telegraph system was supplied by galvanic batteries carried in wagons.
*Top* Newspaper coverage of the Civil War was supplied by correspondents from all the major papers, moving with the army.

against Union vessels which were attempting to close Southern harbors and ports. Twenty-seven Union ships were sunk by such mines, the most important being the *Tecumseh* during the Battle of Mobile Bay.

A variation of the mine was used by both the North and the South. The 'spar' torpedo was an explosive device mounted on a long pole at the bow of a vessel which detonated when rammed into the hull of another ship. However, 'spar' torpedos were generally as dangerous to the craft using them as to the vessel under attack.

One of the principal vessels which employed the 'spar' torpedo was the submersible or submarine. Primarily, the submersible was employed by the Confeder-

The 15,000 miles of telegraph wires set up by the US Telegraph Corps was frequently sabotaged by rebel raiding parties.

acy in the hope that it would prove to be an efficient means of breaking the blockade. They were christened 'Davids' as a reference to their role as 'giant killers.'

The first submersible designed for the South was a vessel which ran just below the surface and was powered by steam. Due to the nature of steam propulsion, the funnel and the hatchway had to remain above the waterline if the ship was to function properly. Intended for night use when visibility was poor, that submersible was armed with a 'spar' torpedo.

That initial 'David' had several flaws. It was extremely unstable and during its trial run was swamped by the wake of a

*Below:* The torpedo mine proved to be an effective defense against the Union blockade.
*Right:* Experiments with submersibles and torpedoes continued throughout the war, although many were impractical.

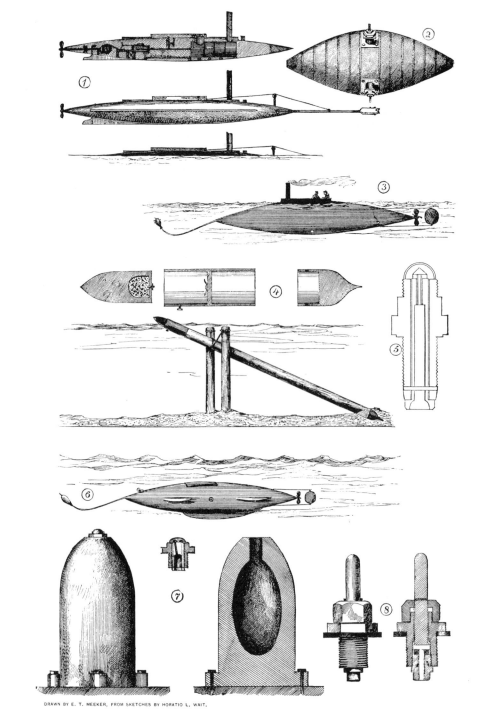

DRAWN BY E. T. MEEKER, FROM SKETCHES BY HORATIO L. WAIT.

1. CONFEDERATE TORPEDO-BOAT "DAVID." 2. CONFEDERATE TORPEDO. 3. CONFEDERATE TORPEDO-BOAT, AS DESCRIBED BY A REFUGEE. 4. CONFEDERATE SPAR-TORPEDO. 5. FUSE OF A BARREL-TORPEDO FOUND IN THE ST. JOHN'S RIVER. 6. CONFEDERATE SUBMARINE TORPEDO-BOAT, AS DESCRIBED BY A REFUGEE. 7. CONFEDERATE VOLCANO-TORPEDO. 8. CONFEDERATE TORPEDO-FUSE.

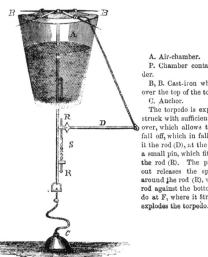

A. Air-chamber.
P. Chamber containing the powder.
B, B. Cast-iron wheel made to fit over the top of the torpedo.
C. Anchor.
The torpedo is exploded by being struck with sufficient force to keel it over, which allows the wheel (B) to fall off, which in falling drags with it the rod (D), at the end of which is a small pin, which fits into a hole in the rod (R). The pin being pulled out releases the spiral spring (S) around the rod (R), which forces the rod against the bottom of the torpedo at F, where it strikes a cap and explodes the torpedo.

passing steamer. The vessel was refloated but the flaw was not corrected. On 5 October 1863 it attacked the USS *Ironsides* off Charleston, South Carolina. The submersible managed to use its spar to blow a hole in the hull of the Union ironclad but did not seriously damage the vessel. However, the wave which resulted from the explosion crashed over the submersible and it was again swamped. Only the captain and two crew members were able to escape.

After that incident, Southern designers looked for an alternate source of power which would allow for the complete submersion of the vessel. The prototype of such a vessel was created by Horace L Hunley. Two unsuccessful designs were built before Hunley was satisfied. Power for the third craft was supplied by an eight man crew who sat and turned a crank which operated the propeller. The submersible was also equipped with a pair of hydroplanes which helped keep it below the water level. Tests showed that the vessel could remain submerged for approximately three hours before the oxygen supply was exhausted. This third vessel was taken to Charleston, South Carolina by rail for further tests. During a trial run in October 1863, she sank. The entire crew which included Hunley went down with the vessel.

She was refloated and a new crew was assembled. In honor of the ship's deceased inventor, the submersible was christened the CSS *H L Hunley*. The *Hunley*'s crew were volunteers from an Alabama infantry regiment and her captain was Lieutenant George E Dixon, also of that regiment. On 17 February 1864, the *Hunley* attacked and sank the USS *Housatonic*. It was the first time in the history of naval warfare that a submersible successfully engaged and sank its enemy. However, the instability of the vessel and the unpredictability of its 'spar' torpedo trapped the *Hunley*. She was dragged under by the sinking Union ship. Many years later,

divers inspecting the wreck of the *Housatonic* discovered the *Hunley* on the ocean floor beside her and nine skeletons encased within. Although the South attempted to develop more practical submersibles, the *Hunley* was the only true success.

Finally, in the light of several other alternatives, the Civil War saw the introduction of an entirely new aspect of war, the prisoner-of-war camp. Throughout the history of warfare certain key figures had been subjected to imprisonment, but the American Civil War saw the first widespread use of camps designed specifically for the purpose of detaining enemy troops for an indefinite time period.

Prisoner-of-war camps rose to prominence shortly after Grant's promotion to General in Chief. As a result of his concept of 'total war' Grant eliminated the customary practice of parole. In such paroles soldiers were made to swear that they would not take part in further hostile activities until they were informed by their government that a 'prisoner exchange' had been made. Records were kept by both the Union and Confederacy of prisoners taken. At various intervals such records were exchanged and those listed were notified that they could again join their regiments for combat duty.

Total war had no place for such 'honorable, gentlemanly' behavior. Specific areas for internment were established in both the North and South for the incarceration of prisoners taken in battle. As the war progressed and supplies dwindled, prisoner camps became a source of punishment and propaganda.

After the war Confederate camps such as Andersonville received notorious attention for their alleged deliberate inhumane treatment of Union prisoners. The North took great pains in making issue of the situation, but a review of the conditions in the Union camps clearly illustrated that they were not without blemish. Records show that more than

Prisoner-of-war camps, such as Andersonville in Georgia, were another innovation, detaining prisoners who might otherwise have been paroled. The Andersonville camp held nearly 32,000 Union prisoners under appallingly bad conditions.

52,000 troops died in Union and Confederate prison camps; that total being almost equally divided. The war of attrition had brought hardships to the Southern people and the Union prisoners suffered as well. There was no grave problem of food and supplies in the North, yet Confederate prisoners at Lookout Point, Maryland were forced to eat the rats which infested the camp to stay alive.

The finger of blame can never be pointed solely at one party or the other, but as has often been the case in war it was the defeated who were held responsible for their 'atrocities' while the victors stood as judge and jury.

The Civil War was the first clear indication that technological advancements and industrial might would have far reaching effect on the wars of the future. Invention would give the soldier more effective weapons with which to practice his profession. The need for industrial capabilities would be demonstrated in that regardless of the apparent advantages, materials for war had to keep pace with the demands.

Warfare had indeed changed. Ideals, principles, and power were outweighed by the evidence that through war and the production, sale and trade of war materials fortunes could be made. Nations could use war to support sagging economies as well as to promote their own self-image to the rest of the world. In the Civil War warfare had gone beyond the soldiers on the battlefields, to foretell of wars of total commitment with the possible end result of the total destruction of a nation militarily, politically, and psychologically. The American Civil War heralded the end of an era and predicted the consequences of modern warfare.

# CONCLUSION

On 14 April 1865, five days after the surrender of the Army of Northern Virginia, President Abraham Lincoln was assassinated by John Wilkes Booth, a personal revenge on the man who had successfully led the Union through the Civil War. With Lincoln died the hope of an honorable peace for the South. His vision of reuniting the states with the least amount of difficulty and pain, 'with malice toward none, with charity for all' would not become a reality. The era of Reconstruction would be a harsh and restrictive one. The powerful Republicans of the new administration wanted revenge for Lincoln's death as well as four years of war. The Confederacy was a defeated state to be subjugated and beaten into submission by her conquerors.

The severe policies of the Reconstruction Congress included occupation by the Northern army. The basic social structure of the South, deprived of the slave economy, was destroyed. The leading citizens of the antebellum and Confederate South were denied all political responsibility because they had served the South. The people of the South were scattered across the nation, to the western frontiers, as they attempted to escape the aftermath

of war. This dishonor, destruction and dislocation were not easily forgotten, as decades passed and the South did not recover her prosperity.

Although the North fought to preserve the Union, the true restoration of the United States occurred only after the senseless urge for revenge had been satisfied. Eventually the destructive application of 'total war' was forgotten, as were the other advances in the art of war. The gallantry and comradeship were remembered, but so were the hardships and the disgrace. The victorious North dictating the postwar conditions fostered fears and hatred which can be detected to the present day. The United States has not forgotten the events of more than a century ago. There are no true victors when men of the same nation take up arms against one another.

*Below:* The assassination of Lincoln five days after the end of the war opened the harsh era of Reconstruction. Had Lincoln lived, there is reason to believe that the United States would have been spared much of the bitterness that was a legacy of the war.
*Right:* The victorious Union army returned home in triumph.

Rebel soldiers were forced to take an oath of allegiance to the United States, administered by the Army of Occupation.

# INDEX

# Acknowledgements

**Bison Picture Library:** 12 top; 48 top; 68; 95 top left and right; 113; 116; 128–129; 130; 140 bottom; 163 and front flap.
**Library of Congress:** 6 center; 7 bottom right; 13 both; 14; 17 top; 33; 61; 63 right; 66 top; 69 bottom; 71 bottom; 75 both; 77 top; 79 right; 109 top; 110–111; 117; 127 top; 139 bottom; 148; 149; 151; 162; 164–165; 166–167; 178–179 top; 183 top; 185.
**The Mansell Collection:** 8–9; 10; 11 right top and bottom; 18; 22 both; 24; 25 bottom; 26 top; 27 top; 28–29; 30; 32 both; 36; 48 bottom; 49 bottom; 50; 52–53; 54–55; 62; 64; 82 top; 83 top; 86; 90; 92–93; 98 bottom; 99 top; 124

top; 127 bottom; 132 top; 134 top; 134 bottom right; 140 top; 142; 143 top; 145 bottom; 150; 152 both; 153 both; 154 top; 158 top; 183 bottom; 184 top left and bottom; 187; 188–189.
**National Archives:** 56; 76 bottom; 94; 103; 157; 170.
**NY Historical Society:** 12 bottom; 186; Front Jacket and back flap.
**Robert Hunt Picture Library:** 45 bottom; 49 top; 51; 57 right; 58 bottom; 59; 60; 62 bottom; 65 top both; 67 bottom; 69 top; 70; 71 top; 74 both; 76 top; 78 top; 80 right; 81 all three; 82 bottom; 83 bottom; 84; 154 bottom; 176; 178 bottom; 182; 183 center.

**Peter Newark's Western Americana:** 6; 7 right; 11 left; 16 top; 17 bottom; 19; 21; 23 both; 25 top; 27 bottom; 31 both; 34; 38–39; 40 both; 41; 43; 44 top; 45 top; 46; 47 both; 53; 57 left; 58 top; 65 bottom; 66 bottom; 67 top both; 72 both; 73 both; 77 bottom; 79 left; 85; 87; 88–89; 91; 96; 97; 98 top; 99 bottom; 100; 101 both; 102; 104; 105 both; 106–107; 109 bottom; 114–115; 119; 120 both; 121 both; 122 both; 123 both; 125 both; 126 both; 131; 134 bottom left; 135 both; 137 both; 138–139; 141 both; 143 bottom; 145 top; 146–147; 155 top; 156 all; 159 both; 160 all; 161 both; 164 top;

168–169; 171; 175 both; 177; 179 bottom; 180 both; 181 both; 184 right.
**Smithsonian Institution:** 80 left; 95 center.
**US Army:** 35; 155 bottom; 158 bottom.
**US Navy:** 26 bottom; 132 bottom; 133; 136; 172–173.

The author and publishers would like to thank the following people for their help:
David Eldred for the design, Richard Natkiel for the maps, Ellen Crampton for the index, Elizabeth Miles for the editing and picture research.